I'd first like to thank Tom Hagley for inviting me to work with him on the third edition of this book. This partnership has been one of the best surprises that life has thrown my way. Tom, I've enjoyed and sincerely appreciated learning from you and working with you. Words can't thank you enough.

My graduate assistant, Scott N. Mitchell, was an invaluable help during this process. Keep writing, smiling, and challenging yourself.

Finally, to my children—Xavier, Jude, and Sydney. You three are the driving force behind all that I strive to accomplish. Thank you now and always for being the fuel to my fire.

— **Rebecca Gilliland**

I have dedicated this book to my lovely, loving wife, Peggy, whose support through the years contributed so much to the success of my professional career, which is the foundation for this publication. I want to acknowledge the comforting companionship throughout this project from our precious little Cotons de Tulear, Truffles (1996–2009), Woodruff, and Latte.

I am grateful to Rebecca Gilliland for her expertise and diligence in contributing to and carrying forward the knowledge in this book that was developed to advance the PR profession. Her dedicated initiative has given a new and updated perspective to what was started as a course packet and then sharpened by student discussions in 21 upper division PR courses at the University of Oregon.

— **Tom Hagley**

D1295279

Writing Winning Proposals
Public Relations Cases

Third Edition

Rebecca A. Gilliland
and Thomas R. Hagley

 cognella® | ACADEMIC PUBLISHING

Bassim Hamadeh, CEO and Publisher
Kassie Graves, Director of Acquisitions and Sales
Jamie Giganti, Senior Managing Editor
Jess Estrella, Senior Graphic Designer
Carrie Montoya, Manager, Revisions and Author Care
Alisa Munoz, Licensing Associate
Kaela Martin, Associate Editor
Abbey Hastings, Associate Production Editor
Bryan Mok, Interior Designer

Cover image copyright © Depositphotos/Rawpixel.

Printed in the United States of America

ISBN: 978-1-5165-1636-0 (pbk) / 978-1-5165-1637-7 (br)

Contents

III: RULES FOR WRITING 10 COMPONENTS OF A PUBLIC RELATIONS PLAN

Foreword

By Glen T. Cameron, PhD

I was pleased with Tom Hagley's invitation to provide a foreword to the first edition of his book, *Writing Winning Proposals: Public Relations Cases*, in 2005, and for a second edition in 2009, and now for this third edition in 2017. The pleasure has been in seeing Tom's continuing resolve to show students how to connect what they learn in class with what will be expected of them in practice.

I first became acquainted with Tom when I was teaching at the University of Georgia, where I schemed whenever possible to get him into my classroom. He was director of public and investor relations for Alumax, a Fortune 200 company located in Atlanta, when he became a favored guest lecturer and internship mentor at the Grady College of Journalism and Mass Communication. In addition to bringing his considerable experience to the classroom, Tom provided the students with structure, guidance, and an opportunity to grow—the same ingredients that make his text a must for our classrooms.

When Tom retired from his distinguished career as an executive in corporate and agency public relations—with a stint running his own PR firm thrown in for good measure—I was teaching at the Missouri School of Journalism. I tried to recruit Tom, knowing that he had spent three decades striving to make the profession better in every way. Tom is committed to embracing innovation as a basis for tempering the metal and sharpening the edge of the profession. Although we competed unsuccessfully with the lures of the Northwest, I feel that we have finally captured Tom by way of his wonderful textbook. It's not the same thing as having an experienced, compassionate, creative professional in our classroom, but it is the next best thing.

His book is a great piece of work. I say that with respect for its contents, but even more so with respect for the author. *Writing Winning Proposals: Public Relations Cases* comes from a person I always believed was destined to take the "real world" to the classroom. I saw that when Tom spoke to my classes at the University of Georgia and here at the Missouri School of Journalism. He has a passion for teaching, coaching, and counseling. He listens, recognizes, shares, encourages, tolerates, and even admits his own mistakes to those he mentors. His internship assignments made students stretch far beyond what they ever thought they could do with so little experience.

It is no surprise that in this book he insists on writing by the rules to develop winning proposals. He comes to academe knowing precisely what executive managers want from PR practitioners.

Glen T. Cameron, PhD

Professor and Maxine Wilson Gregory Chair in Journalism Research,
Missouri School of Journalism
Professor, Family and Community Medicine and Founder and Co-Director,
Health Communication Research Center,
University of Missouri

Foreword

By Christopher K. Veronda, APR

Thanks to his book, Tom Hagley is helping to raise the bar in the PR profession. When I started to review the first edition of this book, I couldn't put it down. *Writing Winning Proposals: Public Relations Cases* addresses one of the greatest weaknesses in public relations. I was so pleased to see someone take a bold step not only to define the components of PR plans, but to establish rules for writing them. Tom's clear delineation of how to put a plan together is engaging and the best blueprint I've seen. Students who master the principles in Tom's text will certainly have taken a big step toward being ready to enter the profession.

This third edition of *Writing Winning Proposals: Public Relations Cases* is a great reference and review tool, even for veteran practitioners. In judging hundreds of Silver Anvil Award entries over the years, I noticed that many lacked quality plans. It was common to find goals confused with objectives and strategies combined with objectives. Plans that suffer such deficiencies don't win, or don't even get implemented.

To student readers of Tom's book, I would say you have an opportunity to distinguish yourselves in the profession by learning to write winning plans and proposals, and to stand out from the crowd of professionals, especially by understanding how you build research and evaluation into any plan. I can't emphasize that enough.

There are no secrets to creating winning plans or winning Silver Anvils. If you develop a good plan, you shouldn't be in a position of having to look around afterwards, trying to identify success indicators that might or might not be attributable to PR activities and claiming them to be measurements of success. It seems to me that too many "plans" are written from a shower of communication activities that happen to rain some indicators that could be claimed as results. Your plan or proposal should be like a business contract that puts research, clear objectives, and means of measurement up front. I am excited for people just starting a career who have a big opportunity to write plans worthy of respect and high recognition.

Christopher K. Veronda, APR
Director of Corporate Communications (Retired), Eastman Kodak Company
Former Chairman, Honors & Awards Committee and
National Board Member, Public Relations Society of America

About the Authors

Dr. Rebecca A. Gilliland, Distinguished Professor of Service Learning and Associate Professor of Communication at the University of Indianapolis, joined Thomas R. Hagley, Senior Instructor of Public Relations Retired, University of Oregon, to carry on the invaluable instruction and body of knowledge in his book, *Writing Winning Proposals: Public Relations Cases*, from its publication in 2005 and its second edition in 2009, to this third edition. Dr. Gilliland has reviewed, revised, and given a new and updated perspective to what started as a course packet developed from Tom Hagley's instruction sharpened from close attention to student learning in 21 advanced classes in Public Relations Plans and Problems that he taught at the University of Oregon.

This book is the only PR case text with specific instructions for writing winning PR proposals and plans. A unique aspect of the text is that it has been written entirely from a client–employer perspective to show students how to give clients and employers what they want in a plan, the way they want it. Tom Hagley, with his critical analysis from 30 years in practice, has challenged the profession to consider improvements in PR plan writing that would be welcomed by plan reviewers and enhance the reputation of PR practitioners.

In the third edition, Dr. Gilliland, based on her expertise in PR education and pedagogy, complements this perspective by adding details to enable students to translate what they are currently learning in the classroom to the language spoken, and best understood, by clients. Her experience in advising more than 80 client campaigns in a successful student-run PR firm fosters this translation, while preserving the foundation and uniqueness of the previous texts' editions—the client-centered approach that will catapult students to an understanding of industry needs, beyond any other textbook.

Writing Winning Proposals: Public Relations Cases gives instructors and students a broad range of choices of diverse cases to study in online community engagement, media, government relations; employee empowerment, crisis, risk, corporate, emergency service, and social media communication; and sports, arts, green, and celebrity promotional event planning. It is a PR case textbook that motivates students to work in teams and develop PR plans and proposals, knowing that their problem solving is with recurring situations that they are likely to encounter as they enter the profession. This strategy-based approach will begin to cognitively train successful practitioners rather than simply feed them information. Moreover, the authors feel strongly that it is quite possible to teach students the necessary information, yet afford them the opportunity to understand that clients—those who are often not formally trained in public relations—need the same information from a different perspective, so that they may best appreciate the benefits of the practice of public relations, and of PR practitioners.

Rebecca A. Gilliland, EdD, APR

Dr. Rebecca Gilliland, EdD, APR, is the Distinguished Professor of Service Learning and a tenured Associate Professor in the Department of Communication at the University of Indianapolis (UIndy). She has taught courses at UIndy in personal branding, PR principles, PR case studies, writing for public relations, and public speaking. In addition, she advises UIndy's chapter of Public Relations Student Society of America (PRSSA), and the student-run PR firm, Top Dog Communication (TDC).

Rebecca's expertise in the area of service learning and student-run PR firms has produced both national and international recognition. She diligently restructured TDC to foster student learning and to produce positive client outcomes. TDC now works to instruct students through real-world experience as students lead and implement pro bono campaigns for nonprofit organizations in the Indianapolis area and beyond. This work includes visioning and implementing full strategic plans, culminating in tactical completion to bring the respective campaigns to fruition.

To date, TDC has initiated campaigns for more than 80 nonprofit clients. Rebecca's dedication to excellence and her students' passion for success has resulted in numerous awards and recognitions for the program. PRSSA named TDC as the Teahan Outstanding Student-Run Firm of the Year in both 2011 and 2013. TDC has also received numerous Pinnacle Awards from the Hoosier chapter of the Public Relations Society of America (PRSA).

Rebecca has been invited to present at conferences and symposiums across the globe, providing strong foundations and careful elaboration on topics like curriculum development, student-run PR agencies, service learning, and evaluative measures. She has shared her knowledge through instruction as a visiting professor at Pepperdine University in California and Auckland University of Technology (AUT) in New Zealand, and has presented to several PR professional organizations worldwide, including PRSA, the Public Relations Institute of Australia, and the Public Relations Institute of New Zealand. She was named a Plank Scholar and worked for the executive team of Sprint. She is also a Fulbright Specialist, having spent time mentoring faculty, visiting PR firms, and teaching at AUT.

She has held jobs in public relations, journalism, and communication for several companies and organizations, including internationally, and has achieved the status of "Accredited in Public Relations." Rebecca holds a doctorate in higher education with a double cognate in communication studies and public relations, and a MA in communication studies. She completed her BA in psychology with a minor in business administration while also competing as a student athlete.

Thomas R. Hagley Sr.

Thomas R. Hagley is Senior Instructor of Public Relations Retired at the University of Oregon School of Journalism and Communication. He is a recipient of the school's Jonathan Marshall Award for innovative teaching in journalism and communication. Tom joined the Oregon faculty full time in 2001. He taught 51 classes in J350 PR principles, J440 (J351) PR Writing, J453/J553 PR Planning and Problems, J452/J552 Advanced PR Writing, J454/J554 PR Campaigns, and J610 Crisis Communication to an enrollment of more than 1,000 students during a 10-year second career.

Tom has a MS and BS in journalism from Ohio University. He is a member of Kappa Tau Alpha, the college honor society that recognizes academic excellence and promotes scholarship in journalism and mass communication. His work as an educator was preceded by 30 years of progressive professional experience as a general assignment reporter with *The Cleveland Plain Dealer*, as publications editor with Newport News Shipbuilding & Dry Dock Co., as an executive with Alcoa, (Aluminum Company of America), Hill and Knowlton, Inc., his own consulting firm, and Alumax, Inc. Tom is the consummate professional with an extraordinary range of perspectives "from all sides of the desk"—as a client served by worldwide PR agencies; as a worldwide agency executive serving international clients; as a corporate executive managing staffs and annual program budgets of $6.5 million, including title sponsorship of an IndyCar racing team and corporate philanthropic annual contributions of $10 million; as director of public and investor relations throughout the spin-off of a subsidiary from AMAX Inc., to its formation as a public entity, Alumax Inc., during a takeover attempt by Kaiser Aluminum, and ultimately through the acquisition of Alumax Inc. by Alcoa in 1998, which formed, at the time, the world's largest aluminum producer.

He is a master of all forms of PR writing, including PR plans, congressional testimony, and executive speeches; a white paper used by the office of the U.S. Trade Representative as the base document in negotiations which resulted in the resolution of an international trade crisis; and persuasive documents, such as a federal grant proposal totaling $1.25 million awarded to a public school district for before- and after-school programs. Tom is author of articles published in business and professional journals, including seven featured in *The Strategist* magazine published by the Public Relations Society of America.

Preface

This book is about showing you how to excel in public relations. As coauthors, Tom and Rebecca have combined the very best of their backgrounds to coach you in making a successful transition from class to practice in ways that benefit you and the profession.

Consider this: As a PR plan developer, you are in a unique position because so much of what happens in practice begins with a plan or proposal. The quality you write into plans and proposals distinguishes you as a skilled practitioner and enhances the profession's reputation. Making improvements in plan writing is a challenge because routines like writing plans become institutionalized and those involved become resistant to change. But we will show you the way to do it, give you a model, work with you as you learn, and build your confidence to continue on your own.

We will show you that the approach to plan writing is most effective and fun when it's done as a collaboration of knowledge and a meshing of working relationships, much more so than as a competition just to win clients and awards.

What distinguishes this book is that its instruction is presented from the perspective of those who review PR plans and communication proposals and authorize the resources necessary for their implementation. In short, it tells specifically what plan reviewers—typically clients or decision makers in a company or organization—want to see in a plan and how they want the information to be presented.

With this book, you will have the opportunity to practice writing plans and proposals to solve problems, seize opportunities, and meet challenges in diverse, real world cases. The cases are representative of what you can expect to be working on when you step into practice.

Use of the cases as teaching resources has been classroom tested to be effective in more than 20 university-level PR plan writing classes.

Something in your interest brought you to this book. Hopefully, you find its worth in showing you how to develop plans with a potential for success.

How to Use This Book

This book is organized into four sections. The first one provides an introduction to public relations planning.

The second section focuses on writing PR plans and proposals. The third section provides new fundamentals and rules for writing PR plans and proposals that can exceed the profession's ability to win clients and employer approvals. It gives a clear picture of the profession's dire need for better plan and proposal writing and how to give clients and employers what they want in plans, the way they want it.

The fourth section presents 20 cases needing, but not providing, solutions. Each case includes learning outcomes as a guide in studying the case and planning solutions. As in the real world, solutions are up to you as a PR plan developer. Each case includes writing assignments for what might be included as tactics in a plan, such as a press statement or talking points. Many cases include a role play in which class colleagues can read from a script and together act out a key part of a case.

A class can take on a single case in four- or five-member teams with the task of developing plans and having each team member choose a different writing assignment following the case. Or teams can take on different cases, depending on the length of the term, depth of assignments, and administrative capabilities.

Teams can present the cases in class, and even in team competition for the best written plan. The cases are real, but the identities of people, companies, and organizations have been obscured to provide the unvarnished truth in all situations.

This book, with its uniquely diverse content, has application by instructors as a resource throughout an entire PR course sequence. For example, for an introduction to PR course, case examples can give students an insightful view of real situations that challenge PR practitioners as they enter the profession. For a PR writing course, the text provides more than 80 writing assignments related to actual case situations. For a PR plans course, the text provides the ultimate instruction with rules for writing the components of a plan. The text gives students opportunities to organize and function in teams, to divide work, to write and present plans that give employers and clients what they want, the way they want it. For PR campaigns courses, the text gives teams guidance in writing plans with the potential to delight actual clients and win awards. Overall, the text is a timeless, invaluable, desk reference for public relations practitioners.

I: Introduction to Public Relations Planning

1. Importance of Planning

Why is it important to learn how to write public relations proposals or plans? Here are three reasons:

One reason is that a plan is the instrument used to propose and obtain approval for executing PR activities. Executive managers who have responsibility for allocating an organization's resources require various methods, such as a traditional business Request for Authorization, that provide a basis for evaluating expenditures. In similar fashion, a PR plan serves as a proposal to spend a certain amount of an organization's time and money on PR activities. The 10 components of a plan provide the information necessary for managers to evaluate proposed PR activities and approve their execution.

Another reason it is important to learn how to write a PR plan is that a plan provides a mechanism for measuring results of PR activities. A good plan provides objectives with measurable outcomes. This provides plan reviewers with evidence that a plan is making progress toward achieving the plan's goal. It also provides a sound basis for evaluating the results of a plan and educating reviewers about the power of public relations.

Another reason it is important to learn how to write a PR plan is that a plan is a product, the quality of which can distinguish its developer as a star among practitioners of all levels of experience. This is because the quality of PR plans throughout the industry leaves so much room for improvement that well-conceived plans easily take on a brilliance that wins approvals and adds credibility to the profession.

Communication professionals who serve as judges for the industry's most prestigious award competition, the Silver Anvil, sponsored each year by the Public Relations Society of America, review hundreds of PR plan entries. Judges are outspoken in saying that many industry professionals need to go back and learn the basics of developing successful PR plans. The criticism is leveled at all but the few plans selected for recognition.

It is important to learn how to write a PR plan because a plan is the instrument used to propose and obtain approvals, it is a mechanism for

monitoring and evaluating, and it is a product that distinguishes true PR professionals.

To fully appreciate how planning relates to public relations, it is necessary to know precisely what public relations is and what can be expected of its practice. There are hundreds of definitions of public relations, some short, most beyond conversational. You will want to settle on one or create your own—one that is memorable and fits comfortably into a conversation.

Challenge yourself to define public relations in two words. Other professions define themselves in two words—doctors practice medicine, lawyers practice law, accountants keep records. People in these disciplines define their work in two words, issue invoices, and get paid accordingly for their expertise.

Not everyone in public relations can receive compensation so readily for their work because many people—yes, many people—in public relations cannot define what they do. And if you can't define what you do, you can't measure what you do. If you can't measure what you do, you can't evaluate what you do. If you can't evaluate what you do, no one will pay for what you do.

To arrive at a two-word definition of public relations, make a list of PR projects and programs and you will see that they were designed to convince people to support, to vote, to consider, to learn, to champion, to follow, to testify, to read, to buy, to trust, to invest, to listen, to become informed, to join, to leave alone, to contribute, to believe, to participate, to think, to work, to authorize, to accept, to welcome, to compromise, to accommodate, to cooperate, to wait, to attend, to decide, and the list will go on and on and on. The common denominator, the two-word definition, becomes perfectly clear. That is, in public relations, we influence behavior. Whose behavior do we influence? The answer for a public corporation, for a private company, and for a nonprofit organization is the same. We influence the behavior of anyone who has or could have an effect—positive or negative—on the organization's ultimate performance and well-being.

That would include, as examples, employees, suppliers, customers, shareholders, industry and financial analysts, labor unions, voters, government regulators, media, special interest groups, and many more.

Is that ethical? Of course it's ethical. The ethical principles applied to public relations are no different than those applied to any other profession. Is it ethical to persuade someone to replace a heart, a tooth, a roof, or a brake cylinder? Certainly it's ethical if something does, in fact, need to be replaced.

How do we influence behavior? We influence behavior through strategic planning and communication. And therein lies the "magic of the profession" that few PR practitioners possess and for which fewer still get proper recognition.

True expertise in strategic planning and communication is the work of masters. That's why you can call it the "magic of the profession." Strategic communication requires knowledge, skills and problem-solving experience in the dynamics of persuasion, human interaction, and communication design.

In public relations, we influence behavior through strategic planning and communication. We define strategic communication as having five characteristics:

1. Skillfully planned and managed
2. Transmission and receipt of information
3. Authoritative
4. Targeted at individuals or groups
5. Specifically designed to influence behavior

How do we evaluate the effectiveness of our strategic planning and communication? The answer, simply: Did we influence behavior or not?

Public relations can be defined as the practice of influencing behavior through strategic planning and communication. Planning is the central function in this process.

2. Understanding the Planning Process

Consider that public relations is the practice of influencing behavior and that planning is the method by which behavior is to be influenced. A plan focuses on a problem, challenge, or opportunity that would significantly benefit its sponsoring individual or organization. The subject of a plan could be the result of an organization's initiative or could arise as a result of circumstances beyond the organization's control. In either case, a plan is required to deal with the subject and derive benefits for its sponsor.

Planning begins with gathering information: first, to understand the problem, challenge, or opportunity; second, to develop ways to accomplish the plan's goal, and third, to track and measure effectiveness in achieving the plan's goal. Planning efforts are likely to fail if the task is approached single-handedly, because effective planning requires a range of knowledge, and information gathering requires gaining the cooperation of many different sources.

One source of information, of course, is yourself, the PR plan developer—and the knowledge you have acquired from study and experience. Depending on the subject of your plan, you also will look within your organization to draw on the knowledge skills and backgrounds of other individuals. They can provide onsite, in-house expertise in law, marketing, product development, finance, sales, human resources, engineering, technology, and other professional disciplines.

You will look to information sources outside your organization, such as industry trade associations, government agencies, nongovernment organizations, and professional and service organizations, and you will tap other sources around the globe through the Internet Gaps in information will have to be filled and assumptions validated through informal (qualitative) or formal (quantitative) research that you recommend in the plan or conduct for development of a plan.

The information you gather must be assessed and funneled into development of the plan's situation analysis. From the analysis you should be able to (a) write a statement summarizing the problem, challenge, or opportunity; (b) establish a goal with compelling reasons for taking PR actions to achieve it; (c) decide what must be done to accomplish the goal, which is the role of objectives; (d) determine the primary focus or target audiences of the plan—people whose behaviors must be influenced to accomplish the plan's objectives; and (e) develop strategies with detailed activities to show how the plan's objectives are to be achieved.

The process of strategically influencing the behavior of individuals or groups of individuals must take into account all dimensions of communication. The process requires careful development of what is to be communicated, selection of channels through which messages are to be conveyed, consideration for how the communication might become obstructed and/or filtered, and regard for how messages will be received by the intended audience, depending on its disposition toward the message and its source.

A plan developer must decide how much of this process can be based on professional experience and intuition and how much should be based on formal or informal research. Another important part of the planning process is providing methods of evaluation for tracking and gauging a plan's implementation, such as use of a regular Progress Tracking Report.

The planning process includes development of a timeline that provides an at-a-glance view of major preparatory steps, deadlines, and milestones leading to achievement of the plan's goal. Finally, a plan provides an estimated budget for its implementation.

The process is complex, but it is an exciting challenge for people who enjoy problem solving, gathering information, investigating, researching, interviewing sources, applying lessons in human behavior, and orchestrating it all into a plan.

Table 1. Planning Process

Introductory Statement Problem ~ Opportunity ~ Challenge		
Situation Analysis		
Goal		
Target Audience	Target Audience	Target Audience
Objective(s)	Objective(s)	Objective(s)
Strategies	Strategies	Strategies
Activities (or Tactics)	Activities (or Tactics)	Activities (or Tactics)
Evaluation	Evaluation	Evaluation
Progress Tracking Report		
Execution Timeline		
Budget		

3. Grasping the Challenges of the Planning Environment

Public relations plans are developed in many different environments—publicly owned and privately owned companies, government and nongovernment organizations, and nonprofit and various other entities. These environments have characteristics that can have a bearing on how plans are developed; whether plans are approved, modified, or rejected; and even whether plans succeed or fail. So planning cannot be done in a vacuum. Planners must take into account the characteristics of their respective organizations, which will enable them to understand how to meet the challenges of the planning environment.

Let's take a look at major challenges of the planning environment relative to an organization, to leadership, to resources and to the expertise of the PR plan developer.

Organization

A publicly owned corporation, for example, can be mission driven or financially driven. Organizations, of course, can and do fall somewhere between these aims, but for our purposes we will look at these as points on opposite ends of the spectrum.

In a mission-driven organization, employees are considered the key to success. When employees are motivated by meaningful work, they invest more than their time in an organization. They work with a purpose that captures their interest and taps their creativity as they reach out to customers with innovative solutions and extraordinary service. By building relationships with customers, an organization grows in sales, profit, market share, and, ultimately, in overall value to its shareholders. In a mission-driven organization, management is interested in investing in PR plans that

- motivate and empower employees to provide innovative, superior service to customers;

- win the loyalty of suppliers;

- build long-term working relationships with all stakeholders; and

- strengthen the bottom line in terms of economic performance, social investment, community involvement, ethical performance, and environment values.

In a mission-driven organization, a plan developer is in competition for resources with other areas, such as operations, marketing, sales, customer service, and research and development. The allocation of resources is evaluated in terms of the organization's mission, rather than short-term financial goals. Management reviews plans for their potential to benefit all stakeholders. The focus is on investing for the longer term.

In a financially driven organization, management tends to take employees for granted and simply goes through the motions of showing respect for other stakeholders. The serious interest is in impressing securities analysts and shareholders with short-term performance improvements—quarterly profits. The focus on profits can be so intense that management will do whatever it takes—acquire this, sell that, lay people off, cut back, borrow more—to obtain an attractive stock price.

Developing a PR plan in a financially driven organization can be a challenge because management in many cases will be inclined to resist plans that

- don't yield an immediate, virtually guaranteed return;

- propose costly benchmarking or other investigative and evaluative research measures;

- require an investment in the long term for building relationships with any of the organization's stakeholders;

- have strategies requiring consistent values, such as telling the whole truth internally and externally and not spooning it out according to the differing tastes of stakeholder groups; or

- offer effective solutions but require added costs of using outside services, such as photographers, graphic designers, multimedia studios, and PR firms.

Leadership

Let's look next at the challenges of the planning environment in the area of leadership. Approval of PR plans is, in large part, under the control of executives who have no academic education in public relations. This paradox deserves a deeper look.

Next to the ability to manage people and budgets, PR skill is the most sought-after attribute in top executives by today's corporations, according to private research by a worldwide human resources organization. Yet few executives have any formal education in public relations and slow progress is being made to equip future business leaders with these critical skills.

Business schools develop leaders for businesses that operate throughout the world. What these leaders are taught has an influence on the daily lives of millions of people—an enormous responsibility that business schools try to address but typically only with the traditional focus on finance, accounting, and marketing.

Examine the dramatic transformation taking place in the role of chief executive officer and one can easily surmise that market demand for formal PR training should be heading toward academe like a high-speed train. Executive leadership today is about building and maintaining trusting relationships with employees, customers, suppliers, investors, analysts, board members, and all major stakeholder groups. It's about influencing the behavior of people through persuasive, strategic communication. It's about showing empathy for others. In sum, it's about public relations. In recessionary times, especially, building relationships with compassion and open, candid communication is imperative for today's business leaders. These core values are critical to corporate America's struggle through traumatic upheavals marked by acquisitions, mergers, downsizings, and restructurings that are leaving employees with feelings of instability, insecurity, and uncertainty about their work and personal lives. More business schools are going to have to expand functional areas with formal PR training.

Meanwhile, living up to public expectations of good corporate behavior remains a continuing challenge for corporation after corporation. The problem sometimes is the character of the CEO. It has been said that CEOs are hired for their skills and fired for their personalities. Sometimes the problem is the CEO who has no formal PR training.

For example, in 1989, millions of gallons of oil spilled from the ill-fated Valdez oil tanker into pristine Prince William Sound. The corporate giant, Exxon, was at fault. At the time, it was the third largest corporation in sales in the world. This oil spill is still considered one of the most, if not the most, devastating environmental disasters caused by humans of all time. As many as 250,000 seabirds, more than 2,000 sea otters, and hundreds of other animals, including bald eagles and orcas, died. The chairman of Exxon at the time, Lawrence Rawl, said jokingly, "We would have liked to recall the oil off Prince William Sound. We called, but it didn't hear us." Exxon, in its corporate arrogance, later brought the Valdez back to Alaska to operate, which served to rekindle memories of great loss and destruction.

Public relations textbooks always have a supply of updated cases of corporate leaders failing to live up to public expectations of trust, compassion, and good citizenship.

For example, Boeing CEO Jim McNerney apologized in a company-wide message for telling analysts that he won't retire after turning 65 because "the heart will still be beating, the employees will still be cowering."

During an event focused on women in technology, Microsoft CEO Satya Nadella blundered into saying women shouldn't ask for raises but rather trust that the system will take care of them.

Martin Shkreli, a hedge fund manager-turned-pharmaceutical CEO raised the price of the antiparasite medication Daraprim from $13.50 a pill to $750 because his company "need[ed] to turn a profit on the drug." This particular drug is named by the World Health Organization as "essential medicine" and is used for life-threatening diseases.

Volkswagen CEO Martin Winterkorn said, "I am endlessly sorry ..." about VW installing elaborate software in 482,000 "clean diesel" vehicles sold in the United States, so that the cars' pollution controls only worked when being tested for emissions. The rest of the time, the vehicles could freely spew hazardous, smog-forming compounds.

Let's consider what can happen, practically speaking, when a CEO has to manage a crisis situation. Without formal training in public relations, a CEO has no basis on which to make self-confident decisions and instead must rely heavily on the advice of others.

In a crisis situation, a CEO often turns to corporate counsel for legal advice. However, some attorneys can be so intimidating about liability issues that they paralyze a CEO into a state of inaction. With solid PR training to balance legal counsel, a CEO might, as one did, say in a crisis situation: "I've been advised by our law department that the company is not responsible, but we are going to act as though we are."

Or a CEO could hire a PR firm with a track record in successful crisis management, but the CEO without PR training could be putting the fate of an entire enterprise into the hands of experts the CEO has little or no skills to evaluate or direct.

Or a CEO could turn to what Warren Buffett calls the "institutional imperative," or the tendency of executives, he says, "... to mindlessly imitate the behavior of their peers, no matter how foolish it may be to do so."

We will continue to see major corporations failing to live up to public expectations of corporate citizenship until the top jobs are filled with executives who have the formal training necessary to feel self-confident in directing the PR function, building trusting relationships through good communication, and leading with compassion.

Developers of PR plans will continue to be challenged to educate senior executives in the practice of public relations. We know that the profession operates on a body of knowledge in the social sciences that has been developed over many years. We practitioners know how to put that experience to work in all areas of public relations. Many executives have yet to learn even the fundamentals of influencing behavior.

Some plan developers are fortunate to have chief executives who are better educated in public relations and the body of knowledge that supports its practice. These enlightened executives enjoy working with plan developers. A plan developer can show a CEO, for example, that by understanding and participating in the creative process, the chief executive can have visions that trigger in all stakeholder groups the conviction to act in support of an organization's mission.

In a *Business Week* article from early 2003, Jeffrey E. Garten, dean of the Yale School of Management, wrote this timeless advice: "Industry can't climb out of its funk just by cutting costs and meeting quarterly goals. CEOs must bet on their vision." Betting on a vision is a risk that many CEOs are hesitant to take. Some prefer to play it safe, managing costs and fine-tuning strategies. Some prefer to mark time, waiting for economic circumstances to improve. Some have promising visions, but lack confidence in their ability to carry them out.

Launching a vision is like launching a ship. If you don't know how to score the champagne bottle so it will break against the ship's hull at the christening ceremony, the result could be an embarrassing clunk, instead of a spectacular splash. In other words, if you don't know how to launch a vision, you could end up with an embarrassing disappointment rather than a shower of accolades.

Let's consider what it is like to launch a vision with a leader who understands the principles of influencing behavior. First, the leader holds someone accountable for developing the vision. The person held responsible is usually a professional communicator, such as the plan developer. Some executives believe that planting a seed with an individual is the same as assigning an individual to the seed's development. It's a safe position for the executive who doesn't want to take the risk of sharing an idea and possibly being challenged, debated, or criticized about its potential or validity. But there's a big difference between sowing a seed and holding someone accountable for the seed's growth and development. Without a process for development and accountability for driving it, a vision will be no more than a pipedream.

There is no inherent certainty that what a leader has in mind as a vision, especially in its embryonic state, is clearly right for the organization. Executives must have the courage to engage in constructive debate. Open, on-going dialogue with others serves to clarify and perfect a vision. A plan developer shows a leader how to share a vision with others, perhaps in a small brainstorming group or among confidants. The developer knows visionary ideas are fragile. They're not complete. They're not perfect.

A plan developer knows how to shepherd delicate ideas through the creative process, and how to pursue all of the pathways of human engineering necessary to energize the interest and action of individuals who have a potential stake in the organization's success. A plan developer is quick to point out that a vision is not a directive. It's not a figment of someone's imagination. It must be an achievable condition, an irresistible state of being with the power to turn belief in an idea into a conviction to act on its behalf.

An enlightened leader will work closely with a plan developer, knowing that conveying an idea is difficult and requires a variety of professional communication skills. A leader can turn to a plan developer for the draft of a vision the same way the executive turns to a writer to request a draft of a speech.

The leader and plan developer know the aim of a vision shouldn't be to shoot for the moon. Its aim should be to orchestrate readily available resources to achieve results that move an organization to a higher level of innovation, competitive strength, market position, and profitability. An experienced PR plan developer has the position and skills to move freely throughout an organization to expose an idea to a broad spectrum of expertise in sales, marketing, law, finance, and research and development, and to meld ideas into a vision with universal appeal.

The leader and plan developer know that a vision must contain appeals to all stakeholders—employees, existing and potential investors, industry analysts, bankers, journalists. Enlightened executives know that to have the power to trigger convictions to act, a vision must have ownership by all of its stakeholders. It is not a one-sided opportunity. It must be a multifaceted, irresistible opportunity for stakeholders within and outside the organization. No one in an organization has a better grasp of the diverse views of stakeholder groups than an organization's experienced PR professional. Research is a cornerstone of the profession and PR professionals who perform the function in developing annual reports, establishing websites, preparing news announcements, and drafting speeches, position papers, and other forms of corporate communication are well equipped with the skills to research and develop the basis for a vision.

An astute leader knows that once crafted, a vision must be delivered, but not by a "town crier." It's not an edict. It's a vision. It's the seed of an idea. It needs time to unleash its power in the imaginations of people it captivates. It needs time to be considered, studied, and evaluated.

As a vision is pursued by the chief executive and plan developer and evidence of its potential develops and is shared with its stakeholders, a vision gains validity. It is assimilated and communicated with personal conviction by its stakeholders. Results of the vision continue to validate its potential and trigger in the minds of its stakeholders the conviction to act in support of the vision. As the process unfolds, it energizes employees to produce, customers to buy, investors to invest, bankers to lend, analysts to recommend, journalists to write, and suppliers to support.

For PR plan developers who are fortunate to have chief executives who are enlightened and willing to explore what can be accomplished by leveraging the credibility of public relations in a vision, the challenge to planning can be an exciting experience.

Resources

Let's look next at the challenges of the planning environment in the area of resources. The plan developer might have a choice of using resources within the organization or outsourcing work to various service firms. Or the plan developer might have to rely entirely on the organization's resources. The advantages of using the organization's resources are that

- people involved have a vested interest in the organization's mission and are likely to have a better understanding and a personal commitment to contributing to its success;

- control of the plan is internal among the people involved with its implementation; and

- expenses are minimized by enlisting the involvement of existing personnel and obtaining support from existing budgets.

The planning challenge increases when the plan developer must outsource work. A plan developer might not have a choice other than to outsource work to a firm already retained by the organization. Whether the developer must use a designated source or select a source, careful management of the source's performance is essential. To illustrate, let's consider what is involved in managing the outsourcing of work to a PR firm.

Generally speaking, PR firms are service driven. However, some PR firms are cost driven. Unless one is prepared to lose one's shirt, it's best to select a service-driven firm.

By selecting a service-driven firm, a plan developer is far more likely to develop and execute a winning plan.

So how might one distinguish a service-driven from a cost-driven PR firm?

Use of time is a major distinguishing factor. A service-driven firm uses time to provide service. A cost-driven firm uses time to cover costs at the expense of client service. Firms become cost driven when the cost of operating—office rent, vehicle and electronic equipment leases, salaries, and other overhead—is so high that meeting those expenses drives the business.

A service-driven firm provides a plan developer with an experienced account representative. A cost-driven firm provides an experienced account representative, initially, then might switch to a less experienced representative, but at the same high billable rate.

A service-driven firm provides a plan developer with the full depth of the firm's expertise. A cost-driven firm limits client service to the experience of the account representative, allowing others in the firm to concentrate on more lucrative business.

A service-driven firm provides a plan developer with high-quality resources for graphic design, photography, video production, and whatever else is needed. A cost-driven firm attempts to use its own, often mediocre resources to keep profits in house.

A service-driven firm drives the plan developer's assignment to completion. A cost-driven firm is less responsive, causing the client to do the account representative's work of staying on schedule and on budget, enabling the account representative, instead, to handle more accounts.

A service-driven firm is willing to tailor its services to a plan developer's own performance criteria. A cost-driven firm insists on its own way of providing service and resists client attempts to manage and evaluate the firm's performance.

A service-driven firm knows how to serve as an extension of a plan developer's staff. A cost-driven firm keeps its independence and functions to its own advantage.

A service-driven firm keeps working until the work meets the plan developer's expectations. A cost-driven firm is in a hurry to collect its fee. It offers excuses for substandard work and sometimes tries to get the client to accept and pay for the PR firm's mistakes, inability to follow directions, poor writing, careless editing, and other unprofessional practices.

To manage a plan that will involve the services of an outside firm, a plan developer must understand the challenges involved in outsourcing and directing various forms of services.

A plan cannot be developed or implemented in a vacuum. The environment in which a plan is developed can present substantial challenges in the areas of organization, leadership, resources, and plan developer expertise.

The Plan Developer

There is one more factor to consider—the PR plan developer. Acceptance of plans that you propose will depend, in large part, on plan reviewers' confidence in your ability to deliver what you propose. Such confidence comes from how reviewers see you as a PR practitioner. So let's consider the matter of professional image.

The traditional characterization of PR professionals suggests that practitioners fall somewhere on a continuum ranging from lower-paid technicians to higher-paid consultants and that the ultimate career position is having the stature necessary to gain acceptance by the leadership of an organization. This characterization suggests that practitioners have a choice to make between being a technician or a consultant, and that if an individual chooses to be a technician, such as a newsletter editor, the individual will not have the esteem of a consultant in the eyes of senior executives.

Here's a different view. Some of the most effective practitioners use unique combinations of technical skills and consulting talents. Practitioners, through their academic training and education and professional experience, develop a professional capability comprising both technical and consulting skills. These practitioners have the ability to confer on situations, from simple to complex, and recommend ways to influence people—even millions of people—to behave one way or another in response to meaningful communication activities. They have the consulting skills to recommend communication strategies and, in addition, all of the technical skills to use communication tools, such as a news announcement, guide it through the review process, reconcile reviewers' differences, disseminate the announcement worldwide, and handle resulting inquiries from reporters, providing more information and/or effectively correcting erroneous reporting errors. A skilled practitioner has the consulting skills to recommend strategic use of online media and the technical know-how to create projects in the cyberworld.

The combination of consulting and technical skills is a great strength. However, young practitioners need to be conscious of the image they project—someone who scurries around with a pencil behind one ear, clutching a clipboard, and dangling a camera from a neck strap is going to have a difficult time being regarded as a counselor rather than a technician. So if you don't want to be seen as a mechanic, don't carry a big wrench.

Young practitioners entering the profession should take delight in acquiring a combination of technical and consulting skills, and enjoy developing that unique professional capability to the fullest extent possible.

4. Writing with Integrity

A student at the University of Oregon was asked in a job interview to identify weaknesses in the PR profession. Unable to think of any off hand, she turned to the interviewer who admitted that she couldn't think of any either. Understandably, we don't dwell on our weaknesses. However, public relations, as an evolving profession, does have vulnerabilities. Practitioners, and particularly plan developers, have a responsibility to be aware of them and to help ensure that public relations continues to grow in practice and in character.

What can we do as plan developers to strengthen the profession? One thing we can do is market and deliver what we do best. We are strategic communicators. A review of Silver Anvil winners in the category of PR tactics showcases the tremendous talent we have in communication.

Public relations is not clearly defined—it has hundreds of definitions, so expectations of results can be wide ranging. It is better to market our core competencies in communication than to promise more than we can deliver. The temptation exists to pursue hot markets with loosely formed but firmly hyped expertise, such as reputation integration, awareness leveraging, brand amplification, content control, blogger outreach, social media management, influencer marketing, and digital market penetration. This tendency oftentimes sets up great expectations among clients, only to be dashed by disappointing results and invoices that make boards of directors resistant to return to the profession for services.

Another thing we can do is bring PR planning into sharper focus, as we strive to do in the classroom and in this book. Because there is limited textbook instruction in developing PR plans, practitioners have almost as many different definitions of goals, objectives, strategies, and activities as there are for defining the profession itself. A PR plan that puts its audience into a state of glazed-over confusion over terms and form brings great injury to the profession's reputation.

Public relations is not an exact science, so we cannot guarantee the outcomes of plans. We can, however, show how we draw on bodies of knowledge in the social sciences and methodically and strategically formulate plans to increase our effectiveness in achieving objectives.

We can also strengthen the profession by ensuring that our practice of public relations is always service driven. Examples exist of PR firms whose overhead costs for expensive office space, furniture, office equipment, and leased cars—instead of quality service—drive the practice, demanding more and more billable hours any way a firm can get them. There are examples of individual practitioners whose work is driven by personal ambitions at any cost, rather than by a genuine desire to provide quality service. These reflections are amplified by popular media, making a true understanding and appreciation of the practice of public relations even more difficult. The profession's reputation cannot afford further missteps, any more than today's corporations can afford their respective tarnishing due to the liberties many have taken with accounting practices.

Being rock solid in upholding the principles of the profession, as enumerated in the Public Relations Society of America's Code of Ethics, is especially important at a time when public relations is heavily engaged in counseling others about reputation management. Public relations has yet to be fully accepted as a true profession. There are no standardized educational requirements. There is no mandatory licensing or certification. There is no effective self-regulation.

When we market our core competencies in strategic communication, when we bring PR planning into sharper focus, when we ensure that our practice of public relations is service driven, we are leading with integrity. We are demonstrating a passion for principles that command respect and develop mutual trust. By leading and writing with integrity, we enable the profession to grow in practice and in stature.

5. Writing with Accountability

It is easy to get caught up in the excitement of developing a PR plan, especially if you believe its creative elements will delight or impress reviewers. However, telling reviewers that a plan is cool, awesome, fleek (excellent) or G.O.A.T. (Greatest Of All Time), could be a serious miscalculation on the part of a PR plan presenter. That's because a plan, regardless of its degree of creativity, must be backed by accountability for cost, completeness, effectiveness, and measurability.

To feel what it's like being held accountable by a plan reviewer, read the following conversation between a PR plan developer and a potential client.

Potential Client: *Let's cut to the chase. Why should I spend money on public relations?*

PR Plan Developer: *Public relations gives you the ability to influence human behavior.*

Potential Client: *What does that mean?*

PR Plan Developer: *It means that public relations can help you motivate people to support, to vote, to consider, to champion, to follow, to read, to buy, to trust, to invest, to listen, to join, to leave alone, to contribute, to believe, to work, to authorize, to accept, to welcome, to compromise, to accommodate, to cooperate, to wait, to decide, and I can go on and on, as you can see.*

Potential Client: *How does it do that?*

PR Plan Developer: *Public relations influences the behavior of people through persuasion.*

Potential Client: *So public relations uses devious means to manipulate people?*

PR Plan Developer: *There are two sides to everything people do—good and bad. Public relations influences behavior honestly and ethically through strategic communication.*

Potential Client: *How does this work?*

PR Plan Developer: *PR plans, one can say, mirror the process of persuasion. Public relations sets objectives to accomplish a goal. It taps into the field of persuasion to design actions to influence an individual, group, or organization toward achieving a goal.*

Potential Client: *Be more specific.*

PR Plan Developer: *Specifically, here's an example of persuasion. Let's say a person, like a stockbroker, takes an action (recommends a stock selection) to a target (potential investor), designed to cause a particular behavior (recommendation accepted).*

An objective in a PR plan is similar to the persuasion process just described, in that it has three parts: (1) an action to be taken; (2) a target, or receiver of the action; and (3) a behavior desired of the target as a result of the action taken.

Potential Client: *Give me an example.*

PR Plan Developer: *Here's an example of a PR objective:*

Action	Inform about skyrocketing cost of medical insurance
Target	Employees
Desired behavior	Willingness of employees to accept an increased share of the cost
Objective	To inform employees of the company's skyrocketing cost of medical insurance so they are willing to share part of the employer's increased cost.

Potential Client: *How do you assess results?*

PR Plan Developer: *Results can be assessed on the basis of performance and effectiveness. Was the PR plan carried out completely, accurately, on schedule, and on budget? What was the outcome of the PR plan: (1) attempts to influence failed; (2) influence attempts got attention; (3) influence attempts got the behavior desired.*

Potential Client: *Are all PR people trained in persuasion?*

PR Plan Developer: *That's a good question to ask when you interview job candidates and PR firms. Many PR people have a good background in persuasion derived from a broad liberal arts foundation in history, psychology, sociology, geography, language, ethics, and philosophy, as well as many of the sciences. In acquiring this valuable knowledge, they have learned to think and read critically, collect and organize facts, and analyze them and form ideas. They have the ability to analyze a situation, the cultures involved, the mindsets of opposing factions, and similar past lessons learned. They also draw upon the profession's body of knowledge of actual experiences. Public relations is the practice of influencing behavior through strategic communication and is a profession that holds itself accountable for cost, completeness, effectiveness, and measurability.*

Put Yourself in the Place of a Plan Reviewer

Plan developers must be aware of the many considerations plan reviewers must take into account when considering plans, for example, "How do I justify this plan in terms of cost, benefits, and need?" In other words, "Will the benefits I expect to derive from the plan be worth the time, money, and energy that has to be put into the plan to accomplish its goal?"

A question of equal importance: "How does the need for this plan rank among all of the other pressing needs of the organization?" A PR plan could require $5,000 to well over $500,000 to develop and implement. A request for such an expenditure, assuming that it is an expense over a current budget, must compete on its merits with all other special requests for authorizations for funds within an organization. That's why a plan's cost and benefits must be made absolutely clear to a reviewer.

With regard to cost, a plan also must be affordable to the organization receiving the proposal. That's not to suggest cutting corners or lowering standards to suit an organization. If a PR action can't be done right it shouldn't be attempted. Fortunately, in public relations, there are many different ways to accomplish communication objectives cost effectively. So a plan must establish a clear need for PR action and must propose a cost-effective orchestration of communication activities that is within the sponsoring organization's budget.

A plan reviewer also could be expected to ask, "What's the basis for your justification of this plan?" With this question, the reviewer is holding the plan developer accountable for completeness. The reviewer wants to see that the plan developer has all of the information necessary for the reviewer to make a thorough assessment of the plan in order to decide whether or not to approve it. That means the plan developer must be diligent in writing each component of the PR plan: (1) problem challenge or opportunity statement, (2) situation analysis, (3) target audiences, (4) goal, (5) objectives, (6) strategies, (7) activities, (8) time line, (9) evaluation, and (10) budget. As you develop a plan, ask yourself if you are presenting all the information a reviewer would require in each area of the plan to enable the reviewer to make an assessment and reach for a pen to approve your plan.

A reviewer also could be expected to ask, "How do you know this plan will be effective?" Most plan reviewers have no formal education in public relations and will be looking for assurances that what is proposed in the plan is what will be necessary to obtain some reasonable measure of success in achieving the plan's goal. It is incumbent on the plan developer to educate the reviewer in knowing that PR plans are based on proven principles of communication and persuasion and on the body of knowledge in the social sciences that has been acquired by the profession over several decades.

Another important way to assure effectiveness is with research. The use of research, despite its immense value, has yet to become fully utilized in the profession. The term *research*, by its own definition—connoting formal, costly, time-consuming study, documented investigation, and examination of a condition existing in one past moment or period of time—retards its use. Heads of organizations who have ultimate control of PR spending have historically resisted spending money on research. With new technologies, however, research is becoming much more affordable and timely.

Measuring effectiveness doesn't always require formal research. The fact is, there are many forms of research that are not costly or time consuming. In the broadest terms, everyone conducts research. We all gather information to find solutions to problems. It is an important function in our daily lives and not as a formal process. Research is vitally important in the development of plans and should not be summarily dismissed.

A plan reviewer could be expected to ask, "What indications will you have to show that your PR plan is, in fact, proceeding effectively toward accomplishing its goal?" With this question, the reviewer is holding the plan developer accountable for measurement. Assuming the plan is being implemented, how can its effectiveness be measured? The answer should be that the plan's objectives—all of them—are measurable. Every one of a plan's objectives should be written to include a desired behavioral outcome that can be measured in qualitative or quantitative terms.

6. Writing with Clarity

As a PR plan developer, you are at the center of action. Developing a plan requires you to communicate clearly and concisely in many forms with a full range of people of varying backgrounds at different levels of expertise. You cannot develop an effective plan off the top of your head sitting in a coffee shop. You must seek out information sources and have the gumption of a researcher, and you must be a good writer.

There's no need to get tense about this. You have more control over your writing than you might imagine. Let's take a practical approach to these requirements. For example, how often have you said to yourself, "This time, what I write is going to be really good!" How often have you been disappointed that nothing much changed, no matter how hard you tried? That's not a reflection of your ability. The old axiom that practice makes perfect is misleading. No matter how hard you try, practice alone can simply reinforce old habits that keep your writing from improving. So let's look at specific tactics under your control that can make your writing more effective.

There are four elements you can control in preparing a message. Be clear—write in plain talk and use details people can visualize. Be brief—write in simple, declarative statements. Be direct—use active verbs and comfortable words. And yes, by all means be human—write the way people converse. If any of these elements seem contrary to the way people in your organization write, be courageous. Set the standard. That's what an organization expects of PR professionals.

There are four more elements you can control. They will enable your writing to connect with people whether you are writing a situation analysis or requesting data. The beginning of every communication should get directly to what your readers want to know. "What's this about?" Provide the big picture, the broad context for your communication. "Why are you telling me?" Give the purpose of your communication—to inform, alert, announce, and the like. "Why should I care?" Pique their interest; tell what's in it for them. "What's your point?" Explain the thesis—the point—of your communication. Try to answer these questions in the opening of your communication.

There is more in your control to improve your writing. So far, we covered preparing the message and connecting with people. Next we'll look at what you must do to maintain the connection with receivers of your message, as well as reviewers of your plan. First is persona—the level of expertise you bring to the subject. Second is tone—the attitude you convey toward the subject. Third is voice—the personality you project. Fourth is style—the distinct or characteristic way you deliver the message (i.e., length of sentences, use of phrases, etc.).

Once you connect with your readers, you must cause them to think about your communication long enough to influence their behavior, to win acceptance of your plan. Make your plan come alive by conveying the elements of the plan through a story—something motivating, inspirational, a situation that makes them wonder what they would do. Issue a call to action. Make an emotional plea—tug at what they care about. Surprise them—seek action through something people haven't thought about. Fill your plan with valid substance—lots of details, convincing research data.

Tactically speaking, you have just discovered 16 ways under your control to improve your writing. Practice can make perfect, now that you know what to practice.

Table 2. Sixteen Controllable Ways to Improve Your Writing

Preparing Messages

CLEAR—plain talk, using details receivers can visualize
BRIEF—simple, declarative statements
DIRECT—active verbs and comfortable words
HUMAN—like a personal conversation

Connecting with Receivers

PICTURE—the broad context of your communication
PURPOSE—why you are communicating; to inform, alert, announce, etc.
PIQUE—what's in it for the receivers; pique interest
POINT—your main point; the thesis

Maintaining the Connection with Receivers

PERSONA—level of expertise you must bring to the message
TONE—attitude you convey toward the message
VOICE—personality you project
STYLE—distinct or characteristic way the message is delivered

Making Messages Stay Long Enough to Influence Behavior

STORY—motivating, inspirational, what receivers would do, call to action
EMOTIONAL—tug at what receivers care about
SURPRISE—seek action, something people haven't thought about
VALIDITY—details, convincing data, third-party endorsements

Image Credits

II: Writing Public Relations Plans and Proposals

Let's begin our study of writing winning proposals and plans with a whimsical presentation we like to call "The Frog." It is titled, "A Public Relations Plan to Influence the Behavior of a Frog."

The Frog presentation will introduce you to 10 components of a PR proposal or plan, illustrate their functions, and show in basic terms what clients and employers want in plans, and the way they want it. The text is written to enable you to translate what you are currently learning in the classroom into the language spoken, and best understood, by clients. The client-centered approach will catapult you to an on-the-job understanding of industry needs and desires beyond the approaches offered in any other textbook. This strategic-based approach will begin to train your thinking as a practitioner, rather than simply feed you information. Moreover, we feel strongly that it is quite possible to teach you the necessary information, yet afford you the opportunity to understand that clients—those who are often not formally trained in public relations—need the same information in a different and unique way, so that they may best appreciate the benefits of the practice of public relations and of PR practitioners.

So, enjoy the "The Frog." We will rejoin you afterwards and will turn whimsy into reality.

1. The Frog: A Whimsical Story to Introduce Components of a Public Relations Plan

Public relations plans should be easily understood and plausible in the minds of reviewers with the appearance of truth and reason, seemingly worthy of approval or acceptance, seemingly credible and believable. This presentation of a plan to influence the behavior of a frog illustrates what clients and employers want in a plan, the way they want it.

1. Problem

There is a problem. We have a frog that refuses to go back into its pond. The bank around the pond is wet and slippery and the safest time to take action would be in daylight hours. If we wait until after nightfall to get the frog back into the pond, we run the risk of slipping unseen into deep water surrounded by a steep, slippery bank and no place to climb out. This problem calls for public relations—the practice of influencing behavior.

2. Situation Analysis

Our analysis of the situation is that the frog will not respond to instructions. We have tried over and over to tell the frog to jump back into the pond. First we tried a friendly, polite approach: "Would you please jump back into the pond?" Next we tried a firm approach: "We want you to jump back into the pond." Then we became frustrated and started shouting orders: "Get back into the pond!" Based on this failed experience, we could only conclude that the frog is stubborn. Not knowing what else to do, we decided to call on a professional—a PR expert who knows how to influence behavior.

3. Goal

A PR expert accepted our challenge to influence the behavior of the frog. The "goal," she said, "is for the frog to be back in the pond." We said, "Yes, that's what we want."

4. Focus or Target

"To achieve our goal, the focus of our effort must be on the frog," said the PR expert. The frog is our target.

5. Objective

According to the PR expert, an objective tells what must be done to achieve the goal and it must have three parts: (1) an action, (2) a receiver of the action, and (3) a certain behavior by the receiver that is desired as a result of the action taken. So the PR expert says that the objective should be: "To make the frog jump back into the pond before nightfall." The action is to make the frog jump. The receiver or target of the action is the frog. The desired result of the action is for the frog to jump into the pond before nightfall.

6. Strategy

The PR expert explained that we need a strategy because that tells how we will achieve our objective. "Our strategy," she says, "will be to lure the frog back into the pond."

7. Tactic

The PR expert says to fully explain how we are going to carry out our strategy we will add specific tactics or activities. She said, "Our tactic will be to lure the frog with a fly connected by a thread to a twig to lead the frog back into the pond."

8. Timeline

The PR expert said our timeline will include four steps: (1) preparing to connect a fly with a thread to a twig of an appropriate shape and length, (2) approaching the frog strategically, (3) beginning the luring operation before nightfall, and (4) and causing a final leap into the pond.

9. Evaluation

The success of our PR effort to influence the behavior of the frog will be determined by observing the frog back in the pond before nightfall.

10. Budget

A proposed budget for PR services includes an hourly rate for personnel, plus out-of-pocket expenses. The total cost of influencing the behavior of the frog is $745.

Personnel Billing	Billing Rate/Hour	Estimated Hours	Estimated # Days	Amount
Account Executive	110	2	1	220.00
Assistant AE	95	2	1	190.00
Expenses				
Photograph				120.00
Report				200.00
Knife to cut twig				12.00
Spool of thread				3.00
TOTAL				**$745.00**

Next, we will turn whimsy into reality.

2. Developing Better Plans

You have an opportunity to excel in PR proposal and plan writing like a shining star above even experienced plan writers. Let's consider why you have this opportunity, how the opportunity developed, and hard evidence to show dramatically that the opportunity exists for you to be a star in plan writing.

You have this opportunity because you are entering the PR profession with an intellectual curiosity not only to learn, but to see things from different perspectives. People in the profession, from educators to seasoned practitioners, are eager to welcome newcomers and assist them in learning how to succeed and develop rewarding careers. The overwhelming support is nice to have, but requires some sorting out because it comes from different perspectives. In the area of writing proposals and plans there are no specific industry-wide guidelines with regard to form and substance, so the helpful support you receive in plan writing will come from people, each of whom has their own idea about how plans should be written.

This book is written from the view of clients and employers that the profession serves—the people who evaluate and pay for plans. The problem is that these reviewers are receiving plans the way the profession thinks they should get them, not the way they would like to get them. Therein lies your opportunity to excel in plan writing. Give clients and employers what they want in plans, the way they want it. That is the core thesis of this book. That is how you can distinguish yourself as a star in plan writing.

Keep in mind, however, that this does not mean that you will toss aside all of your fundamental knowledge of public relations and strategic processes. You will still use that knowledge and make notes relevant to the planning process for yourself—these should be different notes than those that find their way into any plan that is reviewed by anyone other than a PR expert. By doing this, you are simply being a true PR professional in that you are analyzing your audience and delivering the message as it will best be absorbed, understood, and appreciated by the reviewer. It makes a lot of sense when it's broken down in those terms. However, the concept is quite hard for many to grasp. Looking through, and understanding, this non-PR-trained lens is what will set you apart.

How did this opportunity develop? PR proposals and plans fail in classrooms, competitions, and business because of the profession's complacency and ubiquitous insistence on giving clients and employers PR plans the way the profession thinks they should get them, rather than giving them plans the way plan reviewers would like to get them. The profession ignores the need to define even the basic terms in proposal and plan writing, so a different definition of the components of a plan surfaces every time someone says, "That's not how we write them [goals, objectives, strategies, tactics]." Everyone has their own idea of how the components should be written. Many are adamant about using their definitions of terms, but such myopic insistence often creates confusion in the minds of plan reviewers, who say to plan presenters, "I thought you said this was a strategy," or "So what is the goal?" or "I don't think we have a need for this right now, but thank you for the proposal."

Christopher K. Veronda, APR, former chairman of the PRSA Honors and Awards Committee and national PRSA board member, wrote: "In judging hundreds of Silver Anvil Award entries over the years, I noticed that many lacked quality plans. It was common to find goals confused with objectives and strategies combined with objectives. Plans that suffer such deficiencies don't win, or don't even get implemented."

There is a serious need for the consistent use of clear, easily understood terms, such as goals, objectives, strategies and tactics, in PR proposal and plan writing, a need that is addressed in *Writing Winning Proposals: PR Cases*.

There is hard evidence to see for yourself that the opportunity exists for you to be a star in plan writing. The profession's weakness in plan writing is illustrated in the following study of extracts of goals, objectives, and strategies written by award-winning plan developers. After each extract is a brief analysis and model examples of a goal, objective, and strategy written by rules provided in this text that show what plan reviewers want in a plan, and the way they want it.

Which of the following is a Goal?

1. To obtain from public and private sources, including individuals, $5 million.

   No. This statement tells what must be done to achieve a goal. That is the role of an objective. An objective has (a) an action, (b) target of the action, and (c) desired behavior of the target as a result of the action.

2. To conduct a capital fund drive.

   No. This statement is a strategy; it tells how an objective is to be accomplished.

3. To develop a capital fund drive brochure.

   No. This is an activity or tactic providing details for implementing a strategy.

4. To obtain from public and private sources, including individuals, $5 million by conducting a capital fund drive using a capital fund drive brochure.

   No. This statement combines an objective with a strategy and a tactic or activity.

5. For General Hospital to be serving 25 more patients in a new addition to the main building.

   This is a goal. Congratulations! A goal describes a condition or state of being as though it has been achieved. The goal of a PR proposal or plan has four functions: it provides a vision, a target, verification, and measurement.

Which of the Following is an Objective?

1. Work on many levels of the problem simultaneously to deliver a cannon shot impact that is deep and long lasting.

   No. This is gobbledygook; it is totally meaningless to plan reviewers.

2. Promote each member of Smith's family of digital audio players through individually tailored campaigns to maintain market share of at least 30 percent.

   No. This statement does not begin with the infinitive "to." It has no target audience. "Through individually tailored campaigns" tells how an objective is to be accomplished, which is the role of a strategy. Most importantly, public relations is a staff function and has no control over the many factors necessary to promise a market share of 30 or any percent.

3. Collect $5 million in contributions by conducting a capital fund drive.

   No. This statement does not begin with the infinitive "to." No target audience is specified. The phrase "by conducting a capital fund drive" tells how an objective is to be accomplished, which is the role of a strategy.

4. To fully inform the media about the incident.

   No. To be an objective, this statement must indicate a desired outcome. What does the plan writer want journalists to do as a result of fully informing them? Acceptable: To fully inform the news media about the incident to help ensure that their news reports are complete and accurate.

5. To generate publicity that in the minds of Major League Baseball fans strongly links Box of Snaps with baseball and raises an interest in a new "prize inside" series so that more fans buy Box of Snaps.

   An objective is distinguished by starting it with the infinitive "to" and must contain three parts: (a) an action to be taken, (b) receiver of the action, e.g., target audience or individual, and (c) a behavior that is desired of the target as a result of the action taken. It tells what must be done to achieve the goal. This is an objective. Congratulations!

Which of the Following is a Strategy?

1. The campaign strategy is a simple message for the campaign that could be conveyed through all mediums: "When it comes to keeping your water features clear, count on Barley Bob. Bob is an honest country boy who chews on barley and is spokesperson for the campaign."

   No. A strategy must explain how an objective is to be accomplished. A strategy may contain and explain the use of a particular message or slogan and may include the description of a character to deliver the message. However, this statement falls short of explaining the strategic use of the message and the campaign character.

2. Develop key messages and create benefit-focused materials that set a celebratory tone.

   No. This is gobbledygook; it is totally meaningless to plan reviewers.

3. Invite parents to an informational meeting.

   No. There is nothing strategic about this action. There is not sufficient detail to instill confidence that this strategy will accomplish its objective. There is no attempt to use this opportunity to educate plan reviewers on the techniques of persuasion or communication methods, or to elaborate with a message theme or other details.

4. Arrange a luncheon with journalists from *The Wall Street Journal*, *Fortune*, Dow Jones, Bloomberg, and others. Create mailers highlighting the company's financial capabilities aimed at executives whose companies hold synthetic leases. Produce an acquisitions brochure for distribution to senior-level corporate executives.

No. A strategy should describe how, in concept, an objective is to be accomplished. In other words, it should be explained in broad terms with details left to be covered as activities or tactics. These items are, simply, activities.

5. What we propose is making a public announcement through a news conference because it will be big news to the community, it will be difficult to keep secret, and there is considerable information to impart that will require an open dialogue with the media.

    This is a strategy. Congratulations! Strategies describe how plan objectives are to be achieved. Reviewers want to be able to assess methods proposed for achieving objectives, the rationales behind the proposed methods, the feasibility and practicality of methods, and the practitioner's expertise in implementing strategies.

These extracts from actual plans provide hard evidence of the profession's weakness in plan writing. They illustrate a prevailing illusion that clients will accept whatever the profession writes in a plan. Plan writing is serious business. There's no room for gobbledygook. You can be a star when you study the components of a plan and learn to write them by the rules. Give clients and employers what they want, the way they want it.

3. Ten Components of Public Relations Plans and Proposals

Goals, objectives, and strategies are three of 10 components of a PR plan. Following are descriptions of all 10 components.

1. Introductory Statement

The introductory statement summarizes a problem, challenge, opportunity, or situation which, when addressed with PR activity, will in some significant, measurable way benefit the organization you work for or that you have as a client. It should be headed: Problem, Challenge, Opportunity, or Situation without the words *introductory* or *statement*.

2. Situation Analysis

The situation analysis is more than a report of known facts; it is your analysis of the situation. Present the information you have as you understand it and include recommendations for further investigation (informal or formal research) into areas that you believe require clarification or verification. Write it in a conversational, storytelling style.

3. Goal

A plan should have one goal written in one sentence. It should be distinguished by the use of the infinitive phrase *to be*, responding to the question, What do you want the ultimate condition or state of being to be as a result of having executed the PR plan successfully? Example: For the medical center to be serving 50 additional patients.

4. Focus or Target Audience

The focus of a plan, without exception, should be on people because public relations is the practice of influencing behavior through strategic communication. Practically speaking, a plan could not be implemented without the engagement of people. A plan must focus on influencing the behavior of people to achieve the plan's goal. The focus of a plan could be on one individual, on individuals comprising an organization or segment of an organization, on individuals comprising an audience, or an entire public.

5. Objective

Objectives tell plan reviewers what actions must be taken with subjects of the plan to achieve a plan's goal. More than one objective usually is needed to achieve a goal. There must be one objective for each focal point or target audience of a plan. An objective is distinguished by starting it with the infinitive *to* and must contain three parts: (1) an action to be taken, (2) a receiver of the action (i.e., focal point or target audience), and (3) a behavior that is desired of the receiver as a result of the action taken. Example: To inform employees about the company's skyrocketing costs of medical insurance so that they are willing to accept an increased share of the cost.

6. Strategy

Strategies describe how a plan's objectives will be achieved. Plan reviewers want to be able to assess your methods for achieving objectives, the creativity behind your methods, the feasibility and practicality of your methods, and your knowledge of applying the fundamentals of persuasion in influencing behavior.

7. Activity or Tactic

An activity or tactic is what puts a strategy into action. Activities provide the details of a strategy. Plan reviewers want to assure themselves that they concur with the ways in which strategies are to be carried out. More than one activity is required to implement a strategy.

8. Execution Timeline

The execution timeline is a schedule of all activities in a plan. The timeline provides a visual, at-a-glance sequence of actions showing how long each will take to implement.

9. Evaluation

Public relations plans and proposals should be written to enable evaluation in two ways: performance and effectiveness. Simply: Did the plan implementer do what the plan implementer stated would be done? How effectively was it done?

10. Budget

A proposed budget is developed from one of two positions: One position is that you represent a PR firm or agency and your plan is for a client. The other position is that you are an employee of an organization with responsibility for public relations and your plan is for your employer. You must use a budget format that is appropriate for your position.

Progress Tracking Report

Impress plan reviewers by including a Progress Tracking Report in your plan. An employer or client should not have to ask a plan implementer for the status of a project. The implementer is being paid to manage and report progress. The Progress Tracking Report provides an at-a-glance visual check to show the client or employer that activities of the plan are on schedule, on target, on budget, and completed or not. Once a template is formed, the report can be updated easily and submitted to plan reviewers on paper or electronically as frequently as desired. Offering this report shows an employer or client that the plan implementer is taking the initiative to manage the project openly and meticulously.

Table 3. Progress Tracking Report				
Target Audience	Activity	On schedule On target On budget (green cells)	Behind schedule and/or over budget (red cells)	Completed (blue cells)
Donors	Names	�		
	Rainmakers		▓	
	Brochure	▒		
	Memberships	▒		
Grad Students	Briefings			█
Undergrads	Internships	▒		
	Ambassadors	▒		
	Workshop		▓	
	Longhouse			
Community	Inquiry		▓	
	Response		▓	
	Resolution		▓	
	Event	▒		
	T-shirts	▒		
	Award	▒		
	Ceremony	▒		

	Center/City			
	Honoree			
Faculty & Staff	Ambassador			
	Letter #1			
	Letter #2			
	Website			
Donors	Survey			
	Annual report			

4. Creativity in Plan Writing

Public relations and creativity have certain characteristics in common. One is that both have eluded definition since their inceptions. Neither one has a single, authoritative perspective or definition. Research has identified more than 500 different definitions of public relations. As for creativity, the ways in which societies have perceived the concept have changed throughout history, as has the term itself. Despite the ambiguity and multidimensional nature of public relations and creativity, the two concepts are inextricably associated and, together, act as a powerful force in influencing human behavior. Another common characteristic of public relations and creativity is that they are mental and social processes involving the generation of new ideas or concepts, or new associations of the creative mind with existing ideas or concepts. Both are fueled by the process of either conscious or unconscious insight. An alternative characteristic is that both are appreciated for the simple act of making something new or simply spawning something that had not been considered.

Intuitively, public relations and creativity would seem to be quite simple phenomena; however, both are, in fact, complex and deliver quantifiable but never totally predictable outcomes.

So how does creativity manifest itself in public relations? This is such a sweeping question that books could be devoted to answering it. Let's narrow the focus to the application of creativity in the PR planning process. Specifically, we will look at creativity as it applies to writing the 10 components of a PR plan or proposal.

Introductory Statement

The introductory statement or summary of a plan is the plan developer's first opportunity to instill in plan reviewers the confidence that the developer or the planning team has a solid grasp of the problem, challenge, opportunity, or situation as a designer, a skilled agent of making things happen. Did you catch the key word *designer*? To be regarded at the start of a plan with the stature of a designer would be a high compliment to a plan developer because it would recognize the developer as a professional. Such confidence derives from introductory statements written in clear, concise, simple, coherent language. Errors in accuracy, omissions of facts, and abuses of plain English immediately undermine impressions of a plan developer's competence. It would not be an exaggeration to say that reviewers await plans with high expectations of right brain activity, genius, or divine inspiration. Consider the introductory statement a handshake, first impression, connection of mutual respect. The introductory statement should cause a plan reviewer to think with confidence, "I know the task at hand and so do you."

Situation Analysis

What role does creativity play in a plan's situation analysis? The analysis is best presented in story form, right from the beginning, the way a situation has unfolded and led to the need for public relations action. What could be more creative than telling a story? You know what it means to embellish a story. Well, that's what needs to be done here. Describe the situation in detail and embellish the story with information that provides overall context, with research or recommendations for research that validates what is known or needs to be known, and a thoughtful analysis that provides a foundation for the other components of a plan. In-depth information here signals plan reviewers that you have full understanding of, strong interest in, and unquestionable commitment to the job at hand.

Goal

What about a plan's goal? How does creativity figure into developing a goal? At this point you go from analyzing to synthesizing, bringing all the pieces of the situation analysis together into a single, declarative statement. You have investigated. You have thought about the situation from every angle, and now you create a single goal. The study of creative thought underlying this synthesizing process belongs to the domains of psychology and cognitive science. Call it critical thinking, because an error in determining an appropriate goal would invalidate an entire plan or proposal. The goal is the rallying point for every component of a plan and can be assessed, ultimately, by asking, Did we achieve this state of being or condition or not?

Focus

Public relations plans focus on people. To determine the focal points or target audiences or publics of a plan requires a selection process. However, the process needs to be more than logical selection by association with the problem, opportunity, challenge, or situation. The process can be made most effective by thinking intuitively about individuals, groups, and organizations and how they might be related to the subject of a particular plan. Using one's intuition in this way is a dimension of creativity. To adequately identify and describe a target of a plan requires the ability to place oneself in the positions of others, to see what others see, to feel the way others feel. Empathizing, which is what is being described, is the amazing human maneuver of mentally walking in someone else's shoes. To plan to influence the behavior of others, you must know the subjects from the inside out.

Objectives

The objectives of a plan describe what must be done by the plan's target audiences or publics to accomplish the plan's goal. Another aspect of creativity comes into play in the writing of objectives. Creativity is an assumptions-breaking process. Creative ideas are often generated when one discards preconceived assumptions and attempts a new approach or method that might even seem unthinkable to others. An objective, as you will learn later, has three components: (1) an action, (2) a receiver of the action, and (3) a desired behavior of the receiver as a result of the action. The first component is one of a plan's most overlooked places for creativity. Typical of many objectives, the first component so often is an ordinary action, such as to inform, to convince, to provide, to educate. There are, of course, many creative ways to grab people's attention. Actions could be to surprise, to raise curiosity, to violate expectations, to disrupt a pattern, to create a gap of knowledge, to subvert a traditional schema, to tap into, to present consequences, to simulate, to inspire, to provoke. Think of it this way: What do you have to do to get your target audience to drop its ear buds and pay attention?

Strategies and Activities or Tactics

The strategy component of a plan is a creative platform. Strategies describe how objectives are to be accomplished; activities or tactics explain how the strategies are to be carried out. There are different ways to develop strategies. One might be to learn from the successful lessons of others. Another might be to uncover, through research, ideas not thought of by others. Another might be to derive ideas from brainstorming sessions. In public relations, human behavior is influenced by strategic communication. Keep in mind, however, that what influences society's behavior has evolved over the years. People today are in search of meaning and purpose. To be effective, strategies must be more than a simple nudge from Point A to Point B. Strategies must have meaning to people in order to be influential. So when you are developing strategies, you must describe what must be done to make them influential. If your strategy is to entertain individuals with a dinner party, for example, it is essential to describe how you will make the dinner experience meaningful enough to influence your guests to react according to your strategy. Meaning and purpose are motivators, and both can be leveraged with creativity.

Evaluating Plans and Proposals

Here are tactics to help you shine as an expert in evaluating PR plans and proposals. Some senior executives are reticent even to consider the presentation of a PR plan or proposal because their boards of directors have, in their words, "been burned" by spending huge amounts of money on plans that promise something and deliver nothing. So before developing a plan in-house or inviting a proposal from an outside source, it is wise to adhere to criteria that would make a plan acceptable to a CEO and board of directors. You must never, for the sake of your professional integrity, present a plan that you think would cause a reviewer to think or say, "They must know what they're doing." A comment such as this is a clear indication that the reviewer did not feel the plan was coherent, or understandable, or measurable, or achievable, or within the reviewer's experience to critique. Such a comment usually is followed by another: "This isn't quite what we had in mind, but thank you."

Unfortunately, many PR plans, including national award-winning plans, cannot withstand the test given to a standard business Request for Authorization (RFA). And most plan reviewers seem to find it difficult to relate a PR plan or proposal to an RFA. What sometimes happens is a senior executive reviewer, not knowing what to do, approves a major expenditure, gets marginal results for the investment, gets tagged by the board for poor judgment, and then forms a negative opinion of the PR profession.

Public relations is seen by many as a low-growth career area. Perhaps that's because the profession—defined in more than 500 different ways and with a history of poorly developed PR plans and one-time clients—has yet to learn that while there are big clients to win, the number is reduced every time a client experiences the failure of a plan to deliver measurable results. Not only does the profession continue to struggle to define itself, but it also stumbles over itself defining the components of a PR plan. Christopher Verona, a former judge of Silver Anvil award entries wrote: "It was common to find goals confused with objectives and strategies combined with objectives. Plans that suffer such deficiencies don't win, or don't even get implemented."

5. Questions for Evaluating Some of the Components of a PR Plan

1. Does the plan begin with a statement summarizing a problem, challenge, opportunity, or situation which, when addressed with public relations activity, would in some significant way benefit an organization or client?

2. Does the plan present a thorough situation analysis, stopping short of suggesting solutions?

3. Does the situation analysis give plan reviewers solid assurance that the plan developer has a complete and accurate understanding of the situation from which to develop a plan?

4. Does the plan present one, and only one, goal? Is it written in one sentence? Is it written as though the goal has been achieved, stating the ultimate condition or state of being resulting from execution of the plan? Acceptable: For XYZ to be operating as a recognized leader in its field. This is written as though the company has arrived at a new level of esteem, a new state of being. Unacceptable: The goal is for XYZ to become a recognized leader in its field. That leaves XYZ in its current unrecognized position or state of being, trying to become a recognized leader.

5. Is the focus of the PR plan on engaging and influencing the behavior of people, either individuals or target audiences?

6. Does the plan identify and describe each target audience? Does it tell why the target audiences were selected, what each one knows about the subject of the plan, how each one is positioned relative to the subject, and what each one's disposition toward the plan's originating entity is? Does the plan present each of the audiences separately, or does the plan, unacceptably, just list target audiences?

7. Does the plan have objectives that tell reviewers what must be done with each target audience to achieve the plan's goal? Does each objective start with the infinitive *to* and contain three parts: (1) an action to be taken, (2) a receiver (audience) of the action, and (3) a behavior desired of the receiver as a result of the action to be taken? Is each objective written to enable measurement? Example: To provide the media with information so they take an interest in writing articles and that their reports can be based on complete and accurate information. Unacceptable objectives are those that tell how something will be accomplished. That is the job of a strategy.

8. Does each objective in the plan have one or more strategies? Do the strategies describe how, in concept, each objective is to be achieved? Do the strategies include discussions of messages or themes, or creative ideas that plan reviewers have not considered? Are the strategies presented in broad terms, stopping short of giving details as to how they will be carried out, which is the job of the plan's activities or tactics?

A closing thought on the matter of evaluation is that comments can be expected in the PR profession claiming "This is not the way plans are written." That's true in the sense that it's not the way many PR veterans write plans, but it's also true that it is time for the profession to think seriously about giving plan reviewers—employers and clients—what they want in a plan, the way they want it.

6. Model Student Plan: Promotion of Racial, Ethnic, and Cultural Diversity

Following is a PR plan initiated as a class exercise by student teams in the School of Journalism and Communication, University of Oregon, proposed for the Center on Diversity and Community. CoDaC is an applied research center dedicated to advancing cross-cultural dialogue, knowledge, skill, and awareness building, with an emphasis on academic communities within higher education. CoDaC works with individual faculty as well as campus units striving to become more multiculturally inclusive and accessible. The plan is shown here as a model for teaching purposes.

Problem

The Center on Diversity and Community strives to promote racial, ethnic, and cultural diversity on the University of Oregon campus and in its surrounding communities. Some of the marketing challenges the center currently faces include limited financial resources, advertising, and communication that is insufficiently tailored to multiple and specific audiences.

The center's executive committee recognizes the pressing need for a strategic PR plan in its efforts to position the organization to fulfill its mission. Without the success that a plan could provide, which includes a financial development facet, the center could be seriously restricted in its ability to achieve its goals. The center is requesting assistance with these serious PR problems.

Situation Analysis

In spring of 1999, a student publicly made a racially insensitive remark in a large University of Oregon classroom. A heated exchange ensued between the student and others attending the course, which spilled outside the class through violent threats and emails. The incident brought to light concerns of diversity and equity in classroom environments and throughout the University of Oregon campus. The incident led to an approximate 95-person sit-in at Johnson Hall. Students, faculty, and staff demanded the administration address diversity issues on campus in a formal setting.

In the summer of 1999, the president's office created an action staff to produce a Diversity Internship Program Report, a document describing how the University of Oregon could proactively address diversity issues on campus in a formal setting.

The team developed a proposal for the CoDaC, an interdisciplinary research center. Created in October 2001, the center promotes inquiry, dialogue, and understanding on issues of racial, ethnic, and cultural diversity. The center considers cultural diversity to include such identity factors as socioeconomic status, sexual preference, nationality, and language.

CoDaC offers competitive research grants and awards, diversity dialogue and facilitation training programs, public events and workshops, resource guides, and student internships. Its governing body is the executive committee composed of faculty, administrators, and student leaders. Executive committee meetings are held twice a term along with additional subcommittee meetings. CoDaC reports to the Office of the Vice President for Research and Graduate Studies and the Office of the Vice Provost for Institutional Equity and Diversity.

The center is funded by a one-time allocation from the Associated Students of the University of Oregon plus funds from the University of Oregon administration. Its marketing strategies use its website, email lists, three-times-a-year newsletter, posters and flyers, campus announcements, University of Oregon media relations, announcements through local news outlets and websites, and display ads in the *Eugene Weekly*, *Oregon Daily Emerald*, and *The Register-Guard*.

Goal

For the Center on Diversity and Community to be fully institutionalized as an essential, unique, and authoritative resource for diversity education on the University of Oregon campus, and to be making a substantial regional and national impact.

Focus or Target Audience(s)

Graduate Students

Many graduate programs require a research project. The grants offered by the center provide a financial resource for graduate students to complete such research. The completed research acknowledges the center as the funding source and serves as a promotion tool. These students participate in an annual Graduate Research Conference organized by the center.

Potential Corporate Sponsors

The center seeks to receive funding from corporations, specifically Northwest-based and progressive-thinking national companies that value diversity and cultural competency. In an effort to continue the center's operations, the executive committee is seeking corporate or foundation sponsors. This target audience is important because of its potential for funding the center and because many companies seek to increase diversity and cultural competency in the workforce. It is also the most time-consuming audience to research because, to be effective, contact must be made with senior management, one organization at a time, and any such relationship must relate closely both to the center's and to the company's mission and values.

Undergraduate Students

The center is seeking greater visibility with undergraduate students. This audience comprises the majority of the university's population and can be viewed as the most impressionable of all target audiences. Some undergraduates could be experiencing their first meaningful encounter in a culturally diverse environment. The center strives to educate these students on diversity and cultural competency issues to encourage a positive college experience.

Faculty and Staff

The center seeks to improve its visibility with faculty as a resource for promoting and supporting their diversity-related research activities. The center also works with staff on increasing individual and organizational cultural competency.

Community

Despite successful public events and articles in the local press, many Eugene-area residents are not currently aware of the center's efforts, but could benefit from its programs and research. Greater knowledge and awareness of the center throughout the community would give more public emphasis to the program and would lead to more opportunities for obtaining sponsorships.

Potential and Current University Funding Sources

This audience is also important because it has a direct bearing on future funding of the center. The center provides its reporting offices with formal annual reports and informal reports on its activities and successes. Greater awareness of these results and reports may produce greater university funding sources, both potential and current. A critical prerequisite to the recommendations contained in this plan is a suggestion to modify the organization's name. Currently, the center does not wish to change its name due to the recognition it has accrued to date on campus and in the community, but it may consider doing so in the future if its mission were to undergo significant change. Potential funders and others unfamiliar with the organization might confuse CODAC with the Kodak brand. In order to clarify what the acronym signifies and to distinguish itself, the center has contemplated a change in printed appearance and logo from CODAC to CoDaC. No name modifications or changes are suggested in this proposal.

7. Model Student Plan Objectives, Strategies, Activities and Evaluations

Objective #1

To attract the interest of corporations and/or professional and business organizations that would like to raise their public profiles in the area of diversity and to have them become active participants in and financial supporters of the Center on Diversity and Community.

Strategy

The center could better engage potential financial supporters through presentations to professional, business, and civic organizations in the Eugene community and through personal contact with Oregon graduates who are employed by potential sponsors. We recommend implementing this strategy with activities (or tactics) selected from the following:

Activities (or Tactics)

1. Obtain from the Oregon Alumni Foundation the names of graduates who are currently employed by companies that the center has identified as potential financial supporters. Call on these graduates to be rainmakers to help the center establish relationships with their respective organizations.

2. Ask rainmakers to make presentations for support from their respective companies and organizations.

3. Solicit funds at CoDaC presentations with a newly developed brochure of irresistible funding opportunities. The brochure would describe various ways to support the center in a range of marketable packages of opportunities with clearly defined forms of public recognition for the sponsors.

4. For example, one opportunity for funding could be for the design, production, and special packaging of 1000 cast bronze mementos to be known as the center's Diversity Medallion, a symbol of recognition to be earned by individuals and organizations for volunteering time, talent, and energy to embrace diversity. The medallion could have on one side a graphic symbol of the center and a slogan, such as a phrase "We are bound together by the task that stands before us," borrowed with permission from the song "Shed A Little Light." On the other side could be the center's mission, "Men and women dedicated to promoting inquiry, dialogue and understanding on issues of racial, ethnic and cultural diversity." The role of the medallion will become clear as this plan unfolds. The sponsor that provides funds for the medallion could receive public recognition in the form of a credit line on each medallion, such as "Provided by [foundation name]."

5. A range of funding opportunities from $100 to $100,000, each in an irresistible marketing form, like the medallion with clearly defined public recognition of sponsors, would be described in the center's brochure.

6. The center's brochure would be distributed at all CoDaC presentations.

7. Expand the center's executive committee membership or create a community advisory board to include organizational memberships for professional, business, and civic organizations in the Eugene community that would like to embrace diversity more openly.

8. Present each organization that joins the board with a membership plaque featuring the center's Diversity Medallion. The plaque could have a heading borrowed with permission from the song "Shed A Little Light" that says "There are ties between us, all men and women living on the earth, ties of hope and love."

9. Members of the community advisory board would be expected to have their respective companies or organizations host annual CoDaC presentations for support of the center.

10. A CoDaC ceremony could be scheduled to be held during the week of Diversity Walk, an annual commemorative event established by the Eugene City Council, which is described later in the plan. At the public ceremony, selected community leaders could be awarded the center's Diversity Medallion for their efforts and involvement in promoting diversity.

Evaluation

This objective will be evaluated in two areas: performance and effectiveness.

Performance

1. Rainmakers were developed.

2. Rainmakers made CoDaC presentations for support.

3. CoDaC brochure was produced.

4. Diversity Medallions were produced.

5. Community Advisory Board was established.

6. Diversity Walk was conducted.

7. Public Ceremony was conducted.

Effectiveness

1. How many financial supporters were recruited?

2. Who are the individual, company, and organization supporters?

3. How much funding was obtained for the center?

Objective #2

To increase graduate student awareness of competitive research grants available through the center so that more students participate in research on issues of diversity.

Strategy

We recommend that the center strengthen its appeal to graduate students through graduate-to-graduate briefings:

Activities (or Tactics)

1. Organize current graduate student grant recipients to undertake a series of graduate-to-graduate student briefings about the center and its research-funding opportunities. Make this outreach responsibility a requirement for every student who receives a grant in the future. It would be the responsibility of each grant recipient to inform through informal briefings all graduate students in the recipient's particular school of center activities throughout the grant recipient's period of center-sponsored research.

Evaluation

This objective will be evaluated in two areas: performance and effectiveness.

Performance

Were graduate-to-graduate student briefings organized and conducted?

Effectiveness

How many graduate-to-graduate student briefings were conducted?

Objective #3

To heighten interest among students in the center's undergraduate-focused programs and resources so that more individuals participate in the organization.

Strategy

We recommend that the center heighten interest among undergraduates by communicating the benefits of participating in the CoDaC frequently through multiple and familiar channels. Activities (or tactics) to consider are the following:

Activities (or Tactics)

2. Publicize and fill openings at the CoDaC for one or more credit-based internships in specific areas, such as public relations, website development, campus outreach, community outreach, faculty staff liaison, student group liaison, Associated Students of the University of Oregon liaison, and graduate student liaison, and use this cadre of talent to produce promotional materials, such as brochures, newsletters, and fliers. Each student who completes an internship would earn one of the center's Diversity Medallions.

3. Recruit, train, and dispatch a dozen student volunteers who would like to develop their presentation skills as the center's ambassadors by spreading word of the center's mission and events before large lecture classes in business, ethics, sociology, management—any and all areas of study, and before professional student organizations, such as the Society of Professional Journalists, the American Marketing Association, and business honors societies. Students who make a certain number of presentations on behalf of the center would earn Diversity Medallions.

4. Develop a conspicuous presence for the center during the fall student orientation programs, perhaps in the form of a short workshop on conflict resolution or other skill-building activity related to diversity to educate students on diversity issues to encourage a positive college experience.

5. Partner with the appropriate organization for publicizing the up-coming dedication of the $1.5 million longhouse being built on campus to represent Native American students from throughout the Pacific Northwest. At an appropriate ceremony, present the leadership of the longhouse with a piece of Native American

art with the Diversity Medallion embedded in its design and publicize the presentation with a photo news release to all area media.

Evaluation

This objective will be evaluated in two areas: performance and effectiveness.

Performance

1. Internship positions have been established and filled.

2. Students have been recruited and are being used as CoDaC ambassadors.

3. CoDaC workshop has been conducted at the fall student orientation program.

4. Connection has been established with leaders of the longhouse project for future work in diversity.

Effectiveness

1. Interest among students in the center's undergraduate-focused programs and resources (a) stayed about the same or (b) heightened noticeably.

2. Student participation in CoDaC has (a) stayed about the same, (b) increased somewhat, or (c) increased significantly.

Objective #4

To raise the Eugene community's awareness of the center, its role, and its activities in the community and on campus in ways that would motivate community members to get involved and participate in the center and its diversity-related events.

Strategy A

This objective could be accomplished by having the city establish an annual Diversity Walk for the greater Eugene area with proceeds contributed to the center for managing the event. This would require:

Activities (or Tactics)

1. Making an informal inquiry of Councilman David Kelly, who represents the university area, to gage the interest in a possible council action to designate an annual Diversity Walk. If the inquiry receives a positive response, the center would work with Councilman Kelly to draft a council resolution establishing the annual event to promote diversity.

2. Council would pass the resolution and the day following the council meeting the mayor would announce the declaration at a special ceremony at city hall.

3. The center would manage the event for the city and receive part of the entry fees collected.

4. The center would be identified with the city on Diversity Walk T-shirts that would be worn by all participants.

Strategy B

Another strategy for achieving this objective would be for the city of Eugene each year to honor an individual who deserves special recognition for promoting diversity in the community. This could be accomplished in the following manner:

Activities (or Tactics)

1. The mayor and council would select and announce the Citizen of the Year for Exemplary Efforts in Promoting Diversity.

2. The mayor would present the individual with a Diversity Medallion suspended from a ribbon and placed on the honoree in the manner of an Olympic medal presentation. (Some medallions would be produced with an eye through which a ribbon could be passed.)

3. This would be an award made jointly by the center and the city.

4. The honoree would become a special ambassador to the center, would be featured in the center's annual report, and would have a portrait photo displayed at the center.

Evaluation

This objective will be evaluated in two areas: performance and effectiveness.

Performance

1. The mayor and council selected and announced the Citizen of the Year for Exemplary Efforts in Promoting Diversity.

2. The award recipient received a Diversity Medallion from the mayor in a public ceremony.

3. The ceremony was cohosted be the city and CoDaC.

Effectiveness

The honoree has become a special ambassador to the center, was featured in the center's annual report, and has a portrait photo displayed at the center.

Objective #5

To motivate university faculty and staff to take an interest in and actively support the center and its mission on campus and in the community.

Strategy

One way to accomplish this objective would be to enlist the cooperation of the U.S. Ambassador to the United Nations to personally encourage the University of Oregon to advance the cause of diversity among all people for the benefit of world peace. The letter would be sent to the university president who would, in a cover letter to faculty and staff, endorse the ambassador's message and urge campus-wide participation in the center's activities to advance diversity. This strategy would require the following:

Activities (or Tactics)

1. Discuss the proposal with the university president.

2. Discuss the proposal with the ambassador's staff.

3. Send draft letter for the ambassador's review, approval, and signature to the University of Oregon faculty and staff.

4. Draft a cover letter for the university president.

5. Follow distribution of the ambassador's letter one week later with a letter from the center referring faculty and staff to the center's new website with a link to a screen with specific ways in which faculty and staff could support the center and earn a Diversity Medallion for their contribution.

Evaluation

This objective will be evaluated in two areas: performance and effectiveness.

Performance

1. Proposal was discussed with the university president.

2. President's proposal was discussed with ambassador's staff.

3. Draft letter sent to ambassador's staff.

4. Draft cover letter sent to university president.

5. Ambassador's letter distributed.

Effectiveness

Success of this objective will be measured by feedback to the university president from faculty and staff.

Objective #6

To communicate to potential and current university funding sources the achievements in awareness the center has made toward its goal so that donors see progress and are motivated to provide or continue to provide financial support to the CoDaC.

Strategy

This objective could be accomplished through an annual survey of campus awareness with results published in an annual report distributed to potential and current university funding sources. The strategy would require:

Activities (or Tactics)

1. An online campus climate survey developed and conducted by the center.

2. Survey findings would be published by the center.

3. The center's intern cadre would prepare a by-lined, op-ed piece for the director discussing the campus climate survey results and its implications to be submitted in two different versions, one to the *Oregon Daily Emerald* and the other to *The Register-Guard*.

4. The survey results would be included in an annual report published by the center and delivered and discussed in one-on-one visits with the center's potential and current university funding sources.

Evaluation

This objective will be evaluated in two areas: performance and effectiveness.

Performance

1. An online campus climate survey completed.

2. Survey findings published.

3. Findings submitted to the *Oregon Daily Emerald* and *The Register-Guard*.

4. The survey results included in an annual report and discussed in one-on-one visits with the center's potential and current university funding sources.

Effectiveness

Success in achieving this objective will be determined by spot checking feedback from these funding sources through informal conversations.

Execution Timeline

Activities	Target Dates	Responsibility
Rainmakers recruited		
Rainmakers made CoDaC presentations for support		
CoDaC brochure produced		
Diversity Medallions produced		
Community Advisory Board established		
Diversity Walk conducted		
Public ceremony conducted		
Graduate-to-graduate briefings conducted		
Mayor announced Citizen of the Year for Exemplary Efforts in Promoting Diversity. Diversity Medal presented		
Proposal discussed with the university president		
Proposal discussed with ambassador's staff		
Draft letter sent to ambassador's staff		
Draft cover letter sent to university president		
Ambassador's letter distributed		
Online campus climate survey completed		
Survey findings published		
Findings submitted to *Oregon Daily Emerald* and *The Register-Guard*		

8. Model Student Plan Evaluations by Objective

The plan shows evaluation data after each objective. However, an option would be to show all of the information in one section as shown here.

Objective #1

To attract the interest of corporations and/or professional and business organizations that would like to raise their public profiles in the area of diversity and have them become active participants in and financial supporters of the Center on Diversity and Community.

Evaluation

Performance

1. Rainmakers were developed.

2. Rainmakers made CoDaC presentations for support.

3. CoDaC brochure was produced.

4. Diversity Medallions were produced.

5. Community Advisory Board was established.

6. Diversity Walk was conducted.

7. Public ceremony was conducted.

Effectiveness

1. How many financial supporters were recruited?

2. Who are the individual, company, and organization supporters?

3. How much funding was obtained for the center?

Objective #2

To increase graduate student awareness of competitive research grants and conference opportunities available through the center so that more students participate in research on issues of diversity.

Evaluation

This objective will be evaluated in two areas: performance and effectiveness.

Performance

Were graduate-to-graduate student briefings organized and conducted?

Effectiveness

How many graduate-to-graduate student briefings were conducted?

Objective #3

To heighten interest among students in the center's undergraduate-focused programs and resources so that more individuals participate in the organization.

Evaluation

Performance

1. Internship positions have been established and filled.

2. Students have been recruited and are being used as CoDaC ambassadors.

3. CoDaC workshop has been conducted at the fall student orientation program.

4. Connection has been established with leaders of the longhouse project for future work in diversity.

Effectiveness

1. Interest among students in the center's undergraduate-focused programs and resources (a) stayed about the same or (b) heightened noticeably.

2. Student participation in CoDaC has (a) stayed about the same, (b) increased somewhat, and (c) increased significantly.

Objective #4

To raise the Eugene community's awareness of the center, its role, and its activities in the community and on campus, in ways that would motivate community members to get involved and participate in the center and its diversity-related events.

Evaluation

Performance

1. The mayor and council selected and announced the Citizen of the Year for Exemplary Efforts in Promoting Diversity.

2. The award recipient received a Diversity Medallion from the mayor in a public ceremony.

3. The ceremony was cohosted be the city and CoDaC.

Effectiveness

The honoree has become a special ambassador to the center, was featured in the center's annual report, and has a portrait photo displayed at the center.

Objective #5

To motivate university faculty and staff to take an interest in and actively support the center and its mission on campus and in the community.

Evaluation

Performance

1. Proposal was discussed with the university president.

2. President's proposal was discussed with ambassador's staff.

3. Draft letter was sent to ambassador's staff.

4. Draft cover letter was sent to university president.

5. Ambassador's letter was distributed.

Effectiveness

Success of this objective will be measured by feedback to the university president from faculty and staff.

Objective #6

To communicate to potential and current university funding sources the achievements the center has made toward its goal so that donors will see progress and be motivated to provide or continue to provide financial support.

Evaluation

Performance

1. An online campus climate survey was completed.

2. Survey findings were published.

3. Findings were submitted to the *Oregon Daily Emerald* and to *The Register-Guard*.

4. The survey results were included in an annual report and discussed in one-on-one visits with the center's potential and current university funding sources.

Effectiveness

Success in achieving this objective will be determined by spot checking feedback from these funding sources through informal conversations.

Estimated Public Relations Agency Budget

For the 10-week period of January 5 through March 12, 2004
Billing rates in U.S. dollars

Staff	Hours	Billing Rate Per Hour	Amount
Account executive	15	150.	2250.
Account coordinator	30	90.	2700.
Secretary	20	60.	1200.
General manager	5	200.	1000.
		Subtotal	7150.

Expenses		
Description	Amount
Publicity materials	600.
Production of fundraising brochures	500.
Production of presentations materials	450.
Production of workshop materials	500.
Subtotal	2050.
TOTAL	9200.

III: Rules for Writing 10 Components of a Public Relations Plan

You have taken a trip from whimsy to the reality of an actual plan to raise your interest in writing public relations plans and proposals. This orientation is intended to focus your attention on the challenge of influencing behavior through strategic communication.

From what you have read so far, how do you feel about writing PR plans? Is it something you would enjoy doing? Do you believe you have the motivation, basic background, and creative energy to learn rules for writing winning plans?

Let's pursue your possible interest and look at specific rules for writing plans that give clients what they want, the way they want it.

1. Introductory Statement

The first component of a PR plan is the introductory statement. PR plans are presented formally or informally, verbally or as written proposals. Writing the plan in a conversational style is appropriate for all forms of presentation. You will find that in the industry, plans and definitions of their parts vary from organization to organization, from PR agency to PR agency. It's not the lack of standardized form, but rather the lack of common definition that does a great disservice to the profession. The model plan presented earlier has 10 clearly defined components. We will look at each one from the plan reviewer's perspective, from the perspective of the person responsible for authorizing funds to implement a plan.

The introductory statement summarizes a problem, challenge, opportunity, or situation that, when addressed with PR activity, would, in some significant way, benefit the organization you work for or that you have as a client. This part of the plan should be headed Problem, Challenge, Opportunity, or Situation. It is best not to include the word *statement* in the subhead. The introductory statement is important to plan reviewers because it assures them, from the start, that you, as PR plan developer, understand the situation accurately. A lack of accurate understanding on your part most likely would aim the rest of the plan in the wrong direction and render it useless to a reviewer.

Rules for Writing an Introductory Statement

1. Head the statement as a Problem, Challenge, Opportunity, or Situation without including the word statement.

2. Begin the statement by identifying the nature of the case, for example: "We (our organization) have a ..." Or, "As we (our agency) understand, you have a ..."

3. Focus the introductory statement on communicating with people because the aim of a PR plan is to influence behavior.

4. Write the statement in a conversational style. It is a call to action.

5. Show clearly that a situation exists that warrants PR action and the allocation and expenditure of resources.

6. While the statement should provide a compelling argument for taking action, it must stop short of suggesting a solution or course of action, which is the role of other components of a plan.

7. The statement must be brief and accurate.

8. The statement must not be judgmental or place blame.

Example of an Introductory Statement

Option A. We (our company/organization) have a challenge that needs special handling ...

Option B. We (PR firm) understand the challenge you face ...

The company started planning a plant expansion and discovered that a large lagoon on the construction site contains hazardous material. The lagoon has to be cleaned out and closed before plant expansion work can begin. Closing the lagoon will be in public view from the highway and workers seen in hazardous materials safety suits will raise questions. If everyone who sees the activity—news media, community residents, employees, local government representatives, and others—is left to speculate about what is seen, the community could become unnecessarily alarmed. Media reports could exaggerate health risks and call the company's reputation into question. The general public could pressure government for information and generate public meetings about the project. Local government officials could delay issuing permits for expansion. Employees could become outraged about earlier potential exposure of their families to health risks.

You don't want anyone to become alarmed unnecessarily. You don't want expansion plans to be delayed because needed modernization is already costing the company money and inadequate capacity is causing the company to lose market share. This clearly is a potential public relations problem with serious consequences and must be addressed.

Exercise 1: Introductory Statement

For this exercise, use ONLY the information provided below and write by the rules an introductory statement to the following case challenge.

Tasty Products Tries for Distinction

It used to be that food processors could market products for their good taste. Today it is evident that people are more interested than ever before in their health and fitness. When they shop, they want to know what products will do to them, and more importantly, what they will do for them. Health claims on products have an influence on buying decisions. Tasty Products figured that when you have a product that is not only great tasting, but also naturally nutritious, it makes sense to promote the natural health benefits. The company wanted to put a health claim on its Ultra Fine orange juice. It wanted to spotlight the fact that Ultra Fine orange juice contains potassium. The mineral potassium is found in orange juice. The company wanted to point out that in clinical trials potassium has been shown to reduce the risk of high blood pressure and stroke. Tasty Products petitioned the Food and Drug Administration (FDA) to carry the health claim about potassium on its Ultra Fine orange juice label. The company spent months researching and writing the petition and working with FDA employees on drafting the claim's language. The petition was accepted. Now Tasty Products can market the potassium health benefit claim. But so can any juice producer tout the benefits of having potassium in its orange juice. Tasty Products wants to use the health claim, but has to keep other orange juice producers at bay.

2. Situation Analysis

The second component of a PR plan is the situation analysis. Why is this component of the plan important to plan reviewers? It is important to reviewers because the manner in which the analysis is written gives reviewers evidence of your depth of knowledge about the case, the breadth of your experience, your level of professionalism, your understanding of the organization and its needs, the seriousness of your commitment to addressing the situation, and your overall understanding of public relations.

The situation analysis is not an elaboration of the introductory statement. It is a consideration of all aspects of the case. Your job is to gather information necessary to provide an in-depth understanding of the problem, challenge, opportunity, or situation. The analysis should be a focused investigation of internal and external factors, including recommendations for further study and possible research that will support effective strategic planning.

Be judicious in preparing the analysis. Collecting and assembling everything that could possibly relate to a case, including volumes of peripheral information that is marginally relevant, could be seen by a client as a costly, overindulgent, unnecessary expense. Be aware that the profession's use of the proverbial communication audit is often perceived, accurately or not, as a way for a PR firm to charge a lot of extra money for informing itself about a client's case, or for gathering information and doing nothing with it to benefit the client. As a newcomer to the profession, you don't want to be surprised by a negative reaction to the suggested use of an audit. The communication audit can be a useful PR tool, but its misuse has tainted its reputation in the marketplace.

For the situation analysis to be a useful component of a PR plan, it should organize and convey information in a familiar, easy-to-understand manner. What better way could there be to describe a situation than to do what comes naturally, that is, tell a story. To tell a story in this regard is to describe a series of happenings which, when related or connected, enables others to grasp the significance of a problem, challenge, opportunity, or situation. It is up to you in your storytelling to enable others to sift through events, and to understand how and why they occurred and what part they played in creating the case under study.

Storytelling allows you to describe the development of a situation from its origin to its current state based on a thoughtful review of explicit as well as tacit information. In other words, an analysis should involve hard evidence as well as unseen influences that are more difficult to evaluate. It will be necessary to decide to what extent you can rely on intuition to form an analysis and to what extent it will be necessary to conduct and/or recommend primary or secondary research to help validate your story of how the problem, challenge, opportunity, or situation surfaced. Research to be recommended and/or conducted could be, for example, in the form of in-depth interviews, focus groups, field observation, tabulating phone calls, postal and electronic mail, social media, surveys, and content analysis.

Rules for Writing a Situation Analysis

1. Take ownership. This is not a playback of the situation that you got from your client or employer. This is your analysis. Do some homework. Learn more about the case. Identify areas that need clarification and/or verification. Show where informal, qualitative, or quantitative research would be important and give reasons why. Build a case for action, if action is warranted.

2. Write the analysis in a conversational style, as though you are explaining your assessment of the situation to your client or employer in person.

3. Present your analysis in a storytelling format. Begin at the beginning and tell how the situation developed, what you learned about it, what more needs to be known, and how the case reached a point requiring PR action.

4. The analysis should provide a compelling argument for taking action.

5. Be forthright about problems, weaknesses, and mistakes, but do not be judgmental or place blame.

6. The analysis must not include solutions or suggestions for dealing with the situation. Leave that to the rest of the plan.

Example of a Situation Analysis

Employees of two companies have been pleased with the way their respective employers managed the local shops, and provided opportunities for individual advancement and competitive pay. Both companies provided clear visions for employees about their respective missions and goals. A vision of the merged company has yet to be provided. The former visions of each company must be replaced quickly with a common vision so employees can see light at the end of the tunnel.

Executive officers of both companies know that employees are worried that this corporate action could be like a merger of banks, which, for some, created an excuse for closing branch offices and cutting jobs. After all, there's no reason to have Meeting Place coffee shops in proximity to Gathering

Place coffee shops. Executives know there will be short-term pain and that they will have to decide whether to hide it or try to balance potential negatives by describing the long-term payoffs for everyone.

Based on lessons learned about mergers and employee communication from MCI, British Telecom, IBM, Lotus, BellSouth, LG Electronics, UPS, Martin Marietta, GE, and others, the companies realize that the chief executive officers of both entities should champion a common vision and take an active role in articulating it to employees and the news media. It is common knowledge that messages in a merger acquisition must be consistent.

The CEO of Meeting Place Coffee Company, the acquiring company, knows and acknowledges to staff members that she buries herself in her work and is seldom seen by employees. She says the perception employees have of her is probably that what's most important to her are investors. Research makes clear that in times of uncertainty employees want a lot of face time from the CEO and need to be treated with the same intellect and attention given to shareholders, customers, and the media.

There is no empirical data to show that mergers and acquisitions, in any way, guarantee benefits. There is evidence to show that mergers and acquisitions produce unanticipated and, often, undesirable consequences. With respect to employees, it is important to focus on retaining an organization's human capital, which represents a large part of its intellectual capacity and abilities. In an acquisition, a major bank ignored its wealth of human capital by neglecting to assure its most valued employees that they were important to the success of the organization and that their jobs were secure. Consequently, the bank lost many of its most valuable employees, who took jobs with other banks.

Referring to employees as a valuable asset, as so many executives do, puts employees into a category with copy machines, computers, and water coolers. Experienced professional communicators know that employees will not get behind the broad strategy of a merger and acquisition until they know how the merger is going to affect them personally. They must be able to function as participants, not as victims or powerless players. In a merger process, employees can feel like the corporate culture is under siege. They can feel like things are out of control. Suspicions, even a degree of paranoia, get heightened. There is enormous ambiguity. Employees must be made to feel that their interests are being well represented.

Companies that have worked through a merger know that a constant effort must be made to monitor traditional and new media channels of communication and to clear up blurred impressions. Experienced companies know how important it is to constantly revise main messages to respond to criticisms and misinformation. They know how vital it is to help all stakeholder groups keep things in perspective. For example, instead of talking about becoming a $43 billion corporation and the fourth largest telecom corporation in the world, MCI in response to criticism started to point out that, although it would be big, MCI would have only six percent of the market.

Establishing and maintaining two-way communication with employees and all stakeholder groups is essential. Even if there is nothing new to provide, management must stay in close touch with its constituents and reassure them that they will get straightforward information as soon as it is available.

This is a quick analysis of the situation. There is a body of knowledge to draw on in the PR profession that makes it possible to develop an employee communication plan solidly based on the challenges and successes realized by companies that have gone through the merger and acquisition process. This plan is based on the successes of others.

Exercise 2: Situation Analysis

Based on the rules for developing a situation analysis, read the case overview below and describe what additional information you would want to have to do a thorough analysis of the situation. Include in your critique recommended informal or formal research that you think should be conducted to verify certain information and suppositions or to shed more light on the situation.

Shelter Association Pursues Housing for The Homeless

Homeless individuals, mostly men, lived and searched for food on land along the riverfront in downtown Berryton. However, in 1998 the area came under rapid change with the development of expensive homes, a science museum, and an arena.

The Berryton Relocation Task Force was formed by the Shelter Association, a provider of homeless services, to help homeless men who were threatened with being displaced from the riverfront property.

The task force studied the situation and conducted public meetings. It came up with a five-year plan proposing to locate 500 apartments for homeless men throughout the county, building a shelter in an inner-city neighborhood and a facility for alcoholic homeless men. The idea was to reduce homelessness and have the permanent housing and support services replace a variety of emergency shelters.

The plan faced significant challenges. Affordable housing hasn't been popular anywhere in the country, not even Franklin County, which is more tolerant than many other counties. NIMBYism (opposition by nearby residents to a proposed building project, especially a public one, and acronym for Not In My Back Yard) is common. People are not inclined to want to live next door to formerly homeless men, many of whom have mental illnesses and addictions. Shelter Association doesn't know what to do to win acceptance of the plan and to successfully raise money for an unpopular effort.

3. Goal

The next component of a plan is the goal. Why is a goal important to plan reviewers? It is important because the goal in a PR plan has four functions.

One function is to provide a vision of a desired position or condition. A plan should have one ultimate aim. All of a plan's objectives should be directed toward achieving the plan's goal. The goal can be specific to the PR task, for example: for XYZ to be trusted by the community for its safe use of chemicals. Or it can relate to broader organization aims that require plans from other functions, such as human resources, marketing, and finance, for example: for XYZ to be merged with ZYX with the support and understanding of all stakeholders.

Another function of a goal is to provide a target on which to organize resources. A goal gives followers of a plan a point of reference on which to center their efforts. It enables them to set their sights on what is to be the overall result of the combined efforts of all contributors to the plan. A goal should use the infinitive phrase *to be* to distinguish this targeting function. What follows *to be* should be stated as though the position or condition has been achieved. An example: The goal for XYZ is to be a recognized leader in its field. This goal clearly rallies an organization's resources around making it a recognized leader in its field.

Another function of a goal is to provide verification that the plan is focused correctly. By stating the goal, plan developers can demonstrate to plan reviewers that the plan focuses on the correct priority. For example, if the client's goal is for XYZ to be viewed as an essential, unique, and authoritative resource for diversity education on the university campus and in the greater community, the goal would not be focused correctly if it were stated: For XYZ being a well-funded campus organization. Directly stated, when a client's goal calls for everyone to be eating Big Macs, plan developers had better not be writing about Chicken McNuggets. That may sound exaggerated, but sometimes client or employer instructions are not followed explicitly or are overlooked entirely and the experience for them is exasperating because they are putting up major resources to accomplish a specific job that is important to them.

Another function of a goal is to provide a measurement of success. When a desired condition or position is evident as stated in the goal, a plan's objectives have been met. In other words, the fact that a certain condition or position now exists is evidence that the plan's objectives have been achieved successfully. Let's say, for example, the goal is for a hospital to be serving 50 more children. When the hospital is, in fact, serving 50 more children, that is proof, or evidence, that the plan's objective (i.e., to raise $20 million for hospital expansion) has been successfully achieved.

So the goal of a public relations plan has four functions—it provides a vision, a target, verification, and measurement.

Rules for Writing a Goal

1. A plan should have one goal.

2. The goal should be written in a single sentence.

3. The goal should be distinguished by use of the infinitive phrase to be, responding to the question, "What do you want the ultimate condition or state of being to be as a result of having executed the public relations plan successfully?" (Example: For the medical center to be serving 50 additional patients.)

4. The goal should describe a desired, ultimate condition or state of being as though it has been achieved. (Acceptable: For XYZ to be operating as a recognized leader in its field. This is written as though the company has arrived at a new level of esteem—a new state of being. It would be unacceptable to write that the goal is for XYZ to become a recognized leader in its field, because that leaves XYZ in its current unrecognized position or state of being—trying to become a recognized leader.)

5. A goal should not tell what must be done for it to be achieved. That is the role of an objective. (Unacceptable: For XYZ to raise $15 million to expand the hospital. That is an objective describing what must be done to accomplish the ultimate goal—to be serving 50 more patients in a new addition to the hospital. The goal should be evidence that a plan's objectives have been successfully completed.)

6. A goal should not tell how it is to be achieved. That is the role of a strategy. (Acceptable: For XYZ to be a trusted member of the community with its use of hazardous chemicals. Unacceptable: For XYZ to be a trusted member of the community with its use of hazardous chemicals by communicating its safety record.)

Examples of Acceptable and Unacceptable Goals

Note how easily and incorrectly goals get combined with objectives and strategies.

Unacceptable: *To provide eligible families with a smooth transition from Island Health Offspring to Children's Health Insurance Program.*

Reasons: *It begins with the infinitive to, which the rules reserve for beginning objectives. It does not include the infinitive phrase to be followed by an ultimate vision, state of being, or desired condition.*

Acceptable: *For eligible families to be receiving increased benefits from the Children's Health Insurance Program, having made a smooth transition from Island Health Offspring.*

Unacceptable: *The goal of the Clean Teeth campaign is to heighten awareness about the importance of tooth brushing.*

Reasons: *The statement is set off with the infinitive to, which the rules reserve for beginning objectives. It does not include the infinitive phrase to be, which the rules reserve for introducing a goal—a desired condition or state of being. It does not tell whose awareness is to be heightened. The scope of the goal is not defined; the campaign was launched in Gumsport, but apparently intended to target audiences globally.*

Acceptable: *For people around the world to be more aware of the importance of brushing teeth.*

Unacceptable: *To have the public adopt natural garden care by changing certain gardening behaviors.*

Reasons: *It does not include the infinitive phrase to be, which the rules reserve for introducing a goal—a desired condition, state of being, or ultimate vision. The phrase "to have the public adopt natural garden care" tells what must be done, which is the role of an objective. The phrase "by changing certain gardening behaviors" tells how something must be done, which is the role of a strategy.*

Acceptable: *For homeowners, ages 25 to 54, in the Garden Gateway area to be using natural gardening practices.*

Unacceptable: *For ABC Company to become accepted as an economic partner in the community by participating in local service clubs.*

Reasons: *It does not contain the infinitive phrase to be, which is necessary to introduce a desired condition, state of being, or ultimate vision. "To become accepted" tells what must be done, which is the role of an objective. And "by participating in local service clubs" tells how to do something, which is the role of a strategy.*

Acceptable: *For ABC Company to be operating in the community as a full-fledged economic partner.*

Unacceptable: *For Children's Hospital to raise $100,000.*

Reasons: *Raising $100,000 is not the vision, the desired state of being, or condition. Raising $100,000 is what must be done to achieve the vision, which according to the rules is the role of an objective. The vision or goal is for the hospital to be serving more patients.*

Acceptable: *For Children's Hospital to be serving 25 more patients in a new wing of the hospital.*

Unacceptable: *For XYZ Inc. to be closing one assembly plant.*

Reasons: *Closing one assembly plant is not the ultimate vision, goal, or state of being. It is what must be done to achieve the goal or vision, which, according to the rules, is the role of an objective.*

Acceptable: *For XYZ Inc. to be operating more competitively having closed one assembly plant.*

Examples of Acceptable Goals

1. For X to be recognized nationally for its expertise in nubyonics

2. For employees to be accepting greater financial responsibility for their health benefits

3. For customers to be relying on X for its technical expertise and creative solutions

4. For X to be merged with Y and the new organization to be vigorously pursuing a common mission

5. For X to be relocated with a minimal amount of confusion

6. For (person) to be a sought-after expert in launching new ventures

7. For X to be recognized by the community as a leader in economic development

8. For employees to be satisfied with the measures taken to ensure their safety relative to the new hazardous materials operation

9. For X to be serving 50 more patients

10. For (country) to be supportive of adding a new industry to its economy

11. For the community to be satisfied with the level of public participation afforded by X on the proposed energy project.

12. For X to be expanding its operation with the support of local and state governments

13. For X to be regarded by subscribers as the authority on health issues

14. For X to be seen by potential employers and experts in PR planning

15. For X to be increasing membership at a rate of 10 percent a year

16. For X to be approaching strike issues with open communication with Y

17. For members of X to be making appearances on TV shows around the world

18. For all students of X to be supported by individual sponsorships

19. For X to be the most popular website for information about Y

20. For consumers of X to be the preferred customers of Y

21. For wind surfers throughout the world to be aware of the town of Hood River located on the Columbia River as one of the most popular locations for the sport

22. For X to be regarded as the most popular wine-tasting festival in the Pacific Northwest

23. For artisans of the Columbia River Gorge to be discovered and publicized internationally for their unique creations

24. In the acquisition of X by Y, for all employees to be fully supportive of the merger

25. For the new comet-like logo to be seen by employees as a more progressive representation of the organization's identity than the old logo that was fondly referred to as the "flying meatball."

Exercise 3: Goal

Explain why the goals in the following article would not be acceptable according to the rules and write one goal for the museum that would be acceptable.

The Great Museum of Natural History

Museums have to work hard to attract interest and visitors. The Great Museum of Natural History is no exception. However, it decided to break out of the low-attendance crowd by adding a planetarium. It was a $6.9 million project. The museum launched a PR campaign. It had two goals: to generate publicity that would position the museum as a world-class institution and to boost revenue through increased attendance.

The museum set up a promotion team of PR professionals and representatives from local television, radio stations, and newspapers. It used its member resources to help publicize the grand opening of the Space Planetarium. A media teaser campaign was also launched that used puzzles and electronic postcards to visually convey the planetarium's design. Media events for the planetarium were sold out.

The campaign was a complete success with all attendance goals exceeded, sold-out planetarium shows for the first three months, and the museum positioned as a learning center.

4. Focus or Target Audience(s)

The focus of a PR plan, without exception, should be on people because public relations is the practice of influencing behavior through strategic communication. Practically speaking, a plan could not be implemented without the engagement of people. A plan must focus on influencing the behavior of people to achieve the plan's goal. The focus of a plan could be on one individual, on individuals comprising an organization or segment of an organization, on individuals comprising an audience, or an entire public. Focal points of a plan could be a labor leader, the management of a labor union, or members of a nation's trade unions. Focal points could be a business, a community, an activist, a student, or a government leader. They could be the management of a public, private, nonprofit, government, or nongovernment organization. Focal points of a plan could be employees or members of organizations. They could be community residents, journalists, industry analysts, or potential investors. A plan could have multiple focal points, but each one must be treated separately.

Rules for Writing the Focus of a Plan or Target Audience

1. A PR plan must focus on people. (Example: This plan focuses on active and latent patrons of the theater.) Plans focus on people because the engagement of people is required to achieve a plan's goal.

2. People who are at the focus of a plan may be referred to as focal points. Use of the term focal point is appropriate when there is a need to focus the plan on an entity, such as executive management, without having to refer to it as a "target audience." (Example: Our own management is one focal point of this plan.) The terms target, target audience, and target public are also appropriate.

3. In writing the focus of a plan, list the main focal points or target audiences.

4. Do not simply list focal points and assume reviewers know why they have been selected. Describe why each entity is a focal point or target of the plan.

5. Tell what each entity knows about the subject of the plan.

6. Describe the disposition of each entity toward the subject of the plan.

7. Describe the disposition of each entity toward the originator of the plan.

8. Provide demographics of each entity that are particularly relevant to the plan.

9. Write about each entity separately; do not combine entities.

Example of a Focal Point or Target Audience

Parents of Apple Elementary School Children

Parents of students at the neighboring Apple Elementary School are among the most concerned audiences about the use of chemicals at WaferMakers, Inc. Parents are concerned for the safety of their children and want to be assured that the wafer plant operation near the school is not a risk to their children's health or safety. Many of these parents are already highly emotional about the situation and want their questions answered immediately. Parents regard WaferMakers as a good corporate citizen and up until this time were unaware of the company's use of many hazardous chemicals. They are members of the local community and it is important to make sure that they trust and continue to be supportive of WaferMakers, Inc.

Exercise 4: Focus or Target Audience

Based on the rules for describing the focus of a plan, explain why it would be helpful to plan reviewers to have more than just a list of entities identified as subjects or targets of a plan as shown here:

The ABC Transport System Key Target Audiences:

- Landowners

- Local elected officials

- Community leaders

- Media

- State elected officials, and regulatory and administrative staff

- U.S. senators, representatives, and staff from six states

- Federal regulators

- Rural/farm groups

5. Objectives

As students are undoubtedly taught, an objective for a PR campaign is always written with a specific audience in mind, is measurable, and has an end date. For instance, "to increase college-age volunteers within our organization by 35 percent by November 14, 2017" is a straight forward PR objective. Like already mentioned, however, the things that you present a potential client (or plan reviewer) via a proposal sometimes differs from your own internal plan and from textbook teachings. The way that an objective is written is no exception to this rule.

The aforementioned, traditionally taught PR objective fosters evaluation, requires benchmarking, and hopes to prove the value of the PR efforts put forth in the given campaign. Although those are admirable and necessary qualities, they are of more worth to those practicing public relations than to those receiving the results of the endeavors. These types of objectives help PR practitioners illustrate their worth and learn from their campaigns, and they certainly have a place within this process, internally.

However, an objective that is actually pitched to a plan reviewer via a proposal should be a bit different, as the potential clients are the ones decoding this message. It should be more descriptive of the efforts to take place, as clients are generally not as versed in the practice of public relations.

Objectives used in proposals and shown to the potential clients tell what actions must be taken with subjects of the plan to achieve a plan's goal. More than one objective usually is needed to achieve a goal. There must be one objective for each focal point or target audience of a plan.

An objective is distinguished by starting it with the infinitive *to*, and must contain three parts: (1) an action to be taken, (2) receiver of the action (e.g., focal point, target audience), and (3) a behavior that is desired of the receiver as a result of the action taken.

Let's look at examples of an objective's three components.

The first component of an objective describes an action that must be taken to achieve a plan's goal, for example, "To inform about a company's skyrocketing costs of medical insurance."

The second component identifies a receiver of the action. Who do we want to inform about the company's skyrocketing costs of medical insurance? The receiver of the action should be one of the focal points or target audiences of the plan, in this case, employees. A plan's objectives always focus on people because implementing a plan requires the engagement of people and public relations is the practice of influencing human behavior through strategic communication. When an objective is written without a receiver of the action, it is like focusing on a ghost. This exasperates plan reviewers because they want to know whose behavior is to be influenced to implement the objective.

The third component tells what behavior is desired of the target audience as a result of the action taken, for example, "To be willing to accept an increased share of medical insurance cost."

A complete objective would be "To inform employees about the company's skyrocketing costs of medical insurance so that they are willing to accept an increased share of the cost."

Action	To inform about the company's skyrocketing costs of medical insurance
Focus or Target	Employees
Result of the action	Willingness to accept an increased share of the costs for medical insurance
Objective	To inform employees about the company's skyrocketing costs of medical insurance so that they are willing to accept an increased share of the cost.

Rules for Writing an Objective

1. An objective must tell what must be done to achieve a plan's goal.

2. An objective must begin with the infinitive to, distinguishing it as an objective.

3. An objective must focus on people because in public relations nothing can be accomplished without some form of human engagement.

4. There should be one or more objectives for each of a plan's focal points or target audiences.

5. An objective must state an action to be taken with a target audience and a reason for the action, which could be called the objective's purpose or desired outcome.

6. An objective must be written to enable measurement. Measurement is enabled by the third part of an objective—a desired measurable outcome. The first part of an objective is an action, the second part is a receiver of the action, and the third part is a desired measurable outcome as a result of the action. For example, the measurable desired outcome of the objective, "To inform parents of safety measures that are in place so they feel there is no danger in sending their children to school on Monday," would be that parents send their children to school on Monday, which could be measured by school attendance records.

7. An objective should not state a means of measurement; that should be included in the evaluation provision following each objective.

8. An objective may contain a critical deadline or milestone; however, scheduling details are best left for inclusion in a plan's execution timeline.

9. An objective should not claim to have the ability to single-handedly influence areas over which it has partial control, such as sales, productivity, or stock value. It would be dishonest to guarantee a target, such as a 15 percent increase, or claim total credit for reaching a target in areas influenced by many other factors. It would be proper to claim the objective will "assist with" or "contribute to" obtaining a particular result.

It is the third component of an objective that most often is omitted, which is a crucial error because it is this component of an objective that enables measurement.

An objective, for example, might be stated as "To provide the media with information." This is not measurable because it does not tell what the media is expected to do as a result of having been provided information.

Action	Provide information
Focus or Target	Media
Result of the action	What's the desired result?

The reason for providing the media with information cannot be simply assumed. It must be stated. Reviewers who are paying the bill to have a plan implemented want to know what outcomes to expect from every objective. For example, reviewers would be expected to ask, "Why are we spending money to provide the media with information?" To answer the question, an objective must provide a desired behavioral outcome. For example, "To provide the media with newsworthy material so that journalists take an interest in publishing articles and that their reports can be based on complete and accurate information." Articles published can be measured in terms of number and content quality.

Action	Provide complete and accurate information
Focus or Target	Media
Result of the action	Media interest and news reports based on complete and accurate information
Objective	To provide the media with information so they take an interest in publishing articles and that their reports can be based on complete and accurate information.

An objective must be achievable, as well as measurable. It must aim at a result that is possible to achieve cost effectively. An objective can include a deadline or time frame. However, the sequencing of activities is best left for inclusion in the plan's timeline. If an objective includes a milestone or benchmark to be achieved, developers of the plan must have complete control of all factors required to reach the benchmark. A PR plan, for example, should not contain a sales target of, say, a 10 percent increase, unless the plan developers have total control over all factors that affect sales. Plan developers would not want to be held accountable for something over which they have only partial control.

An objective stops short of telling how something must be done. That is the role of a strategy. So a writer must resist the temptation to include in an objective a phrase such as "by holding a news conference;" that tells how an objective would be accomplished and is the role of a strategy.

Examples of Acceptable and Unacceptable Objectives

Unacceptable: *Work on many levels of the problem simultaneously to deliver a cannon shot impact that is deep and long lasting.*

Reasons: *This is gobbledygook; it is totally meaningless to plan reviewers.*

Acceptable: *No way to make gobbledygook acceptable.*

Unacceptable: *Generate publicity that strongly links Box of Snaps with baseball and highlights new "prize inside" series.*

Reasons: *An objective must focus on an audience and it must start with the infinitive to. An objective must include a desired outcome or change in behavior by the intended audience. In this case there is no target audience, nor is there any indication of what the writer of the plan wants the implied audience to do as a result of the publicity. Also, plans should take* *advantage of lessons learned from research on persuasion. A reviewer of this objective might ask, "Have you taken into account that research has shown that messages, especially those presented through the public media, are quickly forgotten if they are not at least moderately reinforced by repetition and that repetition is useful for keeping ideas in the public mind?"*

Acceptable: *To generate publicity that in the minds of Major League Baseball fans strongly links Box of Snaps with baseball and raises an interest in the new "prize inside" series so that more fans buy Box of Snaps.*

Unacceptable: *Promote each member of Smith's family of digital audio players through individually tailored campaigns to maintain market share of at least 30 percent.*

Reasons: *This objective does not begin with the infinitive to. It has no target audience. "Through individually tailored campaigns" tells how the objective is to be accomplished, which is the role of a strategy. Most importantly, public relations is a staff function and has no direct control over marketing—certainly not over all of the many factors necessary to promise a market share of 30 or any percent.*

Acceptable*: Beyond repair.*

Unacceptable: *Collect $5 million in contributions by conducting a capital fund drive.*

Reasons: *The statement does not begin with the infinitive to. No audience is specified. No time frame is specified. The phrase "by conducting a capital fund drive" tells how something is to be accomplished, which is the role of a strategy.*

Acceptable: *To convince targeted donors to pledge by December 1, 2017, a total of $5 million for expansion of the XYZ Medical Center.*

Unacceptable: *To fully inform the news media about the incident.*

Reason: *No desired outcome is indicated. What is expected of journalists if they are fully informed of the incident? In other words, what does the organization want journalists to do as a result of fully informing them?*

Acceptable: *To fully inform the news media about the incident to help ensure that their news reports are complete and accurate.*

Exercise 5: Objectives

Study the objectives in the following article. Critique the way the objectives are written. Explain (don't rewrite) how objectives should be written to be acceptable by the rules.

Potty Palooza and Charmin

To help promote Charmin Ultra, Procter & Gamble conducted a traveling road show. A semi-trailer was converted into a "commode on the road" with 27 private bathrooms. The facilities had hardwood floors, sinks with running water, uniformed attendants and Charmin Ultra toilet paper.

Teaser promotions were sent to local media in advance of each appearance of the Potty Palooza. They included T-shirts with "Potty Palooza 2002 ... It's Loo-La-La" on the front, and on the back was a U.S. map with stars marking each stop on the tour. The shirts were compressed and shrink-wrapped into the shape of an 18-wheel truck. Press releases were sent to local media two days before each festival's opening day. A media alert invited the press to visit the Potty Palooza. The main objectives were to get at least 30 million media impressions, secure at least 30 aired segments on television news, and to drive trial and sales of Charmin Ultra. The objectives were surpassed, with more than 62 million media impressions, more than 45 b-roll news hits, three national news stories, plus print and television coverage in all local market stops. Also, research showed a 14 percent increase in Charmin sales among consumers who used the Potty Palooza. Budget for the program was $300,000 and the agency was Manning, Selvage & Lee.

Table 4. Three Component Parts of an Objective

1. Examples of actions to be taken with a target audience or public in order for an objective to contribute toward the achievement of a plan's goal:

To accommodate	To focus	To present
To address	To forecast	To prove
To advise	To generate interest	To provide opportunities
To alleviate	To heighten interest	To raise awareness
To apprise	To honor	To recognize
To assure	To improve	To reconcile
To attract attention	To increase knowledge	To recruit
To change	To inform	To reduce anxiety
To communicate	To instill	To restore
To compile	To mobilize	To reveal
To convey	To negotiate	To sensitize
To describe	To offer	To share confidence
To diffuse emotion	To organize	To show
To educate	To orient	To simplify
To enlighten	To pique	To stimulate interested pet
To explain	To placate	owners

2. Examples of target audiences whose participation might be necessary to accomplish an objective:

analysts	employees	landowners
backpackers	environmental activists	lawyers
bankers	executives of nonprofits	local elected officials
chamber of commerce	farmers	local news media
college students	fashion editors	news media
commissioners	government regulators	parents
community leaders	government	physicians
council members	representatives	product partners
customers	high school students	professional organizations
development council	homeowners	program directors
educators	investors	prospects

residents	special interest groups	U.S. representatives
seniors	suppliers	U.S. senators
service clubs	talk show hosts	veterans
service providers	teachers	voters
shareholders	trade press	

3. Examples of desired behaviors of target audiences as a result of an action taken:

accept	experience	recommend
apply	help	reconsider
approve	insist	reject
assemble	invest	report accurately
attend	investigate	seek
believe	join	sell
buy	keep	sing
capitulate	lead	start
contact	leave alone	stop
contribute	march	support
demand	participate	sympathize
demonstrate	petition	travel
donate	play	trust
email	promote	try
empathize	publicize	
enroll	question	

6. Strategies

The next component of a plan is the strategy. Why are strategies important to plan reviewers? They are important because strategies describe how you will achieve your plan's objectives. Reviewers want to assess your methods for achieving objectives, the creativity behind your methods, the feasibility and practicality of your methods, and your knowledge of applying the fundamentals of persuasion in influencing behavior.

Every objective must have a strategy that describes how, in concept, the objective is to be achieved. More than one strategy might be necessary to accomplish an objective. A strategy must be realistic; it must take into account the amount of time, energy, personnel, expertise, and financial resources available for its implementation. A strategy can state key themes or messages to be reiterated throughout a campaign.

This component is the plan's stage for creativity. It is a plan's platform on which to showcase imaginative approaches to problems, opportunities, challenges, and all manner of diverse situations. If you don't think of yourself as creative, think again. Creativity is thinking of something that has not been thought of by others. In most cases, it has not been thought of by others because they have not had or taken the time to thoroughly investigate, to thoroughly research, a situation. To a plan reviewer, failure to come up with creative ideas is failure to study a situation in earnest.

When developing a strategy, you will strengthen what you propose by basing it, where possible, on lessons learned by others in the profession.

The strategy component provides a plan developer with an opportunity to educate plan reviewers on communication and persuasion. For example, it might be appropriate in a strategy to explain how the seed of an idea becomes a conviction to act. You might include in your strategy a reference, such as, "experience in the profession has shown that …" Do not refer to a particular experience unless it is totally appropriate to the situation. And be sure not to propose a strategy that is contrary to professional lessons learned, unless you can provide a solid rationale for the recommendation.

Rules for Writing a Strategy

1. A strategy should describe how, in concept, an objective is to be accomplished. More than one strategy could be required to accomplish a single objective.

2. A strategy may include an explanation about the use of persuasive techniques based on lessons learned through research; however, research findings should not be included unless they apply specifically to the situation.

3. A strategy may include a discussion of messages or themes.

4. A strategy is the place in a plan for creativity—a platform for presenting ideas that plan reviewers have not considered.

5. A strategy should be described in broad terms with details left to be covered as activities or tactics.

Examples of Acceptable and Unacceptable Strategies

Unacceptable: *The campaign strategy is a simple message for the campaign that could be conveyed through all mediums: "When it comes to keeping your water features clear, count on Barley Bob." Bob is an honest country boy who chews on barley and is spokesperson for the campaign.*

Reasons: *A strategy, according to the rules, must explain how an objective is to be accomplished. In this statement, the explanation is vague. It says, "The campaign strategy is a simple message …" A strategy may contain and explain the use of a particular message and may include the description of a character to deliver the message. However, this strategy falls short of explaining the strategic use of a message and campaign character. According to the rules, a strategy must explain how an objective is to be accomplished, followed by, in bulleted or numbered form, an elaboration of detailed activities. A strategy should take into account lessons learned by PR professionals. A plan reviewer might ask, for example, "Have you taken into account experience that has shown that humor sometimes can generate a liking for the message source, but can backfire if the audience thinks the use of humor is a manipulative device?"*

Acceptable: *We will accomplish Objective #1 by communicating through a variety of media a message for people to "Count on Barley Bob to keep water features clear." The message promoting the use of barley as a natural way to keep ponds and other water features free of algae will come from Barley Bob, the campaign's spokesperson. Research has shown that humor can be effective if it seems natural and not contrived. Bob is a friendly and believable* *character who delivers the natural care message with a hint of humor. The message from Bob will be conveyed to the region's homeowners through six different activities.*

Unacceptable: *Develop key messages and create benefit-focused materials that set a celebratory tone.*

Reasons: *This is gobbledygook and is totally meaningless to plan reviewers.*

Acceptable: *There is no way to make gobbledygook acceptable.*

Unacceptable: *Invite parents to an informational meeting.*

Reasons: *There is nothing strategic about this action. There is not sufficient detail to instill confidence that this strategy will accomplish its objective. There is no attempt to use this opportunity to educate plan reviewers on the techniques of persuasion or communication methods or to elaborate with a message theme or other details.*

Acceptable: *Contact parents by phone and provide compelling reasons why it is important for them to attend an informational meeting on January 1, 2017. Enlist volunteer parents to make the phone calls to give credibility to the communication. Have parent callers make note of feedback from the calls and have them try to confirm attendance of parents they contact in order to get an estimate of the total number likely to attend the meeting. Have callers stress that "No cases of this health problem have been detected and that the purpose of the meeting is to inform parents how to protect their children from becoming susceptible to the problem."*

Exercise 6: Strategies

Based on the rules, write a strategy for the case below. Use only the information provided in the case summary and stop short of listing the details (activities) of how the strategy is to be carried out.

T. T. Cottonfield LLC Media Campaign

Off-balance sheet financing is what got Enron in trouble, so you can appreciate how any company that provides off-balance sheet financing could easily be associated with such scandalous behavior. T. T. Cottonfield is a leading provider of net-lease financing, a traditional form of off-balance sheet financing. The company worried that when the Enron scandal hit, all forms of off-balance sheet financing would be discredited and considered invalid. The company decided to go on the offensive by launching a media campaign designed to differentiate the company's net-lease financing from Enron's use of special-purpose entities. T. T. Cottonfield wanted to capitalize on the high media interest by educating investors and corporate executives about the advantages of net-lease financing and promoting the company as the best firm to provide such financing.

The company, together with Dice, Dice & Rice Inc. arranged a luncheon with journalists from *The Wall Street Journal, Fortune*, Dow Jones, Bloomberg, and others.

The company created advertisements highlighting its financial capabilities aimed at executives whose companies held synthetic leases.

The company produced an acquisitions brochure that was distributed to senior-level corporate executives.

As a result of these efforts, T. T. Cottonfield was able to complete more than $1 billion in net-lease transactions in 2002, a new record for the company and more than double its 2001 results.

Influencing behavior through strategic communication requires that a message be received, noticed, understood, believed, remembered, and acted upon. The sender of a message must focus on message development, source and channel selection, exposure, and navigation around obstacles and through cognitive filters. Following are factors that should be considered in planning strategic communication.

Table 5. Factors in Communicating Strategically

Source	The source of the communication should be someone who is familiar to the intended audience or public, who is trusted, who is considered knowledgeable and credible, and who normally is looked to for information.	Familiar Trustworthy Knowledgeable Credible
Channels	The message should be sent through one or more channels that are familiar to and relied upon for information by the target audience or public. Selection of channels must be accurate. The channels must be adequate to convey the message completely and accurately. Redundant use of channels may be necessary to penetrate or circumvent communication barriers.	Familiar Adequate Redundant Accurate
Exposure	Day of week, time of day, and frequency with which the message is communicated are important factors in determining message exposure.	Timing Frequency
Obstacles	To be effective, communication of the message must overcome obstacles, such as noise, clutter and competition.	Clutter Noise Competition
Filters	Communication of the message must penetrate a receiver's thinking process, passing through cognitive filters of attitude, culture, experience, affiliations, and needs.	Attitude Culture Experience Affiliations Needs
Target	The intended receiver could be an individual, group of individuals, or a larger audience or public. To be effective, strategic communication must be noticed, understood, believed, accepted, remembered, and acted upon.	Noticed Understood Believed Accepted Remembered Acted Upon

Table 6. Commonly Known Facts About Persuasion

Sources	• People are strongly and quickly influenced by people they feel they can trust and believe. • People give even more credence to someone whose opinions are repeated by respected others. • People don't take seriously what they hear from people they don't trust, but over time they may recall what was said and forget who said it.
Message Structure	• It's usually best to make your argument first, refute opposing arguments, and then restate your position, depending on the complexity of the subject. • The last word is the one most likely to be remembered, especially with less educated people. • It's more effective to give both sides of an argument than to give one side, especially with educated audiences. • A one-sided argument might change attitudes initially, but the effect may fade when another side is heard. • People who hear both sides of an argument are likely to maintain a position even when other arguments are heard later. • It's more persuasive to state a conclusion than to expect people to draw their own. • Repetition keeps issues in the public eye. Messages, especially in the media, are quickly forgotten if they're not reinforced.
Message Content	• People listen to what they like and ignore what they dislike. • People pay attention to messages that favor what they believe and ignore those that don't. • People interpret things the way they think; they see what they want to see. • People remember what they consider to be relevant and forget the rest. • People remember things that support what they believe. • Facts and emotional appeals together are more effective than either one alone. • Messages aimed at the interest of a target audience are likely to get attention. • Trying to incite fear, guilt, or other negative emotions, or to issue threats are likely to turn people away. • The use of fear is more effective when combined with suggesting how to avoid it. • Fear can affect how people think, but not necessarily how they act. • Humor can win the hearts of an audience and alienate people if it seems manipulative.
Media	• Public media are more useful in reinforcing existing attitudes than in changing attitudes. • Print media produce more comprehension, especially with complex issues, than broadcast media. • Broadcast media get more attention than print media. • Face-to-face communication is more effective in changing minds than communication through various types of media. • Verbal communication conveys less but is more readily accepted than written communication.
Audience	• People with low self-esteem are more influenced by unsupported messages and fear appeals than people with high self-esteem. • People with high self-esteem are more likely to be persuaded by well substantiated messages. • People who make a commitment are likely to resist changing their minds afterward. • People who actively participate in making decisions are likely to retain changes in attitude over the long term.

7. Activities (Tactics)

An activity or tactic is what puts a strategy into action. Why is the activity component of importance to plan reviewers? It's important because activities provide the details of a strategy and reviewers want to assure themselves that they concur with the ways in which strategies are to be carried out.

More than one activity is usually required to implement a strategy. Typically, activities include the use of communication tools, such as podcasts and news releases, along with various actions and events. There is, however, nothing strategic about a list of communication tools. Yet, there are practitioners who tell reviewers that a strategy can be carried out, for example, with two brochures, a poster, and a fact sheet. It's the strategic use of communication tactics that reviewers want to see. So, avoid beginning activities with communication tools. It is always better to emphasize a strategic step before the vehicle that will be used to implement it.

Activity Begins with a Strategy Better	Activity Begins with a Tool
Generate interest and excitement about the sponsorship among reporters with a message from Bobby Apple and views of him racing in past competitions by sending them a short, specially produced communication on video or CD.	Send a video to all targeted media outlets to generate excitement about the sponsorship with a message from Bobby Apple and scenes of him racing.
Entice the media to interview Bobby Apple and photograph the show car at the Los Angeles Convention Center during the annual car show by sending them a media advisory loaded with photo op ideas.	Send a media advisory that entices the media to interview Bobby Apple and see the team's show car at the Los Angeles Convention Center during the annual car show.
Announce XYZ's sponsorship of the Indy race car team with attention-grabbing quotes from driver Bobby Apple in print and video news releases.	Send a print and video news release announcing XYZ's sponsorship of the Indy race car team with attention-grabbing comments from driver Bobby Apple.

Every tool must be used correctly by itself and in conjunction with other activities. It would be incorrect, for example, to use a news release in place of a media alert to announce a news conference. A plan developer must realize that plan reviewers at the senior level are not, for the most part, professional PR practitioners. It is likely, for example, that they would not know a white paper from a position paper, a tip sheet from a fact sheet, or a news conference from a news briefing. So when an activity calls for the use of a communication tool, you must describe what the device is as well as its purpose.

Activities should not be a list of routine logistical chores, such as "picking up donuts for the meeting," "copying and mailing letters," "renting a car," etc. Plan reviewers are interested in strategic details.

Also, activities should be comprehensive so that the plan developer does not unwittingly shift the job of development to the reviewer. For example, when an activity is described simply as, "Hold a meeting of faculty members who teach courses related to diversity," it raises questions. Hold a meeting where? When? How many faculty members? How would they be identified? What courses do they teach? How would the meeting be conducted? By whom? For what purpose? Providing answers to these questions is the job of the plan developer.

In summary, activities should provide reviewers with a detailed strategic sequence of moves necessary to carry out a strategy.

Rules for Writing an Activity (or Tactic)

1. Activities are detailed steps to be taken to carry out a strategy.

2. Activities should not be a to-do list of logistical chores (reserve a meeting room, order coffee, bring name tags, etc.)

3. Activities should not be a skeleton list of communication tools (brochure, news release, backgrounder, etc.); each communication tool must have a stated strategic purpose and must be employed in the correct manner.

4. Activities should begin with a strategic move, rather than a communication tool or vehicle.

5. Activities should provide complete information; they should not burden plan reviewers with unanswered questions.

Examples of Activities

1. Provide a company phone number for employees to call to receive information and ask questions about the company's downsizing activities. The phone number will be activated on September 18, 2017, and will be deactivated December 31, 2017.

2. Managers and supervisors will establish, or in most cases reaffirm, their open-door policy so employees will be more inclined to approach management with questions about the company's downsizing activities. The open-door policy will be implemented September 20, 2017, and will continue indefinitely.

3. The company will provide the most current downsizing information in monthly employee newsletters or memos. To increase employee confidence, included will be success stories of laid-off workers who have found new jobs outside the company. The first newsletter or memo will be sent to employees October 31, 2017, and will be published monthly through January 31, 2018.

Exercise 7: Activities or Tactics

Write three activities according to the rules for writing an activity or tactic.

Table 7. Communication Tools

Actuality	Editorial	Media alert
Alerts, Internet	Editorial board briefing	Media interview
Annual meeting	Email alert service	Media tour
Annual report	Email campaign	Memento
Archive video	Email pitch	Memo
Archived Webcast	Email survey	Message board
A-roll	E-newsletter	Mission statement
Background video	Episodic framing	MySpace
Backgrounder	E-tour	NetBriefing
Biographical sketch	Event	News briefing
Blog	Exclusive story	News kit
Booklet	Expert news source	News release
Briefing paper	Facebook	Newsgroup seeding
Broadcast news release	Fact sheet	Newsgroups
Brochure	Factoidv	Newsletter
B-roll	FAQ	Newswire
Bumper sticker	Fax, broadcast	Online media room
Buzz	Fax, on demand	Online newsroom
Byliner	Feature, business	Op-ed commentary
Card stacking	Feature, educational	Opinion actuality
Case history	Feature, personality	Organization profile
Chat rooms	Feature, trend	Personality profile
Circular	Infographics	Phone pitch
Closed circuit TV	Information kit	Photo caption
Collateral publication	Insert and enclosure	Photo news release
Commentary	Instant messaging	Pitch for radio talk show
Communication audit	Interview, print media	Pitch for TV coverage
Communication meeting	Interview, radio	Pocket points
Contingency statement	Interview, TV	Podcast, audio and video
Corporate profile	Intranet	Position paper
Cover letter	Leak	Poster
Dashboard	Letter	Prepared statement
Demonstration	Letter pitch	Presentation
Direct mail	Letter to editor	Print publication
Door hanger	Media advisory	Printcast

Product profile	Social media	Video news release
Product review	Social responsibility report	Video teleconferencing
Public Service Announcement, radio	Speakers' bureau	Virtual conference
	Speech	VO-BITE
Public Service Announcement, TV	Spokesperson tour	Voice mail
	Streaming video	VO-SOT
Publicity event	Syndicated service	Web conference
Publicity photo	Talk show	Web monitoring
Q&A	Testimonial	Web news conference
Quarterly earnings statement	Testimony	Webcast - audio
Questionnaire	Tip sheet	Webcast - full feature
Report	Tours	Webcast - visual
Rolling one-on-one	Town hall meeting	White paper
Safety meeting	Trend story	YouTube
Satellite media tour	TV stand-up interview	
Search engines	Twitter	

8. Execution Timeline

The execution timeline is a schedule of all activities in a plan. The timeline is important to reviewers because it provides a visual, at-a-glance sequence of actions showing how long each will take to implement. Timing has a major bearing on the success of a plan, so it is essential to schedule each activity or tactic to know exactly when one needs to begin in order to be completed on time. Plan reviewers see the timeline as an orchestration of activities or tactics that must be conducted with precision because they know that one weakness of executive management in recent times has been initiating plans and failing to supervise them through to completion. Time for each activity must be allotted accurately, not only for a plan to succeed, but also to show plan reviewers what is involved in preparing to achieve certain milestones. It is unlikely that a plan reviewer would know how much time is necessary to research a speech, design a website, write, review and clear a news release, or produce a white paper. In addition to showing dates, preparatory activities, and milestones, a timeline could provide for assigning responsibilities so that it is perfectly clear who is expected to execute each activity or tactic. The timeline could be in the form of a table, critical path diagram, Gantt chart, or even a calendar.

Rules for Writing an Execution Timeline

1. Plot all plan activities or tactics on the timeline.

2. Allot time accurately for each activity or tactic.

3. Show specific dates or appropriate time increments (hours, days, months, etc.) Think of this as "back-timing" to create a count down toward achieving a plan's goal.

4. Make entries self-explanatory.

5. Do not make the timeline a checklist of logistical chores, such as "Rent meeting hall. Hire catering service. Make table place cards."

6. Include preparatory steps for accomplishing activities or tactics.

7. Show milestones (completed stages of development).

8. Consider assigning responsibilities for activities or tactics.

9. Use an at-a-glance format for presenting the execution timeline, such as a table, critical path diagram, Gantt chart, or calendar.

Exercise 8: Execution Timeline

Develop a timeline for an elegant dinner party celebration. Use your imagination to provide details of the event. Begin with the preparatory steps for setting up the dining room and end at the point where guests are greeted. Include items such as table centerpieces, silverware settings, table place cards, and live music, etc.

Example of an Execution Timeline (Table Format)

Date	Preparation	Execution
July 8	Conduct plant closure planning meeting. Review business rationale and approve Q&A.	
July 12	Notify manager of Cyber of plant closure.	
July 15	Meet with Cyber plant manager to discuss business issues relative to closure.	
July 17–19	Conduct three-day work session with human resources director and Cyber plant manager. Review operational shutdown plan and timetable, identify core staff, develop retention plan, approve communication plan, discuss government regulations, approve news releases, review employment information, develop employment assistance, finalize security arrangements, and approve contingency plan.	

July 26	Notify all plant managers by phone of Cyber plant closure. Notify all functional managers of Cyber of closure. Have customer mailings ready. Deliver by courier information kits to division managers.	
July 27	Have information kits ready for sales representatives, sales managers, and service center managers.	
July 28	Follow up with Cyber functional managers. Notify district sales managers by phone.	
July 29		Plant Closure Announcement • Inform service center managers • Inform Cyber supervisors • Conduct meetings with Cyber employees • Inform community (hand-deliver news release to local media) • Inform sales representatives by phone • Inform Cyber customer service representatives in face-to-face meeting • Notify employees of relocation opportunities • Distribute news release to corporate personnel • Transmit news release to state wires via BusinessWire • Distribute letter from CEO to all employees • Call community opinion leaders • Call or fax local and state officials • Notify key suppliers by phone • Fax news release to trade press • Mail letter and news release to customers • Mail letter and news release to suppliers • Follow up on all communication to ensure complete and accurate understanding by all audiences

Example of an Execution Timeline (Critical Path Format)

A Timeline may be shown in a variety of forms, such as a flow chart. The critical path chart (below) shows preparatory work below the timeline and the main event above the line. Another version could be showing behind-the-scenes work below the line and activities in public view above the line, or preparatory work below the line and milestones (stages of progress) above the line.

Critical Path Chart (On a larger scale fill boxes with text.)							
7/8	7/12	7/15	7/17 to 7/19	7/26	7/27	7/28	7/29

July 8	Conduct plant closure planning meeting; review business rationale and approve Q&A
July 12	Notify manager of Cyber of plant closure
July 15	Meet with Cyber plant manager to discuss business issues relative to closure
July 17–19	Conduct three-day work session with human resources director and Cyber plant manager to review operational shut-down plan and timetable, identify core staff, develop retention plan, approve communication plan, discuss government regulations, approve news releases, review employment information, develop employment assistance, finalize security arrangements, and approve contingency plan
July 26	Notify all plant managers by phone of Cyber plant closure, notify all functional managers of Cyber of closure, have customer mailings ready, and deliver information kits to division managers by courier
July 27	Follow up with Cyber functional managers and notify district sales managers by phone
July 28	Have information kits ready for sales representatives, sales managers, and service center managers
July 29	Plant Closure Announcement

- Inform service center managers
- Inform Cyber supervisors
- Conduct meetings with Cyber employees
- Inform community (hand-deliver news release to local media)
- Inform sales representatives by phone
- Inform Cyber customer service representatives in face-to-face meeting
- Notify employees of relocation opportunities
- Distribute news release to corporate personnel
- Transmit news release to state wires via BusinessWire
- Distribute letter from CEO to all employees
- Call community opinion leaders
- Call or fax local and state officials

- Notify key suppliers by phone
- Fax news release to trade press
- Mail letter and news release to customers
- Mail letter and news release to suppliers

Period Following Announcement

- Follow up on all communication to ensure complete and accurate understanding by all audiences.

9. Evaluation

Public relations plans and proposals should be written to enable evaluation in two ways: performance and effectiveness. Simply: Did the plan implementer do what the plan implementer stated would be done? How effectively was it done?

Performance

A plan reviewer wants a regular means of assurance that a plan is being implemented the way it was proposed—every strategic step executed on schedule, and on target. An implementer of a plan cannot guarantee results, but can be and should be held accountable for performance. Plan implementers must be careful to promise to deliver only what they totally control, and that is their own performance. They are expected to execute a plan to the best of their ability, but because they do not have control over every factor that can affect a plan's outcome, they cannot guarantee results.

Plan developers and implementers should provide reviewers with means to monitor progress and performance in the execution of a plan with a Progress Tracking Report. Once a template is formed, the report can be updated easily and submitted to reviewers on paper or electronically as frequently as desired. See a sample Progress Tracking Report on page 25.

Effectiveness

The relative effectiveness or value of what is done in public relations is determined by measurement. PR measurement involves assessing the success or failure of specific PR programs against predetermined objectives.

More specifically, PR measurement is a way of giving a result a precise dimension, generally by comparison to some standard or baseline and usually is done in a quantifiable or numerical manner. That is, when we measure outcomes, we should come up with a precise measure, for example: number of persons convinced to participate, to contribute, to attend, to accept, to reject, to follow, and to respond, etc. Because public relations is not an exact science and because a plan implementer does not have total control of all factors that influence results, PR practitioners must be mindful not to claim total credit for results, such as increased sales, improved productivity, and rising stock values. It is important to the profession and to the practitioner to make legitimate claims about supporting or contributing to outcomes that are obviously the result of multiple factors, along with PR actions. Boastful, unsubstantiated claims of success serve only to undermine the credibility of the profession, and when observed should heighten the profession's resolve to adhere to the Code of Ethics espoused by the Public Relations Society of America.

Writing plans based on solid research and written to enable measurement are products that distinguish professionals in this field. Every practitioner, to be a true professional, must have a fundamental knowledge of how value is established in public relations.

Rules for Writing the Evaluation

1. After each objective in the plan, describe how it is to be measured. For example:

Evaluation for Objective #1

Success in achieving this objective will be determined, informally, based on feedback supervisors receive from employees indicating employee understanding and support of a need to change communication procedures.

2. Position the main evaluation component of the plan after the plan's Execution Timeline and before the Progress Tracking Report. In the plan, under the heading "Evaluation," explain that the plan is written to enable evaluation in two areas: effectiveness and performance. Refer to the discussion above to develop a general explanation. For example:

Evaluation

This plan is written to enable evaluation in two areas: effectiveness and performance. The objectives in the plan are measurable to enable reviewers to judge the plan's effectiveness in accomplishing its goal. Evaluation details for measurement are shown for each objective of the plan. To show accountability for performance, the plan has a Progress Tracking Report, an at-a-glance visual, to show that activities of the plan are on schedule, on target, on budget, or completed.

Exercise 9: Evaluation

Based on the rules for developing the evaluation component of a plan, explain how the following entry could be improved.

Evaluation: Public Forum

The public forum on February 29 was well attended (300 people). Initial questions regarding the problem shifted to broader questions regarding health policy and were directed to the officials present. The center was not the main focus as before. Media coverage on February 30 and March 2 reported on the forum as well as the court findings of no wrongdoing ... and for the first time in months, things got quiet. The hotline recorded 10 phone calls, many from customers wanting reassurance that their warranties remained unchanged. Employees who had borne the brunt of angry customers were acknowledged with a series of appreciation events, including a pancake breakfast served by the president. Further, anecdotal feedback from community leaders was positive, and the quick resolutions of negative media coverage were great indicators of initial success. The topic, which held the attention of the media and community for nearly four months, has entirely dissipated.

10. Budgets

The budget is of paramount interest to reviewers. One of the quickest ways to have a plan rejected is by proposing a budget that is out of line with the organization's resources. An experienced plan developer will gather the insights necessary to present a budget appropriate to the organization. It is much better to present a budget that is on target than to present one that is out of the ballpark, requiring major modifications, even elimination, of some creative strategies to be acceptable. With public relations, communication objectives can be accomplished in many different ways at different levels of expense. Developing a plan within a particular budget is one of the responsibilities of the plan developer.

Rules for Writing a Budget

1. Use the correct budget format: PR Agency or Company.

2. A proposed budget from a PR agency must show time billing for personnel and out-of-pocket expenses.

3. An estimated budget by an organization's PR function must show only extraordinary expenses—those not covered in an annual department budget.

4. Proposed budgets should be affordable to an organization.

5. Budget items should be self-explanatory.

6. Budget figures must be aligned on a decimal point.

A proposed budget should be developed from one of two positions. One position is that you represent a PR firm or agency and your plan is for a client. The other position is that you are an employee of an organization with responsibility for public relations and your plan is for your employer. You must use a budget format that is appropriate for your position.

Let's look first at a budget format for a plan developed by a PR agency. The budget should have two parts: (1) time billing for agency personnel and (2) billing for out-of-pocket expenses.

For time billing, you must estimate the amount of time required by agency personnel to carry out the work of your plan. The lead person on an agency account usually is the account executive, so most of the work will be done by the account executive and an account coordinator, account assistant, or assistant account executive. Also, a certain amount of administrative or secretarial work is usually required.

Time for personnel more senior to the account executive might be included for their particular expertise or experienced counsel. For a highly complex plan, time might be budgeted for an account supervisor who would be responsible for managing the use of additional expertise and services, such as various forms of research. Following are typical PR agency hourly billing rates for use in developing a budget for case exercises in this book.

Example of a Budget for a Public Relations Firm

Relations Firm or Agency Hourly Billing Rates

President, General Manager, PR Director	$200.00
Vice President	150.00
Account Supervisor	125.00
Senior Account Executive	100.00
Account Executive	90.00
Assistant Account Executive	85.00
Account Coordinator, Account Assistant	75.00
Secretary	60.00

Next, your budget should show out-of-pocket expenses. These are expenses the agency would incur or contract for on behalf of the client, such as photography, graphic design, opinion research, media monitoring, long distance phone charges, photocopies, printing, etc. An estimated budget from an agency should have two components: (1) time billing for personnel and (2) billing for out-of-pocket expenses. Suggested formats:

Estimated Budget (PR Agency)

Time Billing					
Agency Staff	Rate/hour	Est. Hours/Day	Est. Days	Amount	
				Subtotal Time Billing	
Out-of-Pocket Expenses					
Description				Amount	
				Subtotal Out-of-Pocket Expenses	
				Total Estimated Budget	

Example of a Budget for an Organization or Company

Now let's look at a budget format for a plan that you, as the person responsible for public relations, would develop for your employer. One major difference between this budget and one developed by a PR firm is that time for work done by you and various staff members is already accounted for in salaries, and some of the expenses shown in the plan, such as photography, might already be covered in your organization's annual PR budget. So, in this position, the budget should show only items or services for which you must request authorization for additional funding.

The budget format for a plan developed by company PR personnel should be as follows:

Estimated Budget (Organization or Company)

Expenses		
Item Description	Amount	
	Total Estimated Expenses	

Exercise 10: Budget

Develop a proposed budget from a PR agency for pitching a client's appearance on Hello America. Consider accounting for time to develop the pitch, including researching the client's subject, creating and producing visuals for the client (charts, photographs, etc.), writing briefing notes for the client, television monitoring service, and other details using your own imagination.

IV. Public Relations Case Studies

This section of the book features actual case situations with compelling needs for public relations action. What distinguishes the cases is that they are not only real world, but typical of what students can expect to encounter going into the work place. Each case is presented in a different manner, such as a role play of a meeting, a contract for services, a transcript of private meetings, or field notes by an account executive. Each case has a team assignment to develop a PR plan and individual team member assignments to provide written elements in support of a plan, such as a news release, briefing notes for a television show, or pocket point cards. No solutions are offered for the cases because, realistically, in public relations, there are different ways to address situations effectively. Names of people, companies, organizations, and other identifying factors have been hidden to provide a true account of each case. Information attributed to individuals in these cases is true to the extent of their personal knowledge, but not always completely factual.

1. Community Relations: Mysterious Sound in Deschambault

Learning Outcomes

By the end of this case, you should be able to:

1. differentiate between the function of traditional public relations and the activities that could enhance public perception,

2. gain an understanding about varying stakeholders and their priorities, and

3. understand both deontology and utilitarianism and how subscribing to each could change organizational decisions.

Let's visit what was the destination of many memorable business trips. They were made memorable by relationships developed with a welcoming community of residents of the French-Canadian village of Deschambault, located in the province of Quebec on the north bank of the St. Lawrence River between Quebec City and Montreal.

An elderly resident of the village wrote a letter to the manager of a huge plant ramping up to full operation in an industrial park developed by the village. In her letter, she expresses concern about a low-level sound she hears inside of her house. She writes that the sound is audible enough to be annoying and asks if he "would be so kind as to investigate and do something to eliminate it."

A major complication in the case is that technicians from the plant took appropriate equipment to the house, tested for sound at different times and on different days at the direction of the resident, and printed charts that showed no evidence of a low-level sound the resident said she was hearing.

After a thorough investigation was completed, the PR manager believed that, all things considered and regardless of the tests, the company, as a gesture of goodwill, should retrofit the entire cottage with the latest insulating and sound-proofing materials.

The elderly woman is a highly respected member of the community. She has written about the region, has kept local traditions alive, and has supported efforts to improve the local economy. The house is on a road built in 1734 to link the cities of Quebec City and Montreal.

The nearby production plant is a billion-dollar operation built as a global model in the use of the best technology available for the handling and processing of material resources, exceeding all standards of environmental control.

Noise, however, is of concern to some residents. For many years, villagers have enjoyed the country charm and serenity of the lower Saint Lawrence. People who regard the peacefulness of the area as a special value would consider any new noise a disturbing intrusion. But the region is in a state of transition. The Société d'expansion de Portneuf provided an industrial park with a full range of services inviting projects ranging from cottage industries to megaplants. No matter how hard businesses and industries try to integrate their operations with the environment, things will never be the way they were in this agrarian region. These were the circumstances under which the plant manager had to make decisions about this community relations situation.

As you read the case, think about it not in strict business terms, but rather in terms of doing what's right. In public relations, sometimes you need to use your judgment as a human being in addition to your business acumen to solve a problem.

Presume you are from the public relations department of the parent corporation of the plant in Deschambault and that you have traveled there to meet with the plant manager about the mysterious sound and the community relations implications.

Assignment

1. Write a recommendation to the plant manager for dealing with the mysterious sound situation, addressing all of the following questions:

   A. What do you think the plant manager should do?

   • Respond to the resident's letter, defending the plant

   • Deny the problem

   • Argue the cost/benefits of industrial development

- Minimize responsibility with excuses

- Blame the community for inviting industry and not accepting it

- Pay a personal visit and offer an apology

- Something else

B. Should the company try to accommodate the resident's request?

- What does accommodation mean in this case?

- What are the pros and cons of using accommodation in this case?

- What should the company do now that the plant manager has investigated the sound and did not detect with scientific equipment any low-level sound inside the house?

- Should the company, as a gesture of goodwill, retrofit the house with insulation, storm windows, and other sound-proofing methods whether or not a sound is detected?

C. How would you counsel the plant manager in discussing this problem with the elderly woman?

- Is it best to address the emotion, then the facts? Does the order matter?

- What emotions are involved? What are the facts?

D. What about the matter of control?

- What type of control (recourse) does the resident have? What control does the plant manager have in the situation?

- Should control be shared?

- How could control be shared?

- Is control sharing a facet of accommodation?

E. Why would it be important to have a planned approach to addressing this case?

- What are the benefits of planning?

- How would planning serve the plant manager?

- How would planning serve the parent company?

- How would planning serve the community?

2. Briefly research deontology and utilitarianism. How would your approaches and decisions differ if you were to subscribe to one approach versus the other in this situation?

2. Accountability in Event Planning: Getting Nothing for Something

Learning Outcomes

By the end of this case, you should be able to:

1. understand the role that events play within public relations,

2. grasp the necessity or the potential non-necessity of events in different situations, and

3. appreciate the value that community advocates and supporters add to an organization.

This case is about accountability and strategy in event planning. Chances are you have attended an open house and enjoyed the host's generous hospitality. If that was the extent of your visit, you could say that the host spent a lot of time and money and got little in return.

Assignment

The case is an example of holding an event and leaving guests with no more than a nice impression. Read or enact with classroom colleagues the case role play of two retired executive managers and their assessment of an open house to introduce a new job training center to a community. Then write a paper or discuss in class how the following questions will help ensure that you are getting something for your organization's efforts.

1. Is there really a need for an open house, or type of event that you are contemplating?

2. How else could the need be met? Are there better alternatives?

3. How would you pitch such an event to the budgetary decision makers at your company or organization?

4. What are you hoping all of those who are exposed to an invitation learn, whether they accept or decline?

5. What if guests are invited yet nobody or only few people attend? Would it still be worth it? Is there another way to convey your message?

6. How can you ensure that your event is on brand? Think about visual brand and also about the intended messages of your organization.

7. Will the media be interested in such an event? Does that matter to you?

8. What are you hoping that all guests learn from the event?

9. How will you measure the effectiveness of the event? What are you specifically wanting to measure?

10. How will the event foster meeting the overall goals of your organization?

Class Role Play

Cast

Dave—retired executive
Frank—retired executive
Restaurant—Two retired executives, Frank and Dave, are talking over breakfast

Dave

Did you go to the open house yesterday?

Frank

Yes. I went over after lunch.

Dave

Did you meet the director?

Frank

He was the CEO of that chain of methadone clinics. Wouldn't have been my pick for the new center.

Dave

Ironic that in management it's easier for an inadequate CEO to keep his job than it is for an inadequate subordinate. That's what Warren Buffett says.

Frank

Sad, but true. Look at that guy. Not much of a performer and they make him head of a new health care job training center. He'll keep that position forever. Chances are good that he has no specified performance standards from the board. Most CEOs don't.

Dave

Or they're easily explained away. Buffett says too many bosses shoot the performance arrow, then run over to paint a bull's eye around the spot where it lands.

Frank

You like Buffett.

Dave

Yeah. I especially agree with him about boards of directors. He says relations between a board and a CEO are expected to be congenial. Any criticism of a CEO's performance is seen as socially unacceptable as belching. Nothing like that stops an office manager from coming down hard on employees.

Frank

Someone should come down hard on the new director for that open house.

Dave

Why so?

Frank

Well, for one thing, they obviously spent big bucks on food, entertainment and giveaways and what did they get for it?

Dave

Yeah, that was apparent to me too. I left with the impression that it's a nice place with nice people and that's about all. What's the point of spending the money?

Frank

The invitation was an expensive piece, too. And, I would have sent some information with it for people who couldn't attend. At least they would be a little more knowledgeable about the center and the mailing wouldn't be a complete waste of money.

Dave

If I were a board member I'd hold the new director accountable for spending money on an event like that and getting virtually nothing for it.

Frank

I remember an open house we had. Talk about impressions! Our PR woman—boy, was she tenacious!

Dave

Pretty aggressive.

Frank

Aggressive about getting results! Why are we doing this? What's the message you want to give to everyone who attends and to those who don't attend? What's the impression you want to make on the whole community? She kept firing questions then came back with a detailed plan and budget.

Dave

I remember that grand opening. So does the whole community, I'll bet. I shook so many hands that I was sure I'd get a cold that week.

Frank

Yeah. We had greeters, well-rehearsed tour guides, information stations with important points on sign boards, good but not lavish refreshments, and mementos that were useful to keep as reminders. Our PR woman wouldn't have launched the event without a clear, measurable objective.

Dave

Well, I think yesterday's open house showed a clear lack on the new manager's part of making good use of capital.

Frank

The unintelligent use of capital is apparent too often in Corporate America.

Dave

Hey listen, Frank. It's my turn to pay for the eggs. Let's do it again next Friday.

[End]

3. Employee Communication: Quality out of Control

Learning Outcomes

By the end of this case, you should be able to:

1. analyze data to create a potential avenue for a communication strategy;

2. use and apply persuasive principles, specifically in regard to discerning diverging values, beliefs, attitudes, or behaviors; and

3. understand how to creatively reach an audience or a public when electronic communication and social media may not be a feasible tactical solution.

All businesses—service as well as manufacturing—have one objective in common and that is to deliver quality in whatever they have to market. Quality is the cornerstone in building a business, so over the years many different "Q programs," such as TQM, or Total Quality Management, have been used to ensure quality in every phase of providing a product. Those phases include purchasing materials, manufacturing, shipping, and billing. This case points out what many companies have learned: without effective communication, you will not achieve a high standard of quality even if you have checks and balances in every phase of the business.

Better Bags manufactures various forms of paper packaging. The manager of one of the company's plants that manufactures paper shopping bags for grocery stores asks you to meet with him to discuss a problem. At the meeting he says, "I have been talking quality around here for months and it's like talking to a brick wall! Quality seems to be lacking in everything we do and I don't know what more I can do. We're beginning to lose customers. We get reports about handles falling off bags and bottoms falling open. One lady is suing us for letting a jar of Bobos Bread & Butter Chips fall through a bag and break her toe. We have had everything tested and we know the problem is not with paper or glue. It's a problem with how we work together to run the equipment that makes the product. It's a very serious situation. I don't want to reinvent this place at this point in my career. I'm just asking you if, as a PR professional, your expertise in communication can help get my quality message across to everybody."

Assess the Audience

In understanding the psychographics of your different audiences and publics, one must discern where their values, beliefs, attitudes, and behaviors diverge in any instance in which you are trying to persuade. As persuasive messages are a key component to practicing public relations, this concept needs to be learned and understood.

For instance, all parties may say that they value health. There is no divergence there. Therefore, to persuade effectively, one looks to the next level, which is beliefs. I may believe that exercise is good for my health. Another person may not believe this; they may think that it's a false concept. If I find that point of divergence, I then realize that all of my persuasive efforts must begin in that area and combat the perception that exercise is not a necessity for good health—the belief. Had the person who I'm attempting to persuade agreed with me and had our beliefs aligned, I would have moved to attitude. If I have a positive attitude toward exercising, but someone whom I'm persuading has a negative attitude toward exercising, yet our values and beliefs had aligned, then I spend my time persuading them by working to change their attitude. My tactics should be messaged in this way.

To finish the example, if our values, beliefs, and attitudes had all aligned, but our point of divergence was behavior—I exercise many times per week, but they do not—then I spend time working to persuade an actual behavior change. I try to get them to exercise more, and I focus my messages around this. Many times in persuasion, it is our instinct to go straight toward a behavior change when we are trying to convince a person or a group because this is the end goal that we desire. However, this is not the correct way to persuade, as if the point of divergence comes before behavior—in values, beliefs, or attitudes—you can lose your audience quickly. You must find where you differ and address those issues before moving onto the next area.

Assignment

This case focuses on the use of research to solve a production problem. Presume that you conducted and recorded 11 interviews, lasting one hour each, of staff members and the plant manager. That would amount to 11 hours of recorded dialogue to listen to, make notes on, and analyze. Plant production could not be stopped for the research and analysis. You decide to do the interviews and expedite your analysis by asking each person interviewed to summarize their answers to questions in one or two words. The interview results are shown in the chart that follows.

Analyze the results by reviewing the different responses to each question and, collectively, to the plant manager's responses. Determine for yourself why a communication expert was hired to solve the problem. How consistent are the responses among staff members and collectively between staff members and the plant manager?

1. Explain your analysis.

2. Where is the point of divergence (value, belief, attitude, behavior) of each of the interviewees and how would you treat each of these situations differently due to those findings? This may take some inferring, which is fine for this exercise.

3. Explain how you would present your findings to the plant manager.

4. Study the fact sheet about the plant and its operation.

5. Develop a public relations/communication plan based on your research to address the problem and to put your client back in control of quality production. Remember that you may have different approaches to persuasion, due to different diverging areas of your audience members.

6. Decide which avenues of dissemination would be best to communicate each of your intended messages.

Research Findings

First column: persons interviewed.

Top row: questions asked.

1. Is quality one of the plant's main priorities?

2. What seems to be management's main focus?

3. Describe the plant's quality standards.

4. Who sets the quality standards?

5. How well are the standards met?

6. What is the greatest need for improvement in this plant?

	Priority[1]	Focus[2]	Standards[3]	By Whom[4]	Met[5]	Need[6]
Plant Manager	Yes	People	Customers specify	All	Good	Money
Printing Supervisor	I think so	Quality	Don't know	Supervision	Yes	Quality control
Production Manager	Yes	Production	Don't know	History	Reasonably good	Communication
2nd Shift Supervisor	Not sure	Safety	Try to make best product	Supervision	We try	Fix floor congestion
Mechanical Engineer	Used to be	Production	Fluctuating	Supervisor, Production Manager, Superintendent	Pretty well	Communication
Superintendent	Don't know	People	Don't know	Supervision	No	One-on-one communication
2nd Shift Supervisor	Yes	Service	Don't know	Top management	Depends	Resolve personal conflicts
Personnel Manager	Yes	Profit	None	Superintendent Customer Service	Hit & miss	More decisive management
Bottoming Supervisor	Think so	Don't know	Talk quality	Tony	Few rejects	Better communication
Production Scheduler	Used to be	Appease customers	Inconsistent	Top management, Supervisor	Mostly OK	Leadership & Communication
Warehouse Supervisor	Depends	Safety	Fine	Everybody	Not bad for the U.S.	Replace the Production Manager

Business Description: Better Bags Inc., Paperville, U.S.A.

Employees: 230
Product: Paper grocery bags with paper handles
Customers: Grocery stores, both chains and independents
Established: In business since 1972
Manager: Tom Jones, 64; 30 years of service; degree in mechanical engineering from the University of Engineering

Bag operation: The bag operation is automated. Movement of material is along an assembly line of machines that cut, fold, glue, and attach paper handles. The equipment adjusts to changes in temperature. Paper jams are infrequent, but require setup and adjustment time. Although the equipment is automated, it must be closely monitored, which requires diligence on the part of equipment operators, accurate reading of gauges, recording of data by workers, and coordination between shift supervisors. Sometimes the equipment runs 24/7. To reach an optimum operating level that results in efficiencies that produce a margin of profit, managers, supervisors, and workers must operate as a team, focusing on quality standards that are demanding of the equipment and the entire workforce. Similar bag operations in other company locations have shown that to achieve optimum production levels, quality standards must be clearly defined and effectively communicated. It has also been learned by industry that many factors are to blame for poor quality, including company politics, shortsighted thinking, and poor management. However, at Better Bags Inc., product quality at six of the company's plants was improved substantially and measurably just through measures taken to improve communication.

Communication: The plant operates three shifts: (1) 7 a.m. to 3 p.m., (2) 3 p.m. to 11 p.m., and (3) 11 p.m. to 7 a.m. On each shift, employees are given a 20-minute lunch break. Supervisors conduct safety meetings every day at the beginning of each shift. Supervisors also conduct communication meetings once each month. The plant manager talks to employees quarterly by shift. The most effective ways to communicate with employees are (1) through supervisors, (2) by weekly newsletter, (3) by monthly video tape, and (4) by closed circuit television. Employees function in work groups and, for special efforts, in teams. Team members select a team leader. The team effort is coached by the shift supervisor.

4. Media Relations: Charlie Zurlock

Learning Outcomes

By the end of this case, you should be able to:

1. understand the fundamentals of constructive, firm but tactful counseling of individuals resistant to taking advice;

2. understand the importance of, and guidelines involved in, training management and all employees about media relations;

3. understand the importance of, and guidelines involved in, training necessary employees about government relations; and,

4. review Maslow's Hierarchy of Needs and understand how and why this learning theory should be understood by public relations practitioners.

This case is a challenging exercise in media relations. Working with the mass media in seeking publicity or responding to their interests is a major function of public relations. This case requires more than establishing and maintaining a good working relationship with the media. It involves counseling a company owner whose lack of understanding of how to work with the media has resulted in an unending saga of negative publicity.

The challenge is to educate the client on the basics of media relations, take immediate steps to end the negative publicity, and provide the client with measures that will begin to restore and establish external relationships that will serve to reduce the chances of generating negative publicity in the future.

The case also involves addressing relationships with government and with company employees. Details of the case unfold in a script that can be used as a classroom or professional workshop role play to show how the company got into an adversarial relationship with a newspaper reporter. Assignments and additional case materials appear after the script.

Class Role Play

Cast

Narrator
Dorothy—Secretary
Student's Name—Reporter
Robin Jackson—Plant Engineer
Jessica Murray—Director, Department of Ecology
Charlie Zurlock—Owner
Dr. Emerson—State Physician
Nancy White—Secretary, Human Resources
Dan Peopleton—Director, Human Resources

Narrator

In the newsroom, a reporter lifts the telephone receiver, calls Custom Parts Company, and asks for the owner. The secretary answers.

Secretary, Human Resources

Charlie Zurlock's office, this is Dorothy. How can I help you?

Reporter

Hello Dorothy. This is (your name) with the MESSENGER. I'd like to speak to Mr. Zurlock about your pollution problem.

Secretary, Human Resources

(instructively)
Mr. Zurlock said if anyone calls about that citation, they should talk to our plant engineer. Would you like me to transfer you to her line?

Narrator

The reporter, somewhat concerned about the owner's refusal to speak to the media about environmental health and safety, agrees to talk to the plant engineer.

Reporter

Yes. What's his name?

Secretary, Human Resources

(boldly correcting the reporter)
HER name is Jackson. Robin Jackson. Just a minute please.

Narrator

The phone rings. Robin Jackson answers.

Plant Engineer

(sounding annoyed)

Hello. Robin Jackson here.

Reporter

Hello, Ms. Jackson. This is (your name) with the MESSENGER. Your title, is it plant engineer?

Plant Engineer

That's right. What do you want?

Reporter

I'd like your reaction to the DOE's announcement. The agency said it appears that five out of every 10,000 people living around your plant stand a good chance of getting cancer.

Plant Engineer

(defensive; takes a shot at the DOE)
There are plenty of ways that government bureaucrats can interpret its data. We've conducted our own health studies of our workers. There's been no increased incidence of cancer.

Reporter

(aggressively interjecting)
But the DOE ...

Narrator

The plant engineer tries to impose the results of a company-funded study that minimizing the health risk but that has yet to be completed.

Plant Engineer

(interrupts)
Listen. We just launched a new study. And we are predicting that by year's end, the findings will show that our emissions pose no more risk than smoke from a cigarette in an auditorium.

Narrator

Aghast, the reporter thinks this engineer must have a crystal ball, since she seems to know the results of a study before it's conducted, and wonders how much the company is paying to get the findings it wants.

Reporter

If you're so sure your emissions are harmless, why did the DOE target your operation for an impact study?

Narrator

The plant engineer attempts to sidestep the issue by taking another shot at the DOE and pointing a finger at other companies.

Plant Engineer

They're picking on us because we're nearby. We're just on the outskirts of town, you know. Practically under their office window. Hey look, we're not the only plant around here with emissions. The other plants like ours are tuned into this issue. You can bet on that! Sorry, I've got to take another call.

Narrator

The reporter, irritated with having been cut off, calls Jessica Murray, director of the DOE, and tells her what the Custom Parts engineer said about the pollution fine and the DOE.

Reporter

Hello, Jessica, this is (your name) with the MESSENGER. I tried to talk with Custom Parts about the pollution citation and fine that it got from you. The plant engineer, Robin Jackson, disagrees with you. She says their emissions pose no health risk. She implied that your agency is manipulating the data. She said the DOE is picking on Custom Parts because the plant is conveniently close to your offices.

Narrator

Upset with the accusation that her government agency is lazy and manipulative, the DOE director strikes back with a sweeping, unsubstantiated but quotable opinion.

Director, Department of Ecology

I think we're going to be able to show that emissions from that plant, and every plant like it, pose a substantial health threat.

Narrator

The reporter ends the call to the DOE and then calls Custom Parts, this time getting through to the owner, Charlie Zurlock.

Reporter

Hello, Charlie Zurlock?

Owner

Yes, this is Zurlock.

Reporter

I'm (your name) with the MESSENGER. I'm doing a story on your plant and yesterday's announcement by the DOE. I talked earlier with your engineer, Robin Jackson. But I have a few more questions.

Owner

Get on with it. I've got a busy schedule.

Reporter

(not about to be rushed)
The DOE thinks it's going to be able to show that emissions from your plant, and plants like it, pose a substantial health risk to employees and people living around your plant. Exactly how much toxic material is your plant emitting?

Narrator

Ignoring the public's legal right to know about toxic emissions, the owner hesitates, then responds.

Owner

(clears throat)
I can't recall the amount. Even if I could, I wouldn't want to tell you.

Reporter

(disgusted with the owner's arrogance)
Aren't you even a little concerned that your emissions might be endangering the health of your own employees and the community?

Owner

(tries to minimize the risk)
I'm telling you … Our emissions are no more harmful to the human body than smoke from a wood-burning stove.

Narrator

The reporter calls the Department of Health and reaches the state physician.

Reporter

Hello, Dr. Emerson. I'm (your name) with the MESSENGER. I just spoke with the owner of Custom Parts Company. He claims that their emissions are no more harmful than smoke from wood-burning stoves. How harmful do you think the effects really are?

Narrator

Not pleased to hear the company minimize a health risk, the physician offers an unsubstantiated but quotable opinion and refuses to let the company off the hook.

State Physician

I think there is occupational exposure at the plant causing more cases of cancer. At this point, I can't tell you what it is—whether it's the emissions or other toxic chemicals. But I am working on a lot of different possibilities.

Reporter

You mentioned the increased incidence of cancer. How many cases have been reported?

Narrator

The physician offers an opinion based on hearsay that is quotable.

State Physician

Over the past several years, I've heard of at least nine workers at the plant who had cancer of the blood-forming organs. But this information came to me by word of mouth.

Narrator

The reporter calls Custom Parts and this time, for some unknown reason, is referred to the human resources department. A secretary answers.

Secretary, Human Resources

Human Resources. Nancy White speaking.

Narrator

The reporter tries to speak to the owner.

Reporter

I would like to speak to Charlie Zurlock. I'm (your name) with the MESSENGER. I'm doing a story on your plant. We understand that at least seven employees at the plant have been diagnosed with cancer of the blood-forming organs over the past several years. I'd like Mr. Zurlock to confirm this.

Secretary, Human Resources

(acting as though she is an authorized spokesperson for the company)
Well, I'd like to help. But we have NO COMMENT.

Reporter

I'd like to speak to Mr. Zurlock.

Secretary, Human Resources

No way, José

Narrator

The reporter, upset with the brush-off, calls the DOE and describes the company's arrogance.

Reporter

Hello, Jessica? This is (your name) at the MESSENGER. We spoke earlier about the Custom Parts plant. I'm not getting much cooperation from them. I understand that your agency has ordered the company to do emission studies to determine the possible threat of cancer to employees and those living near the plant. How severe is the threat of cancer?

Narrator

The head of the DOE offers the strongest statement yet of unsubstantiated but quotable opinion.

Director, Department of Ecology

The risk of getting cancer to employees and people outside the plant could be substantial.

Narrator

The reporter tries once again to reach Charlie Zurlock.

Director, Human Resources

Hello, Dan Peopleton, Human Resources.

Reporter

I'm (your name) with the MESSSENGER. We're doing a story on your plant. I am trying to reach the owner, Mr. Zurlock. According to the DOE, your plant's emissions are jeopardizing the health of workers and community residents. I need to know more about that.

Narrator

The human resources director also thinks he has psychic powers and predicts the results of a study yet to be done, and then takes a shot at state government.

Director, Human Resources

Sure, I'll be happy to comment. We're confident that at year's end our research will show that any cancer cases were not caused by working at the plant. Hey look, Clark Kent, if you want some advice, don't pay much attention to the DOE. They haven't done a thorough job of studying our emissions.

[End]

Team Assignment

Charlie Zurlock, owner of Custom Parts Co., has hired your team, a local PR agency, to help with a situation created by his company's poor handling of media relations that is diminishing the reputation of his family-owned business in his home community. Charlie is accustomed to telling people what to do within his organization. However, he has yet to learn that his authority does not extend to the media or to any level of government, as you can see by his demands of your agency.

He said, "I want you to put an end to the negative publicity we're getting and see to it that it never happens again. I want you to set state government straight on this health issue. And I want you to keep my employees from getting overly excited about so-called health risks in the workplace." Charlie believes that the media can be controlled, that state government can be told what should or should not be investigated, and that employee relations is a matter of giving everyone a glazed ham for the holidays.

Your team must develop a PR plan for Charlie Zurlock that is responsive to his objectives. However, the plan must provide for educating Charlie in the basics of media, government, and employee relations. In the situation analysis of your plan, you must identify the company's short-comings in dealing with the health issue, but the rules for writing the analysis are clear about not being judgmental or attributing blame to individuals or to a company. Consulting in public relations requires firm but tactful criticism and advice.

Individual Team Member Assignments

Suppose that your agency decides that the company's management of relationships requires special guidance to raise standards and, as part of your plan, you offer guidelines. Each team member is to complete a different one of the following items that might or might not be included in the design of your plan.

1. Draft for Charlie a memo to employees establishing guidelines governing the company's working relationship with the news media. The memo should explain how the company is to work with the media and how varying employees should respond to inquiries from journalists. Because this is intended to be general company policy, there should be no reference to the company's current situation with the media. Use memo format:

    From: Charlie Zurlock

    To: All Employees

    Re: You and the News Media

    Be sure to look up several credible sources on how to work with news media and cite the sources in your memo as additional readings.

2. Create an infographic to accompany the aforementioned memo as a concise, yet detailed, visual aid.

3. Draft for Charlie a memo to his staff about how the company is to work with all levels of government—local, county, state, and federal. Use memo format:

From: Charlie Zurlock

To: Management Staff

Re: Working with Government

Be sure to look up several credible sources on how to work with all different levels of government and cite the sources in your memo as additional readings.

4. Create an infographic to accompany the aforementioned memo as a concise, yet detailed, visual aid.

5. Develop a backgrounder on effective employee communication. Use various sources to include some of the latest research on how today's employees want to be treated. The backgrounder might be used by your PR firm in counseling Charlie.

6. Draft an outline of contents for a new company website and provide reasons for what is proposed.

7. Propose how the company can initiate community relations programs. Research what other companies do and prepare a document with at least four different examples.

8. Draft a media advisory addressed to editors and news directors of print and broadcast media calling their attention to an upcoming event commemorating the startup of new environmental control equipment at Custom Parts Inc. and launching of the company's new program, Clean Air Awareness. You make up the details for writing the advisory that must answer the journalist's Ws—who, what, when, where, why?—and describe an irresistible photo/video opportunity (photo-op) for the media.

9. Draft an e-news release announcing the hiring by Custom Parts Inc. of a director of public relations. Assume that you are the new director. Make up the details of the announcement to include job experience, professional awards, education, and major job responsibilities. Write two quotes from you as the new director that would be especially appreciated by local journalists. In other words, write something about wanting to work with reporters as partners and in regard to improving community relations.

10. Develop an information sheet providing an overview of the state's environmental protection agency. It is to be used to brief Charlie and his staff on the agency's director, the director's views on air quality, the agency's mission and goals specifically related to clean air, key staff members, and other background information to promote a better understanding of working with the government role toward common goals. For purposes of illustration, use any state's environmental protection department.

11. Look up several sources on Maslow's Hierarchy of Needs. Create an infographic about this theory and also write at least one page describing the hierarchy. Then, discuss with your group how it relates to this case and why it is relevant to the actions that should be taken to properly address the audiences involved.

Business Description: Custom Parts Company (CPC)

Custom Parts Company (CPC) is located in Capital City, U.S.A. It produces custom parts for industrial machines using steel, titanium, and various carbon composite materials. It employs 231 people. The workers, about 198 people, are members of a union represented by the All Trades Council. CPC is privately owned by the Zurlock family and run by Charlie Zurlock. Its products are marketed throughout the United States. The company itself is not involved in the local community, but Charlie's wife, Helen, is a major donor to and board member of the Women's Association.

The company has been in operation for 28 years and has a record of eight citations by the state Department of Ecology (DOE) for air pollution. The DOE doesn't make a special effort to publicize its fines unless the subject of a fine fails to cooperate and adhere to environmental regulations. On March 1, 20XX, the DOE cited CPC for exceeding toxic emission limits once a week since the beginning of the year. DOE fined the company $20,000 and mandated that an independent study be conducted, at the company's expense, of worker health and of the health of residents living within two miles of the plant. It is true that the company had excursions of toxic emissions once each week from the beginning of the year to the end of February. No excursion lasted more than 10 minutes, but each time expelled more than two tons of fowl-smelling particulate matter into the air. The emissions were big in volume and highly visible. It's true that the company has not been responsive to the government.

New control equipment has been ordered, but for some reason not in time to meet regulatory deadlines. It has not as yet arrived and no one seems to have even an estimated delivery date. Meanwhile, company engineers have tried to fine-tune existing controls, but the effort has not produced consistent results. The company maintains that the worker environment is absolutely free of any health risk. However, the company is in the process of hiring an independent laboratory, True-Test Labs Inc., to conduct a health study of employees and local residents. It is true that the company does not have a perfectly clean record for environmental control. However, Charlie has updated the company's pollution control equipment, once in 1970 at a cost of $2 million and again in 1990 at a cost of $6 million. Employees are loyal to the operation, not because of the glazed ham their families get from Charlie and his wife each year, but because their skills are specialized and limited to Charlie's operation. In other words, they couldn't get work anywhere else.

The local newspaper was informed of the citation and fine in a news release issued by the DOE. The reporter contacted the company for a statement. The reporter talked with several different people (refer to classroom/professional workshop role play) who seem to have an adversarial attitude toward state government and newspaper reporters. Reports of the company's alleged cancer-causing emissions have alarmed employees and have resulted in two weeks of negative publicity for the company. Employees feel that "just because Charlie says it's safe doesn't mean that it's safe."

5. Crisis Communication: Community Alarmed

Learning Outcomes

By the end of this case, you should be able to:

1. appreciate how the credibility of the person communicating a message will affect the public perceptions in a crisis;

2. grasp how to control a message in a crisis situation by utilizing the appropriate channels with prepared speaking topics and transparency, but not information overload;

3. identify all stakeholders who must receive information, including the type of information, information channel, and appropriate verbiage;

4. understand why a public relations professional must be up-to-date on current events in the world; and

5. comprehend the inverted pyramid and how its use in informational writing needs to be understood by a public relations professional.

Crisis is a time of great danger, a time of serious trouble. It's a decisive time, a crucial time. Most importantly, a crisis is a turning point because its outcome will determine its consequences. Answers to how an organization should handle a crisis can be found in a plethora of books. However, it is the court of public opinion—with its own set of expectations—to decide if a crisis was best handled. That perception is the ultimate judge of crisis management. It doesn't matter if the crisis is real or perceived: the situation must be managed as a crisis. In this case a reputable company is about to be thrust into the public spotlight for its use of hazardous chemicals.

A series of unexpected events creates a crisis situation for Wafermaker in Oakleaf, U.S.A. As you read the news reports that follow, imagine how quickly emotions must begin to intensify among community residents. Consider how easily a company's hard-earned reputation can be seriously damaged. Try to empathize with Wafermaker management as they contemplate a situation with which they have no experience. Share management's feeling that at any minute issues can come into the public eye, and Wafermaker, with its sterling reputation as a model corporate citizen, can be put on the defensive by the same people who earlier welcomed it to the area with open arms.

The region had aggressively recruited electronics plants, considering them to be safe, clean and nonpolluting, a preferred alternative to traditional basic industries. There were no known reasons why such plants could not be integrated into the community in business parks and on property sharing borders with stores, schools, and residences. However, an incident in India focused world attention on industrial hazards, and an incident in Oakleaf brought the matter of concern even closer to home.

Team Assignment

Your team has been hired as a PR agency by Wafermaker Inc., one of many silicon wafer manufacturers, to develop a PR plan to address mounting concerns among community residents about health and safety risks associated with the company's use, storage, and transportation of hazardous chemicals.

Tensions are so high among residents that the company expects its association with hazardous chemicals to surface in the news media at any time in a way that could put the company on the defensive and possibly tarnish an otherwise sterling reputation as a corporate citizen. Following the case details are individual team member assignments.

Day 1: Gas Kills 300 in India

Gas from a pesticide plant escaped into a city in central India this morning and killed at least 300 people and injured thousands more.

Day 5: Top Executive Arrested, Then Freed

The chairman of an American company whose plant was associated with a gas leak that killed more than 1,600 people was taken into custody by India police today. He was released later.

Day 7: Death Toll in India Hits 1,900 from Gas Leak

The official death toll from a poison gas leak at a pesticide plant rose to about 1,900 yesterday.

U.S. Company's Reputation Severely Damaged

Reputation of the U.S. company with a majority ownership in the pesticide plant in India, where leaking of a deadly chemical cost more than 2,000 lives, has suffered substantially in the eyes of the American public.

Day 9: Fire Damages Wafermaker Plant

A fire today damaged the Wafermaker plant in Oakleaf. Firefighters entering the plant were sprayed by what at first was feared to be chemicals but instead was water from the plant's sprinkler system. Damage was estimated to be about $1 million.

Day 10

Mention of chemicals in news reports was the first time that the community became aware of the use of chemicals in electronics plants, such as Wafermaker. Parents of the 500 children enrolled at Parks Elementary School located near the Wafermaker plant were particularly interested in the reference to chemicals. When parents talked about the plant at home, their children told how they looked through the school windows at people in baggy suits moving big barrels behind the plant. They told about how trucks bring barrels and take barrels away.

Day 12

Phone calls began pouring into the principal's office at Parks school. Parents wanted to know more about the school and its safety procedures should there ever be a chemical accident at the Wafermaker plant. Phone calls of community residents to the silicon wafer manufacturer also increased and became more emotionally intense as callers pressed for information about chemical use.

Day 14

Wafermaker management requests professional public relations advice.

Business Description: Wafermaker

- Wafermaker employs 700 people at its Oakleaf plant

- Wafermaker makes silicon wafers for the computer industry

- The fire caused about $1 million damage, according to company officials

- Cleanup work is under way

- The company does not expect any of its employees to be off the job because of the fire

- About 30 people will be used in the cleanup operation; another 50 to 75 workers will move their operation to a nearby warehouse while duct work is replaced at the plant and soot and dust are cleaned up

- The fire was started by a malfunctioning electrical switch

- Most of the damage was from smoke; about 20,000 of the plant's 200,000 square feet were affected by the fire; damage to walls and equipment was minimal

- The cleanup process will affect the silicon wafer polishing area, final inspection area, and the packaging operation

- Some machinery has already been moved to temporary quarters

- The plant manufactures silicon wafers used in making computer chips

- Numerous chemicals are used at the facility, but none of the chemicals were burned or released during the fire

- The fire was nearly out by the time firefighters arrived, but it produced extensive smoke

- Wafermaker operates in an ultra-clean environment; manufacturing the wafers and maintaining the clean environment involves the use of chemicals; because of possible chemical contamination of workers, the facility has safety showers; a worker who is accidentally contaminated can enter a shower, which releases a large volume of water to promptly wash off any chemicals

- Wafermaker said the majority of chemicals used there are hazardous, but are safe if handled properly

- Employees handling chemicals are required to wear protective suits to prevent any possible harm to themselves

- Wafermaker said a worst-case scenario would involve liquefied hydrochloric acid; if it escaped all safety systems, a gaseous cloud would form and, depending on the weather, could hang over the area; people would know to move away because of the odor; prolonged exposure could be harmful to people, according to the company

- Wafermaker said it takes every possible precaution and safeguard to protect its employees, the environment, and neighbors

- The company spent more than $5 million on environmental control systems for the plant

- Fearful of the chemical hazard, some parents wanted to keep their children from going to the Parks Elementary School near the plant

- Leaders of the Parent Teacher Organization began contacting local, county, and state government agencies to learn more about the plant's use of chemicals

- Most chemicals are stored in tanks in an area that has concrete walls and floors painted with an acid-proof resin; pipes carry the chemicals to work areas through a concrete tunnel also painted with the acid-proof resin; wastes are piped through the tunnel to a treatment facility in a similarly secure area, according to Wafermaker

- Acid and bases are neutralized and piped into the city sewer system; nothing is disposed of on plant property except purified water used in the manufacturing process

- A chemical spill is highly unlikely, according to the company

- The company emphasized that the plant was planned to operate in close proximity with a community, so was designed with the best available safety systems; plant managers and workers live in the community and have children who attend area schools

- Wafermaker was aware that its use, storage, and transportation of chemicals was under intense scrutiny by the community, that rumors were rampant, and that the company could expect media attention any day, at any minute

Individual Team Member Assignments

Each team member is to complete a different one of the following items that might or might not be included in the design of the team plan.

1. Your agency is asked by Wafermaker to draft a letter from Parks Elementary School Principal Henry File to parents inviting them to an informational meeting to be held at the school (you select a date). School officials and officials of Wafermaker Inc. will be at the meeting to provide information and to answer questions. You are to draft the letter for the principal's signature.

2. In deliberations with your agency team, Wafermaker officials consider calling a news conference or briefing. In considering such an event, Wafermaker officials discuss what they might say in opening remarks at a conference or briefing to set the tone and tenor for their response to what is sure to be an intense community

demand for information. You are to write 90 seconds of opening remarks for George Sanders, Wafermaker vice president for manufacturing, for a news conference or briefing. You decide if it is to be a news conference or briefing and what Sanders should say to put the company in the best light before the media and the community. In your remarks you will want to welcome reporters and thank them for coming, tell them why you called the meeting, briefly recapping the fire incident, the mention of chemicals in news reports, and resulting concern in the community, especially among parents of children attending nearby Parks Elementary School. The remarks are to lead up to a briefing by company representatives about its use, storage, and transportation of chemicals. Set the tone of the conference by making known the company's desire to provide complete and accurate information, and touch upon the company's standing in the community and how it wants to uphold its reputation by being completely open and forthright in its communication with the public. Be careful not to try to persuade the media of anything; let the information presented in the meeting stand on its own merits to provide a convincing argument that living near Wafermaker is an acceptable risk. Your remarks should close with the line, "And now I would like to present the staff members who will provide you with a briefing."

3. In deliberations with your PR agency team, Wafermaker officials discuss possible communication with customers. Assume that it is decided to contact customers. Draft a letter from George Sanders, Wafermaker vice president for manufacturing, to customers. Assume that Sanders told you to acknowledge the incident and assure customers that it would not have any bearing on the scheduled shipments of their orders or on the quality of the silicon wafers. The same letter is to be sent to every customer but will be addressed to individuals. In the letter you will want to acknowledge the fire so that customers learn about it firsthand from Wafermaker, but you will not want to provide details that will unnecessarily cause concern among customers.

4. In deliberations with your PR agency team, Wafermaker officials agree that you should develop a fact sheet listing the chemicals that it uses with two or three practical, common, worthwhile applications for each chemical. For this assignment, you will have to research the uses for the following: acetic acid, hydrochloric acid, hydrofluoric acid, nitric acid, sulfuric acid, ammonium hydroxide, potassium hydroxide, sodium hydroxide, sodium sulfide, methanol, trichlorethane, trichlorosilane, argon, nitrogen, hydrogen, hydrogen chloride, oxygen, diborane, phosphine, hydrogen peroxide, chromium trioxide, potassium dichromate, isopropyl alcohol, and silane. Create a QR code for the most credible and encompassing Internet source found to be used on appropriate printed materials.

5. In deliberations with your PR agency team, Wafermaker officials request that you develop a list of all questions (including rude ones) that might be asked at a news conference or briefing. The list is to form the basis of a Q&A sheet.

6. Wafermaker officials ask your agency to develop a one-page backgrounder describing silicon wafer production in terms that can be used easily by journalists. (Search the Internet for information.)

7. Create an infographic to accompany the above mentioned backgrounder.

8. Explain how you would develop a digital dashboard and an alert system to monitor social media and Internet findings for dialogue about the plant situation.

9. Draft a list of messages that would be important for Wafermaker to communicate to each of its stakeholder audiences.

10. Research the inverted pyramid used in journalistic writing and create a fact sheet encompassing an originally designed diagram of the pyramid to share with your group. Since you are to be using factual information and you need to ensure readers' attention, critique selected above pieces using the concept of the inverted pyramid.

Additional Notes

In developing communication to parents, the media, and customers, it is best not to make assumptions about what people know or how they feel. Also, it is best not to try to persuade anyone of anything. Rather, provide complete objective and factual information and firsthand experience that will enable people to persuade themselves—much like journalistic-style writing. For example, you might begin your communication as follows: "On Friday, January 11, Wafermaker had a fire that was believed to be caused by a faulty heater," "No one was injured," "Damage was estimated," and so forth. Resist the temptation to promise more than you can deliver (e.g., "students are perfectly safe"); to make assumptions, especially negative ones (e.g., "no reason that the plant might have to be moved"); to presume what people know or don't know (e.g., "many of you think …"); to guess how people feel (e.g., "many of you are afraid"); or to speak on behalf of something over which you have no control (e.g., "You can rest assured that Wafermaker operates safely").

6. Celebrity Image Building: Superstar Entrepreneur

Learning Outcomes

By the end of this case, you should be able to:

1. understand how to interact with news media through mutually beneficial relationships;

2. understand how several different types of mass media outlets can be used as vehicles to reach a large number of people and build awareness and acceptance of an entrepreneur;

3. comprehend and differentiate news values, writing styles, and contact preferences for various outlets;

4. grasp Agenda Setting Theory and its practical use in public relations.

This is a case of image building and centers on a superstar entrepreneur. Much research has been done in attempts to characterize entrepreneurs. Many are driven by the desire to make a lot more money than they could with some other application of their skills and energy. What every entrepreneur must decide is whether the rewards of their respective enterprise will justify the cost, sacrifice, and risk involved in achieving some degree of success.

George Bernard Shaw said, "The reasonable man adapts himself to the world; the unreasonable man attempts to adapt the world to himself. Therefore all progress depends upon the unreasonable man." The character of the superstar in this case lies somewhere between reasonable and unreasonable. As you study this case using the PR file notes that follow, you will want to think about what makes this superstar tick and how the personality traits of this entrepreneur can be put to good use in building a business.

Team Assignment

For this case, assume that your team has been hired by superstar entrepreneur Jan Overbrook. Your superstar has a tenacious spirit that has enabled her to turn some ideas into profitable ventures. Your team has collected information about Overbook and has a file of interview notes that reveals secrets behind your client's successes and failures. Overbrook has hired your team to develop a PR plan spanning 12 months that will promote her image as a superstar entrepreneur in ways that will propel the expansion of her latest business venture, Wellness Advocates Inc. (WAI). Overbrook wants to use her entire promotional budget on leveraging the credibility of public relations to expand WAI services, initially throughout New York—in Albany, the Bronx, Vahalla, Brooklyn, Buffalo, Stoneybrook, and Old Westbury. Following the case details are individual team member assignments.

Client File Information: Jan Overbrook, Facts and Interview Notes

12/05/20XX

Observations: Overbrook seems to be a pro at getting things done. She obviously likes to run the show and make things happen. Her energy is boundless. We [the agency] had better be as precise about organization and detail as she is. When she goes for a goal, it's done cost effectively and on schedule. If there's one thing we learned at the last meeting, it was to be prepared; she makes decisions! She's analytical and objective. She's also quick. And what we present had better be logical. Forget pitching theory and any abstract ideas. Overbrook wants practical applications; she cares about what's here and now. She's outgoing and sociable; she's also matter-of-fact and direct.

Random quotes from the interview with Overbrook: I know I'm analytical and that can seem impersonal and uncaring to some people. So, I have to remind myself to think about how others think and feel. I've been successful, and I tend to get caught up in the success of things. I've surrounded myself with talented people, and I have to remember to credit them and make sure they know they're appreciated. If this relationship [with the agency] lasts, you'll see that I make rapid-fire decisions. I know I should spend time listening more, so if I get too far out in front I want you to tell me. Don't let me jump to conclusions when you have stuff that I should know. When the work is good, we'll be fine. When it's not, brace yourself because I don't pull punches when it comes to criticizing.

Client's story of what inspired the new business: My latest venture is Wellness Advocates Inc. I started it a year ago, on January 1. The idea for it was inspired a year before that. A dear friend of mine, Jason Adams, drove himself to City Hospital as he was having a heart attack. He had been videotaping a friend's wedding and left the camera running so as not to disappoint his friend. He was transferred to General Hospital where they put a double stent in one of his arteries. Another artery was 80 percent blocked, but they decided to treat that with drugs. Bad decision.

Seven months later, on August 8, Jason had shortness of breath and chest pains. He was rushed to General. The double stent had failed but vessels near it had regenerated. A chemical-release-type stent was placed in the other clogged artery. No one volunteered to tell him the condition of other arteries and he finally had to press hard for answers before leaving the hospital.

On August 15, Jason awoke with tremendous pains in his chest. Off to General once again. Jason waved to friendly faces as he was wheeled on a gurney to critical care. The welcome got serious when they started the heart catheterization treatment. He said it was like some medieval torture chamber. Narrow bed. Doctors and nurses outfitted like Martians to fend off the radioactivity. A sharp jab in the groin with a long metal stick. Big cameras pointing down as he strained to hold the pose for 30 minutes. A shot of morphine eased the pain, but Jason begged for more and more. Meanwhile, down in accounting, the figure in the ledger was reaching into a sixth column.

He awoke to the voices of heart surgeons who said his heart was "fine." Jason said, "Great, so why all the pain?" They told him it must be his lungs or stomach. He said it was obvious their area of expertise and interest was the heart; stomachs and lungs were someone else's area.

Jason was released and sent to cardiac rehab at County Hospital. For half an hour he walked a treadmill, rode a stationary bike, lifted weights, then passed out. His blood pressure fell to 64 over 50. He was rushed to ER. Another battery of blood tests. By now his arm was numb from all the blood taking.

"Jason, your heart is fine," the doctor said. "The problem might be your liver." Liver? Lungs? Stomach? Heart? Totally exasperated, Jason's wife said, "Enough is enough!" She called the family doctor, told him the situation, and without seeing Jason at General, he told her to take Jason back to City Hospital and have them insert a scope to look at his stomach.

Jason had nothing to wear because he had thrown up on his clothes on the way to ER. So he had to wear his General Hospital gown to City. A security guard at General saw Jason in his gown and hassled him because he thought Jason was trying to leave the hospital without permission. Finally he was admitted to City. They insisted on another full examination routine, telling him his heart was fine but that they could not perform the scope procedure right away because he needed to fast for 24 hours.

By this time Jason just wanted to go home. Enough doctors, hospitals, IVs, and blood tests. His weight dropped from 269 at the time of his first attack to under 200 and was continuing to decline.

Finally, the family doctor told Jason that his most recent attack was from acute acid reflux. Jason had never heard of it. Some of the symptoms are the same as those of a heart attack—chest pains, heavy breathing, nausea, even passing out. He was told more pills. More exercise. Better diet control. Better diet was a joke to Jason. He hadn't eaten anything of substance for the past three weeks.

The doctor scheduled the scope procedure at still another hospital, Parkview, for September 23. But Jason decided he needed a new family doctor. He wanted a coordinated approach to his problems. He wanted someone to take a holistic look at his physical condition, to review the list of drugs (and potential interactions) that had been prescribed by a battery of different physicians. He wanted to see details of the many examinations. He wanted to know if he was in a life-threatening situation. He wanted better advice about diet and exercise and dreaded the thought of passing out again on some piece of equipment. He wanted to know more about acute acid reflux.

It was the experience of this very dear friend that inspired me to establish Wellness Advocates Inc.

Client comments on the mission and operation of Wellness Advocates Inc.: The mission of WAI is to show clients how to take responsibility for their health and wellness. At WAI we have a staff of facilitators. They are not medical advisors. Their job is to show clients how to overcome any feelings of trepidation for white smocks and stethoscopes and become medically conversant about their health and wellness. That means suggesting sources of information and teaching them how to ask questions and insist on satisfactory answers. It means showing them how to stay current on the latest developments in medical discoveries, new procedures, medicine, and research. It means showing clients how important it is to take a personal interest in everything they put into their bodies—from food to pharmacy products. It means showing clients how to take a holistic approach to their health and wellness and find qualified medical professionals who subscribe to such an enlightened view.

At WAI we show clients how to create and maintain a personal medical file, what health indicators to track and record, what records to include, and how to obtain them.

We also provide support so that when client feels like they are being led down a blind alley, we can help them avoid an experience like Jason's by showing them how get complete and honest information to enlighten themselves and ensure they are on the right course.

WAI has a staff of six facilitators who collectively are educated in a full range of medical subjects from diet to drugs. We have offices in New York City, Syracuse, and Rochester. We have over 700 clients. The fee for our service is $48 per month. We have a website. We have the private financial backing necessary to begin expanding the business nationally. We have an information kit that explains everything for potential clients. We have a stellar reputation. We are not widely known yet, but those who meet us and become acquainted with our mission in nearly every case become clients. Our service becomes so valuable that when we get together with a client the meeting always begins with a big hug.

Observations and random client comments on managing a business: When we first started I tried to do everything, because I feel better when I have complete control. Then we started to expand, and I hired people who could carry out my ideas and my ways of working with clients. I've had other ventures, like a chain of gift shops in New York hospitals, a wellness newsletter published nationally, and a florist in Old Westbury that specialized in patient bouquets that were delivered by volunteer care givers who spent five to 10 minutes talking with each hospital recipient. But WAI has, by far, been the most successful and most rewarding venture. What I love is meeting people, getting acquainted, and getting hired.

Trying to control everything is a real challenge, especially when I don't like the nitty-gritty accounting work and being involved in meeting all of the regulatory and other administrative requirements. Dividing my attention between serving clients and managing the business gets real stressful. But I'm determined to do this no matter what it takes.

I have an exercise routine and I try to spend time outdoors. But I hate the thought of taking time for a vacation. I love to work. I was married once and have two children. They were my primary interest. My husband died and the children are grown. I couldn't have ventured into my own business while they were growing up. I remarried. My husband, Banks, manages a venture capital firm. Convenient arrangement! Not really. The businesses are kept separate. He's a workaholic too. But we both plan to expand operations, hire staff, and quit killing ourselves. I feel good about the business. I have done well and I've been rewarded for a tireless effort.

Client's views on secrets of her success: I'm results-oriented in a tenacious way. When I set a goal, nothing discourages me from reaching it. When I make a commitment, it is rock solid; you can count on it. You'd be surprised at how tough I can get. And I make good decisions. You have to be a risk taker. I have a good sense about things and know just how far to go. One way to uncover business opportunities is to look for dissatisfaction among consumers. Finding effective ways to eliminate dissatisfaction can lead to a viable business venture, just as Wellness Advocates responds to Jason's frustration with the medical community. I think you also have to know how your talents, interests, background, and values combine with your particular personality to enable you to do what you are most suited to do. Did I tell you I have a book about to be published called, simply, *Wellness Advocates Inc.*?

Individual Team Member Assignments

After reading the preceding notes, each team member is to complete a different one of the following items that might or might not be part of the design of your team's plan. As a group, decide upon a few key messages for WAI and ensure that they are in the following elements.

1. Draft a personality profile of the superstar. Use photos and design elements. If possible, use InDesign, specifically.

2. Research your own local media and decide, if Overbrook were to need promotion in your area, to which outlet(s) would you pitch WAI, and to whom at those outlets would you specifically contact. Create which tool you decide to contact that person with (research and see how he or she prefers to be contacted).

3. Write a phone pitch script to an assistant program director to get television coverage of the superstar. Each member of the group needs to practice the pitch, out loud.

4. Write an email to the superstar client proposing an unusual attention-getting book-signing event/tour.

5. Write a pitch to bloggers to generate interest in the entrepreneur.

6. Draft a concise description of Wellness Advocates Inc. and the superstar for use on a website.

7. Write a prompting sheet for the superstar to use for a television talk show. Describe Wellness Advocates and its purpose. Use short conversational phrases. Illustrate how WAI helps people take responsibility for their health using acid reflux disease as an example—describe what it is and list questions that a patient should ask the doctor about the condition and its treatment, as well as how to avoid the problem. Arrange the information in the order it might be asked by the talk show host.

8. Draft an op-ed article about the need for people to take more responsibility for their own health.

9. Create a social media plan that will promote the brand image of the superstar. The social media plan should incorporate most of the other tactics created, i.e., "Excited to meet Ellen and discuss my new business on her show tomorrow."

10. Create and edit a one minute video about Overbrook to be used on social media to increase awareness and interest about her. Research how to best embed the video on different social media outlets.

11. Research Agenda Setting Theory. Create a fact sheet and an infographic about it that will be shared with your group.

12. As a group, assemble a media kit using the items created above. Discuss if any desired elements are missing.

13. Also, as a group, discuss how Agenda Setting Theory is relevant to the case.

7. Community Relations: Contaminated Lagoon

Learning Outcomes

By the end of this case, you should be able to:

1. understand the concept and importance of becoming a topical subject matter expert in areas as necessary per needs within your company or organization;

2. predict questions that may arise from interested or concerned publics regarding matters of importance to them;

3. understand the concept of two-step flow of communication and how it can foster a positive outcome in situations where the message is better coming from a third party, rather than your own company or organization.

Introduction

This is a case of a contaminated lagoon. Plans were being made for the expansion of Industrial Products Inc. in Douglas, U.S.A., when management discovers that a lagoon on plant property is contaminated with hazardous chemicals. The hazard must be removed before plant expansion work can begin. Industrial Products decides that it does not have the expertise necessary to handle public communication regarding the hazardous waste site cleanup and calls on the PR staff at corporate headquarters for assistance. A staff member is dispatched to meet with the management of the subsidiary operations in Douglas.

Details of the case unfold in a dialogue between the headquarters PR staff person, Kelly O'Connel, and management staff at Douglas. The conversation is in the form of a classroom role play. More detail is available in Kelly O'Connel's handwritten field notes that follow the role play. The article, titled "Community Relations Can Facilitate Corporate Growth," provides a broad perspective on the value of good community relations.

Team Assignment

Your team assignment is to develop a public relations plan to coincide with closing and dealing with the contaminated lagoon. You and your team are staff members of Rockover Inc.'s PR department. Rockover Inc. is the owner of the subsidiary operation, Industrial Products Inc. Industrial Products, Inc. is located in Douglas, U.S.A. The goal of your plan, stated by the operations manager, is for Industrial Products, Inc. to be expanding its facilities with minimal delays from the lagoon closure.

Each team member is to complete a different one of the following items that might or might not be included in the design of your plan.

1. Write a statement to the news media to be used only if reporters inquire about the project.

2. Write the script for a podcast presented by the plant manager and accessed from the plant's website.

3. Write a memo from the manager of human resources to employees responding to their health and safety concerns with regard to the contaminated lagoon.

4. Write a Q&A for management personnel to use in discussing the cleanup project with people within or outside the company.

5. Write a letter to government representatives (David Hall, mayor, or Randy Don, county commissioner) apprising them of the project so they are prepared to answer questions from their constituents.

6. Write a fact sheet on the cleanup project with construction scheduling information. (See field notes.)

7. Construct an infographic to better illustrate the contents of the fact sheet above.

8. Write a one-page backgrounder exclusively on the subject of polychlorinated biphenyl (PCB). Provide information that would be useful to and understood by journalists, not to chemical engineers.

9. Write a pocket point card for management (all levels through supervisor) with information on both sides with talking points about the lagoon project.

10. Construct a social media plan to apprise the community of the situation at hand. Be sure to populate the content in accordance with the schedules found in the notes later in the chapter.

11. Create a QR code to drive publics to at least one credible, third-party website, with content about PCBs, so readers may further understand and do their own research. Said QR code should be embedded in many of the tactics above.

12. Research and understand two-step flow of communication and how it should play a part in this scenario. Write a fact sheet on this concept.

Class Role Play

Cast

Narrator
Kelly O'Connel—PR Assistant
Bob Elwood—PR Director
Sam Seabert—Operations Manager
AJ Detweiler—Production Manager
Jordan Slagel—Environmental Engineer
Terry Trobaugh—Safety Manager
Sharon Duncan—Administrative Assistant
Case Dilena—Manager, Human Resources

Narrator

At the PR department, Corporate Headquarters, Rockover Inc., the PR assistant approaches the PR director for assignment.

PR Assistant

Good morning.

PR Director

Hi Kelly. Ready to work?

PR Assistant

(not knowing what to expect)
I'm ready!

PR Director

That's good. I'd like you to make a plane reservation to Douglas. They're expecting you for a meeting tomorrow morning.

PR Assistant

(clearly caught off guard)
Douglas! Who's expecting me?

PR Director

(privately amused by her reaction, but totally confident that she can handle the job)
I would have handled this myself, but I've got a speech to write for the chairman.

PR Assistant

So, who's the meeting with?

PR Director

The manager of Douglas operations and members of his staff.

PR Assistant

What's it about?

PR Director

A lagoon. They have to deal with it before they can proceed with their expansion plans.

PR Assistant

(half joking)
A lagoon needs public relations?

PR Director

You need to hear the whole story firsthand. The lagoon is contaminated.

PR Assistant

Are they worried about publicity?

PR Director

That's part of it.

PR Assistant

What else are they worried about?

PR Director

Employees. Sorry, Kelly, I've got to see the chairman.

PR Assistant

I'll make the reservations.

Narrator

At an altitude of 37,000 feet heading for Douglas.

PR Assistant

(musing to herself)
I can't believe this. My first assignment. A polluted lagoon. That's all right. I can do this.

Narrator

At the Douglas Operations conference room, Kelly has been introduced and the meeting is under way.

Operations Manager

Thanks for coming, Kelly. We were making plans to expand our operations and in the process we discovered that we have a polluted lagoon. We need to be undertaking the expansion with minimal delays from the lagoon closure. That's our goal.

Environmental Engineer

(interjecting)
We tested sediment in the bottom of the lagoon and found a significant concentration of PCBs. PCBs are …

PR Assistant

(interrupting)
I know, Jordan. Polychlorinated biphenyls. Not very friendly to people. I did some quick research before I left headquarters. So how did the PCBs get into the lagoon?

Production Manager

We think it happened years ago with the old forming operation. They mixed water from the lagoon with a petroleum-based lubricant for cooling. The water was recycled back into the lagoon, and PCBs probably floated to the bottom and settled into the sediment.

PR Assistant

(mentally starting to shape a message)
So, we can say that the pollution isn't the result of any of our current operations, but that we're taking full responsibility for cleaning it up.

Operations Manager

Yes. And it will be closed. The lagoon will be closed as part of our overall plant expansion plan.

PR Assistant

What do you mean, closed?

Environmental Engineer

It will be lined and used as a storm water retention basin.

PR Assistant

How big is this lagoon?

Environmental Engineer

Surface size of the lagoon is about 37,000 square feet.

PR Assistant

That's a small lake.

Administrative Assistant

(abruptly interjecting in a tattletale tone of voice)
It used to be a picnic area for employees. With tables, and benches, and …

PR Assistant

(interrupts Sharon with the dreaded thought that employees may have been exposed)
Don't tell me … a place where families could play in the water? Are employees at risk?

Manager, Human Resources

No. Fortunately, the lagoon has always been fenced off. We're confident that no one is at risk, but employees might not be easily convinced of that.

Environmental Engineer

PCBs are heavy. They don't float. They're in the sediment, not the water.

PR Assistant

(Kelly wonders how assured she would feel as an employee who worked for 10 years or more around a hazardous waste site)
Where is the lagoon?

Administrative Assistant

(she exclaims in her tattletale tone of voice)
That's easy! Don't ya know? It's in plain sight of the whole world!

Manager, Human Resources

Get a grip, Sharon. It's behind the finishing and forming operations. Unfortunately, drivers coming into town in the morning look directly at it from City Expressway. You could read a billboard in the time it takes to pass by.

Safety Manager

The lagoon will be designated a hazardous materials area and workers will be wearing hazardous materials suits.

PR Assistant

You mean … moon suits?

Safety Manager

They do look like space suits.

PR Assistant

(thinks to herself there's a lot of communicating to do)
Who knows about this situation?

Operations Manager

The state Department of Environmental Resources.

PR Assistant

And the media?

Operations Manager

No, not yet.

PR Assistant

What about employees?

Operations Manager

No, but when they do, the long-time veterans are going to be concerned. They'll remember the picnic grounds.

Administrative Assistant

(admonishing the company)
You bet they will! They'll remember all right!

PR Assistant

I would think so. Not the best place to eat hotdogs.

Administrative Assistant

(emotionally charged)
Listen, Kelly. Just the mention of toxic chemicals and some people will go into orbit! Know what I mean? Do you know what I mean?

PR Assistant

What about government? City and county officials? Do they know?

Operations Manager

No. And there's a potential problem. We don't have the best working relationship with local and county government. It's not bad. It's just that … well, we just don't have one and we need their support to get construction permits on schedule.

PR Assistant

Jordan, when is work supposed to start on the lagoon?

Environmental Engineer

May 15th.

PR Assistant

Today is May 1st. We have precious little time to do a lot of communicating.

Production Manager

(grumbling about headquarters' involvement)
What's the big deal? It's not like we're into a meltdown. Why do we need public relations? The facts will speak for themselves. All's we need to do is get the contractor in here and get the job done.

Operations Manager

Not so fast, AJ. Let's think about this. Douglas is about to discover that it has toxic waste on the edge of town. Rush hour drivers coming into town are going to see workers in moon suits. Veteran employees are going to be fearful of possible health hazards to themselves and their families. Local and county officials could get flooded with phone calls from residents wanting to know what's going on. And who knows how the media is going to play this.

Production Manager

(grousing to himself about getting public relations involved and unable to keep to himself)
Come on, Sam. We've been a good company to work for, for years. I don't know why people have to meddle in our affairs.

Operations Manager

(realizes that some people are more sensitive about public relations than others; ignores AJ's comment and turns to Kelly)
Kelly, we obviously need some help from the PR department.

PR Assistant

I'm here to help, Sam. Could we take a few minutes to go over the plan so I have an idea of what's ahead?

Operations Manager

Sure. We hired BBEO Remediation and Construction Company to close the lagoon.

Production Manager

(straightening up and trying to be a constructive participant)

It's a Jersey company. They have experience in cleaning up hazardous waste.

Environmental Engineer

The state Department of Environmental Resources is overseeing the cleanup.

Production Manager

Our engineers and the BBEO staff have a detailed closure plan. First the water will be pumped out of the lagoon.

Environmental Engineer

It will be treated, tested and discharged into a connecting stream. The sediment will be excavated from the bottom of the lagoon. It will be pressed through a filter to get rid of excess water. Then it will be tested and stored in sealed containers.

PR Assistant

What happens to the containers?

Environmental Engineer

They'll be loaded on a train and taken to a regulated disposal site. We'll cover the area with a liner and it will be used as a storm water retention basin.

Safety Manager

The entire work area will be fenced in. Only authorized workers will be allowed access to the site. There will be strict safety rules. Workers will have to wear protective gear that will be cleaned and properly disposed of daily throughout the process.

PR Assistant

(testing the accuracy of what she thought she heard)

So we can say the water will be pumped out, tested, and discharged into a connecting stream. The polluted sediment will be excavated, stored in leak-proof containers, and shipped by rail to a regulated disposal site. The area will then be lined and used as a storm water retention basin.

Operations Manager

That's correct, Kelly. The project will take about six to eight weeks. After BBEO brings in its heavy equipment, the area will be closed. No company equipment will be used. Workers will wear protective suits, gloves, boots, and respirators that will be cleaned or disposed of each time they leave the site.

PR Assistant

Is there any health risk to people around the site?

Environmental Engineer

The chemicals are in the sediment, not in the water. PCBs are not airborne, so there's no chance of contact with employees or plant visitors or area residents.

PR Assistant

(Thinking to herself: Employees will wonder, if there's no risk, why do workers have to wear moon suits? I need to know more about PCBs, like what are the effects of PCBs on people? She thumbs through her notes; Sam hands her a project schedule)

Sam, how will closing the lagoon affect your expansion plans?

Operations Manager

The project might delay our plant expansion work, but it's essential that we clean things up properly, and safely.

Narrator

The meeting adjourns and Kelly returns to headquarters to draw up a PR plan.

[End]

Work Schedule and Initial Research Notes

Kelly's Work Schedule from Sam

The plan has three phases:

1. Mobilization and site preparation: BBEO brings and sets up equipment; start date is May 15 and finish date is May 24.

2. Site remediation activities: lagoon dewatering starts May 25 and finishes June 16; sediment removal starts June 1 and finishes August 9; belt press dewatering starts August 8 and finishes August 23; post-removal sampling starts August 24 and finishes August 30; preparation for structural backfill starts August 31 and finishes September 4.

3. Demobilization and closeout activities: removal of temporary facilities and controls starts September 5 and finishes Sept. 11; demobilization starts September 12 and finishes September 13; closeout meeting is on September 20.

Kelly's Initial Research Notes

Polychlorinated biphenyls, or PCBs, are a class of compounds consisting of two benzene rings joined together at one carbon on each ring ... the rings are then substituted with one to 10 chlorine atoms ... developed in 1929, they have been used as electrical insulating fluids, fire-resistant heat transfer and hydraulic fluids, and lubricants, and as components in elastomers, adhesives, paints, pigments, and waxes ... PCBs were very attractive in industrial use because they are nonvolatile, nonflammable, chemically stable, and good electrical insulators. Because PCBs are very stable, they do not break down in the environment; therefore, they are environmentally unsuitable ... in 1976, Congress enacted the Toxic Substance Control Act, which required the Environmental Protection Agency (EPA) to establish rules regarding PCBs ... production ceased in 1977 ... in 1979, the EPA published the PCB ban rule which prohibits the manufacturing, processing, distribution in commerce, and use of PCBs except in a totally enclosed manner. Concentrations of PCBs 50 parts per billion or over fall under EPA regulations and must be disposed of under EPA guidelines ... PCBs can affect the body if inhaled or swallowed, or if there is contact with the eyes or skin ... they may cause irritation of the eyes, nose, and throat and an acne-like skin rash ... they may also cause liver disorders that would result in such effects as fatigue, dark urine, and yellow jaundice ... studies on laboratory animals showed the chemicals caused liver, reproductive and gastric disorders, skin lesions, and tumors.

Meeting Notes: Operations Manager Sam Seaberg and Staff, Industrial Products Inc.

Douglas, U.S.A., subsidiary of Rockover Inc., May 1.

What is the situation at Douglas?

We were in the process of planning plant expansions; discovered that a small lagoon on our property was polluted.

How small?

A lagoon approximately 37,114 square feet in surface size.

Where?

Located behind the finishing and forming operations.

What kind of pollution?

Tested sediment in the bottom of the lagoon; found a significant concentration of polychlorinated biphenyls (PCBs). The PCBs likely entered the lagoon as a result of the old forming operation ... the water was mixed with a petroleum-based lubricant for cooling ... the water was then recycled back into the lagoon ... PCBs likely fell to the bottom and settled into the sediment. The lagoon will be closed as part of the overall plant expansion plan. It will be lined and used as a storm water retention basin.

Did the company dump PCBs in the lagoon?

The PCBs are not a result of any of our current operations. We're taking responsibility for cleaning and closing the lagoon.

Possible quote: "The pollution is not a result of any of our current operations at the plant. But we will take full responsibility for cleaning it up."

Note to self: What are PCBs? Research. [Later: PCBs are a class of compounds consisting of two benzene rings joined together at one carbon on each ring ... the rings are then substituted with one to 10 chlorine atoms ... developed in 1929, they have been used as electrical insulating fluids, fire-resistant heat transfer and hydraulic fluids, lubricants and as components in elastomers, adhesives, paints, pigments, and waxes ... PCBs were very attractive in industrial use because they are nonvolatile, nonflammable, chemically stable, and good electrical insulators.]

Is this a health hazard to employees? Or to area residents?

The chemicals are settled in the sediment. They're not in the lagoon water. There's no possibility of contamination to any plant employees or visitors, according to plant staff members. The PCBs are not airborne; there's no chance of contact. The situation poses no danger to plant employees or residents. Possible quote: "Although we are dealing with hazardous waste, we want to assure the public there is no danger to residents, to plant employees, or to the surrounding environment. Our primary concern is to have this project done in the safest manner possible."

What are the best ways to communicate with employees?

The plant operates three shifts: (1) 7 a.m. to 3 p.m., (2) 3 p.m. to 11 p.m.; and (3) 11 p.m. to 7 a.m. On each shift, employees are given a 20-minute lunch break. Supervisors conduct safety meetings every day at the beginning of each shift. Supervisors also conduct communication meetings once each month. The plant manager talks to employees quarterly by shift. The most effective ways to communicate with employees are (1) through supervisors, (2) by weekly newsletter, (3) by monthly video tape, and (4) by closed circuit television. Sometimes project teams are formed with a leader selected by each team. Supervisors oversee and coach the teams.

Note to self: Why are PCBs a problem? Is there a legal limit? What are the effects of PCBs on people? Research. [Later: Because PCBs are very stable, they do not break down in the environment; therefore, they are environmentally unsuitable ... in 1976, Congress enacted the Toxic Substance Control Act which required the Environmental Protection Agency (EPA) to establish rules regarding PCBs ... production ceased in 1977 ... in 1979, the EPA published the PCB ban rule which prohibits the manufacturing, processing, distribution in commerce, and use of PCBs except in a totally enclosed manner. Concentrations of PCBs 50 parts per billion or over fall under EPA regulations and must be disposed of under EPA guidelines. ... PCBs can affect the body if inhaled or swallowed, or there is contact with the eyes or skin ... they may cause irritation of the eyes, nose, and throat and an acne-like skin rash ... they may also cause liver disorders that would result in such effects as fatigue, dark urine, and yellow jaundice ... studies on laboratory animals showed the chemicals caused liver, reproductive and gastric disorders, skin lesions, and tumors.]

So how did the PCBs get there?

The lagoon has been used as part of our overall water management plan and has never been used for the disposal of any industrial chemicals or wastes. In the 1960s and 1970s, the lagoon water was used for cooling baths in the old forming operations We believe the contaminants were released when the cooling water was recycled back into the lagoon. The forming operation has since been relocated and an oil/water separator has been installed, so there is no danger of further contamination.

We can say tests of the lagoon sediment revealed the presence of PCBs ... that company engineers believe the lagoon was contaminated during the 1960s and 1970s when its waters were mixed with a petroleum-based lubricant for cooling metal in the old forming facility ... that this facility has been closed for 14 years, so there is no danger for further contamination. The lagoon was constructed in 1959 to be used as cooling water for molds in the old metal forming operations. This was discontinued in 1981 when forming operations moved. The lagoon is currently used as fire water for the sprinkler system and also for the discharge of cooling waters from the current forming operation.

What's the plan to deal with the situation?

The company hired BBEO Remediation and Construction Company to close the lagoon. This New Jersey-based company has experience in cleaning hazardous waste, including PCBs. The state Department of Environmental Resources is overseeing the cleanup. Work will begin May 15 to clean the lagoon.

Our engineers and BBEO personnel have developed a detailed closure plan. The water will first be pumped from the lagoon. It will be treated, tested, and then discharged into a connecting stream. The sediment will then be excavated from the bottom of the lagoon. It will be filter pressed to remove excess water, tested, stored in sealed containers, and removed by rail for disposal. The area will then be lined and used as a storm water retention basin.

Possible quote: "Work is scheduled to begin May 15 to clean the lagoon. The area will be closed, and strict access and safety guidelines will be followed during the project. Workers will be wearing protective gear that will be cleaned and disposed of daily throughout the process."

So, we can say the water will be pumped, treated, tested, and then released. The polluted sediment will then be excavated, stored in leak-proof containers, and removed by rail for disposal. The area will then be used for storm water retention.

Let's go over the plan once more.

BBEO Remediation and Construction has been contracted to close the lagoon ... they have previous experience in dealing with PCBs ... work will begin May 15 ... the project is expected to take six to eight weeks ... after bringing in their equipment (no company equipment will be used), they will close off the entire area ... only select BBEO and company personnel will be permitted to enter the cleaning site ... workers will wear protective suits, gloves, boots, and respirators that will be cleaned and/or disposed of each time they leave the closed zone surrounding the lagoon ... the water will be pumped, treated, and released into a connecting stream ... the sediment will then be excavated, filter pressed to remove excess water, tested, stored in sealed containers, and removed by train for disposal … the area will then be lined and used for storm water retention.

Will this operation present any kind of safety hazard?

The closure plan includes strict safety guidelines. Throughout the project, access to the lagoon site will be allowed for authorized BBEO and company personnel only. All equipment, materials, and safety gear will be either cleaned or disposed of immediately after use.

Do employees know about all of this?

Employees are not yet aware of the discovery of PCBs in the lagoon.

Who knows about it outside the company?

We are working with the state Department of Environmental Resources, but city and county government officials don't know about the discovery yet.

What kind of relationship does the company have with the city and county government?

Distant, at best. We need their cooperation to complete permits for our expansion plans. But we haven't done much in the way of building relationships. They're going to get a lot of questions from the public.

How's that?

The lagoon is visible from the City Expressway that leads into the city. People working on the site will be wearing "moon suits" or hazardous materials protective gear and will be seen, especially during rush hours, by people entering and exiting Douglas.

The plan has three parts or phases:

1. Mobilization and site preparation: BBEO brings and sets up equipment; start date is May 15 and finish date is May 24.

2. Site remediation activities: lagoon dewatering starts May 25 and finishes June 16; sediment removal starts June 1 and finishes August 9; belt press dewatering starts August 8 and finishes August 23; post-removal sampling starts August 24 and finishes August 30; preparation for structural backfill starts August 31 and finishes September 4.

3. Demobilization and closeout activities: removal of temporary facilities and controls starts September 5 and finishes Sept. 11; demobilization starts September 12 and finishes September 13; closeout meeting is on September 20.

Will taking care of lagoon slow down the plant expansion work?

Possible quote: "The project might slow plant expansion work, but that will be resumed right after the lagoon is closed." Also: "Our expansion plan is important and will give a boost to the local economy. But our first interest is cleaning up the lagoon."

When all of this gets communicated, who is going to field questions?

Casey Dilena, Manager of Human Resources. (717) 393-9433.

8. Social Media: Uncharitable Bloggers

Learning Outcomes

By the end of this case, you should be able to:

1. understand the concept and importance of environmental scanning, especially as it relates to being privy to negative press (both traditional and untraditional) toward your own company or organization;

2. gain an understanding about business concepts and terms (such as overhead and expenses) and how to relate those to your company or organization; and

3. understand the Diffusion of Innovations Theory and how it is utilized when trying to foster adoption of a concept or an idea such as the one in this case.

This case is based upon the proactive questions about philanthropy and the nonprofit sector, courageously raised by Dan Pallotta in his book, *Uncharitable: How Restraints on Nonprofits Undermine Their Potential*, and expounded upon in his TED talk entitled "The Way We Think About Charity is Dead Wrong and The Dream We Haven't Dared to Dream." Pallotta, the founder of Pallotta TeamWorks, the company that invented the AIDS Rides and Breast Cancer 3-Day Events, fundamentally reinvented the paradigm for special event fundraising in America. The aforementioned events drew more than 182,000 participants and raised over $500 million, while netting $305 million over the course of nine years. The company had more than 350 full-time employees and was the subject of a Harvard Business School case study.

Pallotta's approach argues that society's perceptions of what a nonprofit organization should and should not be allowed to do hinders them from achieving big goals for the respective causes that they serve. He gives several powerful arguments that are contrary to popular belief about how those things that are negatively deemed as overhead, such as reasonable compensation for those who run nonprofit organizations and paying for advertising and/or marketing to effectively promote events, can substantially increase a nonprofit organization's capacity to gain donors and donations. Pallotta contends that current nonprofits get rewarded more for how little they spend, rather than for what they achieve toward their respective missions. Basically, Pallotta's main point is that if we as a society can abandon these archaic perceptions of nonprofit organizations, we can dramatically accelerate the progress on the most urgent social issues of our time, via nonprofit organizations. More of his ideas can be found on the following chart.

Against Change	For Change
"People who want to work in the nonprofit world should be more interested in the good they do than in the money they can make."	"If we allow charity to compensate people according to the value they produce, we can attract more leaders of the kind the for-profit sector attracts, and we can produce greater value."
"Charities should not take risks. They are taking risks with earmarked funds. They should be cautious."	"The more that charities take calculated risks, the better the chance that they will break new ground."
"Charities do not have the luxury to think about the future. Donated money should be spent immediately to alleviate the suffering of others."	"The more we allow charities to invest in the future instead of only the current fiscal year, the more they will be able to build the future we all want."
"Charities should not waste money on expensive advertising. It is money that could otherwise go to the needy."	"Advertising builds consumer demand. The more that charities are allowed to advertise, the better they can compete with consumer products for the consumer's dollar, and the more money they can raise for the needy."
"Charities should not make mistakes. A mistake means a charity is wasting money and waste is immoral."	"The more mistakes a charity makes in good faith, the faster it will learn and the quicker it will be able to solve complex problems. This is the only path to solving problems—one must 'fail upward.'"
"Charities should maintain a low overhead percentage. This is the only way to know that any good is being done. Low overhead is moral. High overhead is immoral."	"A charity's overhead percentage doesn't give you any data about the good it is doing in the world. If charities focused more on solving the world's problems than on keeping overhead low, more of the world's problems would be solved."

Dan Pallotta, Excerpts from: *Uncharitable: How Restraints on Nonprofits Undermine Their Potential*, pp. 6-7. Copyright © 2010 by University Press of New England (UPNE). Reprinted with permission.

Charity Description: The Society for Little Children

A charity we will call The Society for Little Children has organized a three-day marathon run we will call Run for the Little Ones. Three months before the event, the charity enlisted the pro bono support of your public relations agency. While the charity is operating within legal bounds, it has pushed the envelope on what the public regards as ethical and moral behavior for nonprofit and philanthropic endeavors.

The charity is using some of the tools, such as advertising, that are freely available to the for-profit sector, but frowned upon by the public for use by nonprofits. The charity's use of advertising, hiring of a highly experienced event management company, taking the risk of rallying participants to a first-of-its-kind event for the town, incurring an above-average administrative cost for the event, and investment in event logistical equipment to be used in future marathons is beginning to be debated among bloggers. The controversy has not yet appeared in the traditional media.

The event is expected to attract about 500 participants, who are expected to raise $1.6 million in donor contributions. Expenses in support of participants for three days and two nights are estimated to be $275,000. Expenses for marketing and raising awareness of the event are expected to be about $112,000. The fee for an event coordinating company will be $140,000. The contribution remaining for direct charitable service would be about $1,073,000 or 67 percent of total funds donated. Because of the nature of the event, there is no other way to significantly reduce expenses.

Assignment

The charity is concerned that becoming the center of a fire storm of discussion among bloggers over society's ethics for nonprofits is going to reduce participation in the event and damage the reputation of the charity. Your job is to quickly quell the negative cyber buzz and prevent undermining of the potential fundraising success of Run for the Little Ones.

Each team member is to complete a different one of the following items that might or might not be included in the design of your plan.

1. Develop a social media news release announcing that Run for the Little Ones is expected to raise more than $1.5 million based on early registrations. Include links to items such as reports, backgrounders, and financial statements that would help quell the developing negative cyber dialogue.

2. Write a persuasive email message to area bloggers involved in the nonprofit/for-profit discussion, inviting them to an informational meeting with the charity's director (make up name) to discuss their concerns about the charity's use of funds.

3. Write an email news release to editors of the traditional area media announcing that Run for the Little Ones is expected to raise more than $1.5 million based on early registrations and calling their attention to the social media news release on the charity's website.

4. Research information about how the performance of nonprofits is to be judged and write, with a reader-grabbing headline, a compelling blog of about 150 words in favor of giving nonprofits more latitude in using the tools available to for-profit organizations in planning, promoting, and implementing fundraising events.

5. Create an infographic to illustrate the key points of the blog above.

6. Write a memo from the charity's president to staff members calling their attention to the growing debate among bloggers about nonprofit organizations' use of donated funds, and how the charity and its marathon run could become the center of a fire storm of negative publicity online and in the traditional media, and stating a policy directive that no one but the director is to engage in the discussion online or with the traditional media because even personal

comments by employees could be reported as statements by the charity. Of course, still be directive and offer to help. "No comment" is never an answer.

7. Describe the electronic tools that could be used in analyzing and monitoring the debate on the Internet over the use of donated funds by nonprofit organizations. Research how to effectively use these tools. Include alerts about your own organization.

8. Create, in diagram form, a crisis communication page for the charity's website. Include buttons or links that take visitors to information that would be responsive to criticisms of the charity identified. This would not be titled a "crisis communication" page because it isn't a crisis yet, and you don't want visitors to see the situation labeled a crisis. Use an appropriate title. Show how you want this gateway to information to look and what you want it to include.

9. Create a social media plan involving several platforms that will create buzz and change public perceptions about how funds are being used for Run for the Little Ones. Links to the website, stories, and pictures should be included.

10. Research the Diffusion of Innovations Theory. Create a fact sheet on this theory and understand how it relates to the adoption of the idea of nonprofits having more business latitude, as proposed in this case.

9. Promotion and Volunteer Recruitment: International Art Exhibit

Learning Outcomes

By the end of this case, you should be able to:

1. understand the research associated with and the details found within a client contract,

2. understand the importance of volunteerism and the basics of how to best recruit and serve volunteers, and

3. understand Social Learning Theory and how it is utilized when trying to do things such as engage volunteers.

This is a case of promoting the premier showing of Nihonga art in the United States. The exhibit comprises a world-class collection of 50 contemporary works of Japanese masters. The exhibit was arranged by the mayor of Townsville, U.S.A., for the purpose of promoting greater understanding of the Japanese culture in a community attracting businesses based in Japan.

To the Japanese, Nihonga exemplifies the solidly traditional merged with the new. The name *Nihonga* essentially means Japanese style of painting, as distinguished from Chinese style or Western style, and describes a blend of graphic style from the Chinese with the Western-influenced use of perspective. The imagery shown in the exhibition illustrates how the Japanese are able to reconcile old and new, to adapt a traditional discipline to embrace new ideas.

Assignment

For this case, assume that your public relations firm has competed for and won a contract with Townsville. The contract, shown later, has specific requirements for your firm in three areas. Your challenge is to develop a PR plan that meets the city's contract requirements: (1) to promote attendance at the exhibit, (2) to foster community involvement in three exhibit programs, and (3) to recruit volunteers to help operate the exhibit. The city is not looking to create a festival of activities. It has a primary purpose for hosting the Japanese art exhibit. It is imperative to focus your plan on the mayor's primary purpose for hosting a Japanese art exhibit. All elements of your plan must be in support of the mayor's primary purpose. So, develop your plan with only one goal (the condition the mayor wants to achieve for the community), and three objectives, spelling out what must be done in three areas required by the contract to achieve the mayor's goal. Under the heading Further Research, you will find guidance in the area of recruiting volunteers.

Team Member Assignments

Each team member is to complete a different one of the following items that might or might not be included in the design of your plan:

1. Write for the town a news release announcing that Townsville will host an exhibit of Nihonga art. See case information for dates, cost of admission, and other details. Assume that visitors to the exhibit will receive a designer-type ticket with a large souvenir portion to be retained that features a Nihonga painting; that they will be greeted and guided through the exhibit by one of more than 150 docents trained by the Townsville Art Museum director, Ron Hawkins; shown a five-minute video tape; and given a four-color brochure about Nihonga art.

2. Write instructions to a webpage designer for an event page featuring the Nihonga exhibit. Include an outline of content and suggestions on how said content could facilitate the learning of those who eventually visit the exhibit.

3. Write a post of at least 150 words to the city's event blog, recruiting volunteers to serve as docents (knowledgeable tour guides) for the exhibit. See the article titled "How to Attract and Retain Volunteers" under the heading Further Research.

4. Write briefing notes for Mayor David Green to use in talking about the exhibit of Nihonga art on a local television talk show. Prepare the mayor's notes in the form of sound bite responses to questions in the order they are most likely to be asked by a talk show host. Answers should be short and conversational. Every response should work to entice people of all ages to see the exhibit and participate in exhibit activities. Responses should be organized with labels so that topics are easy to spot.

5. Write a letter of invitation from the mayor to major donors. Assume that the mayor decides to precede the public opening of the exhibit with an exclusive dinner (paid for by private sources) and a private showing of the exhibit for 16 donors who made major contributions in support of the exhibit. The event is an expression of gratitude from the mayor on behalf of the town, so use your imagination to describe in the letter an elegant affair in terms of location, guest transportation, menu, entertainment, and, of course, the private presentation of Nihonga art.

6. Write a persuasive letter for Mayor David Green's signature to superintendents of public school districts encouraging them to make the Nihonga Classroom Experience program available to schools (kindergarten through 12th grade) throughout their respective districts. The president's letter must have compelling reasons for superintendents to use the programs, including bus tours to the exhibit.

7. Research your state's teaching guidelines for the respective grades mentioned and see if there is an angle at each level as to how the materials could be promoted as meeting those guidelines to teachers, who may potentially adopt the ideas. Create appropriate fact sheets based on your findings.

8. Write a storyboard for a video exclusively on Nihonga art, drawing on Internet sources for information.

9. Write a news release for Townsville to announce that it is accepting applications for volunteers to be trained to serve as docents for the exhibit. The release should center on quotes from the mayor that present this volunteer experience in irresistible terms. For ideas on what motivates people to volunteer their time and energy, see the following article. The city needs to recruit 150 docents to staff the exhibit. Volunteers are required to complete training provided by the Townsville At Museum. It will include five one-hour lectures on Nihonga art, instruction on the correct approach to conducting tours, and a bibliography of readings. The cost of training will be covered by the law firm of Swallow, Finch and Robin, one of the exhibit's major sponsors. For their service, docents will receive commemorative gold pins in the form of the Japanese alphabet characters for "Nihonga."

10. Write a public service announcement for radio promoting the exhibit.

11. Create an event plan based on the information and dates disclosed in this case. Do this calendar style, and embed all of the aforementioned components into the plan.

12. Oftentimes, Social Learning Theory has been directly paired with volunteerism activities. An understanding of this theory would help those on your team to better engage in volunteer recruitment and engagement. Research this theory and make the necessary connections. Create a factsheet to present about the theory and its connection to volunteerism.

Class Role Play

Cast

Narrator
Clarissa—Vice President
Katie—Account Executive
Danielle—Coordinator
Abby
Robert
Hilary
Chad
Erin
Kelsey
Zoe
Elizabeth
Zachary
Sara
Amanda
Stephanie

Narrator

Members of the account team and other staff members assigned to the Nihonga program assemble in the PR firm's conference room for a preliminary information dump on the new account assignment and to prepare for the first client meeting with Mayor David Green.

Vice President

Let's go over our plan for tomorrow's meeting with the mayor. Close the laptops. I want your full attention.

Account Executive

(asserts herself)
So what does the mayor expect?

Vice President

OK. Let's start from the top. We won the contract from the city. Now we need to make absolutely sure that we understand the assignment.

Coordinator

It's spelled out in the contract.

Vice President

Yes, but it's important to think about what the mayor is asking for and what we can realistically deliver. Abby, you did some preliminary research.

Abby

There's no question, Townsville's growth in the past three years has come from an increasing Asian population. About a 22 percent increase: 5600 to 7000.

Vice President

The city is developing relationships with incoming Japanese firms faster than towns-people are developing relationships with their new Asian neighbors. It's this growing culture gap that concerns the mayor.

Robert

And he wants to use the arts to bring everyone together.

Vice President

Yes, and not just the arts. He's bringing to Townsville a world-class, first-of-its kind exhibit. He has managed to put Townsville on the premiere, international showing of Nihonga art.

Hilary

How did he manage that?

Vice President

One of the Japanese companies here is half-owner of the art collection.

Narrator

The conference room door opens, and a secretary enters and hands Clarissa a note.

Vice President

It was the mayor. He says we need to talk tomorrow about a news conference to announce the exhibit.

Chad

The media will love this. The project is loaded with firsts.

Vice President

What do you have?

Chad

Well, it's the first of its kind ever assembled. It will be shown for the first time in Tokyo, Yokohama, Osaka, and Nagoya. Townsville will be its premier showing in the United States, and that will launch its premier showing in Europe—London, Paris, and Barcelona. It's the first major activity our town has had with its sister, Japan City.

Erin

So our job is to promote the exhibit.

Vice President

That's just part of it. I want everyone to read the contract with the city very carefully. Who has a copy?

Kelsey

I have one.

Vice President

Read assignment number one.

Kelsey

Number one. That our agency will promote (exclusive of the use of paid advertising) exhibit attendance among people of all age groups throughout the Greater Townsville Area. That we will secure publicity about the exhibit and prepare all of the materials necessary to work with the news media, such as a fact sheet, back-grounder, and news announcements. And that we will work with Townsville staff and elected officials on all questions or issues involving the exhibit event.

Vice President

Thanks, Kelsey. So, how far do we go with the promotion?

Zoe

Just Greater Townsville. But why not the region? Or national media?

Vice President

Good question. What's the mayor's main objective?

Elizabeth

To address a situation in Townsville.

Vice President

Exactly. What about contract Item #2? Zachary, answer your emails later, please.

Zachary

Sorry. What was the question?

Vice President

What is the second part of our assignment from the city?

Zachary

We're supposed to get the community to participate in three programs: Nihonga Artists on Location, Nihonga Classroom Experience, and Nihonga Town Seminars. Should I read each one?

Vice President

No. But everyone needs to read the details before our meeting with the mayor tomorrow.

Sara

The third part of the assignment is right here—to help the town recruit about 150 volunteers as tour guides, gift shop keepers, program coordinators, and others to assist with the exhibit.

Vice President

Thanks, Sara.

Amanda

I just read two good articles about recruiting volunteers.

Vice President

Why don't you make copies for everyone, Amanda. Let's see. Yes, Stephanie.

Stephanie

The contract says that we are to help the town recruit volunteers. Does that mean just publicizing volunteer opportunities? Or do we have to get names?

Vice President

I like that. You think like an attorney. Danielle talked about that with the mayor's assistant.

Coordinator

I did and here's what they want. It's not just publicity. The mayor wants a campaign to get people to sign up to help. We need to rely on some good research about what entices people to volunteer. The city estimates that 150 volunteers will be needed to setup and operate the exhibit. We need to incite a recruitment epidemic!

Vice President

That's something to think about. OK, let's get ready for our meeting with the mayor. Danielle, you just did that.
[Meeting adjourns.]

Nihonga Art Exhibit Classroom Experience

Nihonga Art Exhibit Contract

This is a contract between Townsville, U.S.A., and (Your Public Relations Firm) by which your firm agrees to provide certain public relations services to Townsville in connection with an exhibit of Nihonga art.

WHEREAS Townsville will be host to an exhibit of Nihonga art from July 1 through September 14;

WHEREAS the exhibit was assembled and offered for display by Japan City, sister city to Townsville;

WHEREAS this collection of 50 contemporary Japanese paintings in traditional style—known as Nihonga—will be shown for the first time in Tokyo, Yokohama, Osaka, and Nagoya, then on to its premier showing in the United States at Townsville, launching its world tour that will include London, Paris, and Barcelona;

WHEREAS this first-of-its-kind collection assembled by a sister city and provided by masters of the art is seen by citizens and officials of Townsville as an effective way to promote greater understanding and appreciation of the Japanese culture in a town that is growing faster in its relationships with businesses on the Pacific Rim than in its personal relationships among citizens of communities with an increasing Asian population;

WHEREAS to prevent the widening of a culture gap, citizens and city officials set as their objective the showing of a world-class exhibition of Nihonga art in Townsville as a stimulus for local residents and people throughout the area to learn more about the history, customs, and national character of Japan;

WHEREAS the public, of which 50,000 visitors are expected, will be able to view the Nihonga art from 10 a.m. to 6 p.m. daily at the Townsville Art Museum;

WHEREAS for the exhibit event to be the success that it should be, it has been and will be necessary to contract with a public relations firm to promote attendance and community involvement in the exhibit and to recruit volunteers, and (Your Public Relations Firm) is qualified and willing to provide such services.

NOW, THEREFORE,

IT IS HEREBY AGREED AS FOLLOWS:

That (Your Public Relations Firm) will promote (exclusive of the use of paid advertising) exhibit attendance among people of all age groups throughout the Greater Townsville Area, securing publicity about the exhibit, preparing all of the materials necessary to work with the news media, such as a fact sheet, backgrounder, news announcements, and cooperating with Townsville staff and elected officials on all questions or issues involving the exhibit event and public relations.

That (Your Public Relations Firm) will generate community involvement in the exhibit specifically by promoting three educational programs, each of which is described in the Attachment to this contract:

Nihonga Classroom Experience
Nihonga Town Seminars
Nihonga Artists on Location

That (Your Public Relations Firm) will help the town recruit approximately 150 volunteers as tour guides (docents), gift shop keepers, program coordinators, and others to assist with the exhibit.

For services under this agreement, extending from this contract date to September 14, (years intentionally omitted), (Your Public Relations Firm) will present Townsville with invoices and proper vouchers documenting time spent on such services at standard public relations rates for total compensation not to exceed $100,000, plus documented out-of-pocket costs not to exceed 10 percent of such professional fee. Major promotional items, such as direct mail pieces, video productions, and classroom materials, are to be presented separately and will be approved as funding sources are secured. (Your Public Relations Firm) is to begin its work by providing Townsville with a public relations plan for promoting attendance for the exhibit and community involvement in the three aforementioned educational programs, and for helping the city recruit 150 volunteers to help with the exhibit. The plan should include a proposed budget. Major promotional items should be shown as line items marked TBF (To Be Funded) in place of a cost estimate.

DATED this 10th day of December.

TOWNSVILLE, U.S.A., a municipal corporation

By: _____

David Green
Title: Mayor

_____

T. Tom Plumb, Town Clerk
By April Rostkemper, Deputy Town Clerk

_____

(Your Public Relations Firm)

Approved as to form:

_____

Alfred A. Apple, Town Attorney

Attachment

Contract
   Attachment A
   Nihonga Artists on Location

Townsville Art Museum will host the visit of four Nihonga artists. The purpose of this program is to give people an opportunity to converse, informally, (through an interpreter) with students of Nihonga and learn about the history of the art, the painting techniques used, and the way in which the artists select and approach their work.

The student artists will be in residence for six weeks beginning the second week in June. The artists' programs will include workshops and demonstrations of painting techniques; informal discussions with American artists; visits with educators and summer workshop students; studio time for the artists to work on a current or new painting and for visitors to observe; and time for the artists to produce artwork of their own to take back to Japan, possibly inspired by the greater Townsville environment. The schedule will be developed cooperatively between the artists and the museum staff member responsible for the Nihonga Artists on Location program.

Question to ponder: What kind of local potential partnerships would be productive for this endeavor?

Activity Description

The Nihonga Classroom Experience is a student lesson using Japanese art to generate interest in learning more about Japan—its culture, history, and national heritage. Lessons are being prepared for students in three groups: ages 4 to 6 years, 7 to 11 years, and 12 to 18 years. Instruction packets for each age group will contain a teacher's lesson guide, appropriate classroom activities, video, and Nihonga brochures, all enclosed in a program folder imprinted with a sponsor's name. Instruction packages could be available to all public school buildings. The classroom program will have a potential audience of 55,000 children.

Curriculum units for the classroom lesson and summer workshops are being developed, professionally, as follows:

Purpose: To promote a better understanding of the Japanese people—their customs, culture, and national heritage.

Curriculum units are being designed for children of ages ranging from 4 to 6 years, 7 to 11 years, and 12 to 18 years. Each unit will include three activities. Individual activities will take one to three hours each. These activities will include the following components, which emphasize instruction and content that promote greater understanding of the Japanese culture.

(a) Instructional Components

   i. Goals and objectives.

   ii. Good, clear directions so that nonspecialist teachers can readily translate the materials.

   iii. A range of activities that appeals to different learning styles.

   iv. Activities that stress collaborative learning.

   v. Activities that foster higher level thinking skills.

   vi. A concluding activity that engages students in evaluation of their own work and/or their peers' work.

   vii. List of materials, specific.

(b) Content Components

   i. A general background and history of the activity as it relates to Japanese culture as expressed, for example, in Nihonga.

   ii. Introduction to the appropriate Japanese words that relate to the activity.

   iii. A geographical orientation to the activity, i.e., Where in Japan does this activity take place/originate.

iv. An introduction to stories, music, dance, art, drama, and/or games of Japan that enhance the activity.

v. An exploration of Japanese life surrounding the activity, i.e., Where would students find this—at home? In school? For what age group is it appropriate?

Each curriculum unit will be packaged in folders appropriate for each grade level and will be used during the Nihonga children's workshops, as well as in regular classrooms. A curriculum director has been retained to develop the lessons, to provide in-service training for area teachers, and to help with summer workshops.

Nihonga Town Seminars

The Nihonga Town Seminars will be designed to introduce mature students and adults to a broad range of subjects. They include: Tea Ceremony, Japanese Cuisine, Japanese Flower Arranging, Raising of Koi, Bonsai Demonstration, Myths and Customs of Japan, Japanese-American Woman, Kimono Demonstration and Fashion Show, and Japanese Business Etiquette.

Each seminar will be presented by a qualified leader. There will be a different seminar each Monday evening at the Townsville Art Museum, and possibly other locations, during the exhibition. There will be six to eight seminars in the series.

Additional funds are being sought to enhance the stature of the seminar series by featuring a Nihonga artist for one of the sessions.

Each of the seminars will be videotaped for use by colleges, universities, and civic and professional organizations.

The following sources have been contacted for help in identifying qualified seminar leaders:

- Japan American Society

- International Examiner

- Asian Arts Council

- Council General of Japan (state office)

- California Institute of the Arts

- School of Music and the Arts

- San Francisco Art Institute

- United States International University

- Western State College

- World Affairs Council

- Japan-American Society (state office)

- University of Washington

- Regional art institutes

- Regional art museums

- Academy of Art College San Francisco

- California State University Los Angeles

- Pacific Northwest College of Art

- University of Southern California

- University of California

- University of Hawaii

- Others

Question to ponder: What kind of local potential partnerships would be productive for this endeavor?

Notes About Nihonga Art

- a technique whose roots extend back more than a thousand years

- a term created in the 19th century to distinguish traditional Japanese painting methods from Western-influenced art

- often synonymous with art of the past

- incorporates time-honored materials, such as silk, rice paper, ground semi-precious minerals, and gold and silver leaf

- employs only materials fully derived from natural sources (brushes, paper, Chinese ink, mineral pigment, and animal glue)

- paintings retain close harmony with nature

- technique has become one of the principal art forms of Japan

- one distinctive feature of this medium is the subtle control of detail that it allows; fine variations in line thickness and nuances in color attainable in Nihonga require painters to maintain close observation of their subjects

- once seen, paintings remain in the heart, creating a feeling of internal peace that originates with the painter's own clear conception of the subject

- rock pigments come from natural minerals; hues differ according to the fineness of the grains

- *Nikawa* (glue) is used to affix pigments to silk or paper on which artists paint

- the *eginu* silk used in Nihonga is woven from unglossed, raw silk strands; there are three or four different types of silk material, graded by strand thickness

- a large number of types of paper are used in Nihonga; choice of a particular type depends on personal preferences and an artist's intentions for the painting

- a wide variety of brushes in many sizes is used and broadly classified into brushes for drawing lines and brushes for coloring

- a distinguishing feature is the use of gold and silver foils

- artist usually begins by sketching a rough image

- more difficult to convey a lifelike subject in Nihonga than with oil painting

- subject matter classified broadly into landscapes, flowers and birds, and the human figure

- landscape paintings are traditionally referred to in Japan as *sansui-ga*, or paintings of mountains and water

- paintings of the *kacho-ga* genre generally have flowers and birds as their themes

- there are *kaki-ga*, featuring only flowers, and *sochu-ga*, with butterflies or other insects instead of birds

- genre also includes paintings of animals as well as birds

- figure painting is in portraits and in *bijin-ga*, images of famous beauties

- Nihonga artists look beyond the surface of their subject

- have a reverence toward nature

- appreciate the inherent beauty of nature in themes they portray

Further Research: Volunteer Recruitment

Attract and Retain Volunteers

Does your organization rely heavily on the use of volunteers? If so, are you finding it more difficult to maintain a full complement of them? Perhaps it's time for your organization to start a recruitment epidemic. By creating such an epidemic you should be able to attract and maintain volunteers at a consistent level.

What is a recruitment epidemic? I created the phrase by borrowing from the term *epidemic* as popularized by Malcolm Gladwell in his best-selling book *The Tipping Point*. I define a recruitment epidemic as a phenomenon in which an individual has an exceptional volunteer experience that results in feelings of joy and gratification that the individual feels compelled to share. The volunteer speaks to others with contagious enthusiasm that infects and motivates them to pursue the same experience. The cycle repeats itself in the form of an epidemic, demonstrating that the best recruiters are satisfied volunteers. Interestingly enough, we don't often see such epidemics in our local communities because conditions must be right to spark an epidemic.

Why do you need to start an epidemic? The main reason is that lifestyles have changed dramatically and individuals' discretionary time has become a precious commodity. Lack of time seems to be the largest reason for not volunteering.

Formally, previous studies on campus at the University of Oregon conducted by five student teams clearly indicated lack of time as a deterrent to volunteering, while also indicating no lack of interest or desire to participate in volunteer activities. This means that organizations must work even harder to attract and retain volunteers. In fact, organizations should generally elevate volunteerism in their hierarchy of social responsibilities because it's a material factor in the strength of the nation.

The Bureau of Labor Statistics reports that about 62.6 million people volunteered through or for an organization at least once between September 2014 and September 2015, spending a median of 52 hours on volunteer activities within that one year period. Teen participation remains relatively high, with 26.4 percent volunteering. Overall, 24.9 percent of adults gave to their communities by way of volunteering during the aforementioned time period.

Creating the Right Conditions

Many organizations launch recruitment efforts with an advertising or PR campaign when, in fact, engaged volunteers seem to be the most effective force. According to a previous Bureau of Labor Statistics report, only two in five volunteers became involved with the main organization for which they did volunteer work on their own initiative. Almost 43 percent were asked to volunteer, most often by someone in the organization.

We don't see recruitment epidemics because of another missing condition. It has to do with context or the environment in which an organization operates. The context of an organization (i.e., how people treat each other, the norms and values they share, the way they relate to people outside the organization) is shaped by the executive director. It's the head of an organization whose policy direction fashions the organization and makes volunteers feel at home, respected, and appreciated.

Once accountability for volunteerism is established, then it is necessary to ensure that policies for its engagement are effectively managed. Volunteerism is not something for an executive simply to recognize and relegate to the human resources or PR department. In their book *Execution*, Larry Bossidy and Ram Charan maintain that delegation of responsibilities to others with no executive follow-through or oversight has been one of the greatest management pitfalls in recent times. An executive manager must see that an organization has the discipline necessary throughout the process to get things done.

Another reason for lack of success is due to a lack of resources—having in place all that enables a volunteer to have an exceptional experience.

First and foremost, a volunteer's time must be put to good use. Assignments should be well-defined, interesting, and relevant to a volunteer's personal interests and needs. They should give individuals an opportunity to accomplish something. Volunteers want to see direct results from their personal efforts.

What a Volunteer Needs

An exceptional volunteer experience has several important elements:

- a job description stating tasks to be done, work standards, measurements, and reporting relationships.

- a job title for résumé use

- introduction of volunteer to staff

- job orientation

- work area and tools to operate

- list of coworkers with job titles, phone numbers, and reasons why they are important to the volunteer

- important publications and documents to read

- a conversation about how assignments contribute to the volunteer's professional goals

- periodic critiques of the volunteer's performance

- notes of praise that the volunteer could include with a résumé

- the experience should provide a volunteer with meaningful recognition that exceeds a mere thank you note; a word of encouragement or praise for something specific is powerful, as are grateful comments from someone served

- a volunteer experience can offer personal growth, give a person a chance to gain new skills, and foster one's own development capabilities; the resulting personal growth can be tremendous.

- a volunteer experience can also be a valuable outlet for developing relationships; it can be a place for meeting new friends while providing a feeling of belonging and an opportunity for making social connections

- the recruitment epidemic increases by word-of-mouth and enables an organization to attract and maintain an adequate complement of volunteers

10. Empowering Employees: The Bridge

Learning Outcomes

By the end of this case, you should be able to:

1. brainstorm functionally and productively within a group while considering others' ideas via critical listening and analyzing skills,

2. decipher creative avenues to potentially meet more than one objective at a time—even for two different audiences,

3. understand and appreciate others' thoughts while effectively finding potential flaws in all ideas presented,

4. know and recognize all elements of a public relations pitch for business, and

5. feel prepared and comfortable in answering questions about your own thoughts and ideas.

Business Description: XJS Communication

This case is about a large cellular communication company, XJS Communication, that recently hired an external consulting organization to conduct research and analyze data to determine what their consumers and employees thought about the company, its products, and its services. Findings revealed that the newer customers felt much more positive about XJS than did those who had been with the company for a longer term. The same also held true for the employees. This was consistent with the company's recent push to improve internal employee relations, as well as customer service. It was recognized that the newer customers and employees had only interacted with the company under the recently improved employee relations and customer service, hence their satisfaction was higher. Upper management felt that it was necessary to begin more programs that would keep the newer consumers and employees engaged and feeling positive about their respective experiences with the company. Carried forward, this would continue a positive upswing in both groups' perceptions. One major finding was that corporate employees wanted more input and control; they wanted to have opportunities to impact the consumers' experiences. Ironically, another finding was that consumers wanted more transparency from XJS—transparency that corporate employees could potentially provide. Therefore, ways for the newer headquarters employees to potentially interact with consumers needed to be conceptualized. Jobs within XJS headquarters include accounting functions, public relations, sales, service and shipping, technical support, product development, bookkeeping, marketing, and more. These people, with the exception of those in public relations, never really got to develop interpersonal relationships with customers who were using the company's services, enjoying the use of its products, looking forward to new developments, and wanting recognition for their loyalty to the company. Users, who were becoming patrons of the company, wanted more of a relationship with the company than what little attention they were able to get from the customer service department. Your team might discover some useful thought starters for a brainstorming session in the following transcript of a conversation between the authors of this book, Rebecca Gilliland and Tom Hagley.

A Conversation between the Authors, Rebecca and Tom

Rebecca

I think this cellular communications company's use of research is a wonderful invitation to creative thinking. I also credit the company for thinking in terms of employee empowerment rather than traditional employee relations or employee communication.

Tom

I like the idea of building a bridge to facilitate two-way understanding and interaction among individuals.

Rebecca

The company's research reveals needs that beg for more than communication. Employees feel a need to associate with customers and customers feel a need to associate with employees.

Tom

You used the term *customer*. How does the company refer to people who use their products?

Rebecca

I suppose you could call them users, consumers, subscribers, customers …

Tom

Could they be called patrons?

Rebecca

What are you thinking?

Tom

I think the term *patron* has a much deeper meaning than the more common terms. I saw that the company is deliberately keeping its customer relations folks out of this process.

Rebecca

I think that's part of the broader aim to empower all employees to be responsive to the needs of customers, or patrons. Maybe this shows that organizations have become too organized, too compartmentalized. When you have a customer relations department, you are telling all employees that the company has people designated to deal with customers, that it's no one else's responsibility. I suppose you could say the same about a public relations department.

Tom

The more we talk about this case, the more I think about an experience I had in the hospital.

Rebecca

What?

Tom

A couple years ago I had major heart valve surgery at the Cleveland Clinic in Ohio. Part of the experience was being in the clinic's program of putting patients first. From the moment I entered the hospital, I saw evidence everywhere—in the attitudes and actions of employees, in all of the optics of the physical environment, in the printed documents—that patients come first.

Rebecca

Somehow, the entire organization was empowered to put patients first.

Tom

The screen savers on every computer in the lobbies, waiting rooms, labs, and doctors' offices display a logo with "Patients First." Think of what that says to all employees and patients!

Rebecca

You are on the edge of wanting to say "Patrons First" for the communications company.

Tom

On its website it states Cleveland Clinic was the first major academic medical center to make patient experience a strategic goal and to appoint a Chief Experience Officer, and one of the first to establish an Office of Patient Experience.

Rebecca

So where are we going with this?

Tom

Maybe we can use this with this case to provoke discussions.

Think about how the clinic's program could be modified to provide a framework for empowerment by the communication company, as well as other organizations.

For Cleveland Clinic, Patients First is:

- Safe Care

- High Value Care

- High Quality Care

- Patient Satisfaction

As the clinic points out, Patients First "requires more than world-class clinical care—it requires care that addresses every aspect of a patient's encounter with Cleveland Clinic, including the patient's physical comfort, as well as their educational, emotional, and spiritual needs."

Every employee of the clinic is encouraged to add best practices to enhance Patients First in every functional area of its operation.

Rebecca

One might wonder, initially, why the communications company would want to spend resources on employees in a headquarters operation that would seem to have little contact with customers scattered across the country. But the idea is to create a culture that empowers employees to put patients first in everything it does.

Team Assignment

Your PR firm has been hired by XJS to develop ideas and programs to foster relationships between company employees and the company's consumers. Keep in mind that management's end goal is to have in place a relational bridge that will facilitate interactions between XJS employees and customers to overcome challenges and share the joys of success. Strategies in the suggested plans should consider that consumers are spread nationwide, while XJS' corporate offices and headquarters are centered in the Midwest.

Separate into groups for this task. Treat this assignment as a competition for winning this account.

1. Brainstorm three possible programs to meet the challenge above. Talk about all three, as a group, and make a list of at least five challenging questions for each potential program. Talk through the respective questions and brainstorm answers. Try to find deficiencies in each suggested program.

2. Determine which of the ideas will best meet the needs of the employees' desire for empowerment/contact with consumers while also helping consumers feel positive about the company. Debate this choice until a group consensus is made as to which idea is the best plan of action.

3. Create a professional pitch for your idea. Create a PowerPoint, Prezi, or other visual aid.

4. Each group should present to the class its respective idea. Each member should speak during the presentation. This should be a persuasive pitch to sell your group's idea as the best course of action.

5. Each group should be allowed to ask one question (or more, if agreed upon) to the other groups upon pitch completion. These questions should be challenging and, again, attempt to illustrate deficiencies in the competing groups' plans. Any group member may field the question(s) posed.

6. After pitch completion, a group winner should be determined. The instructor could choose, or each class member can vote (but not for one's own group), or outside professionals could be used as judges if arranged in advance. Judges should take into consideration how persuasive the pitch was, as well as how creative the proposed idea is at building the desired bridge. Finally, the ability to think quickly and aptly when answering questions should also be considered.

11. Public Information: Black Crater Fire

Learning Outcomes

By the end of this case, you should be able to:

1. understand the essential elements of crisis communication, including how to use direct and persuasive language through mass communication channels to spur people to action, avoid sensationalism, and ethically relay information to communities;

2. experience, vicariously, how a PIO would feel trying to anticipate communication needs of a community threatened by a raging wildfire; and

3. understand communication cycles and the necessity for feedback channels, even, and especially, in a crisis situation.

On Monday, July 24, 2006, vacationers with plans to enjoy the wonders of Central Oregon drove into their destination town and became victims of a raging forest fire, which, in a matter of days, required state, regional, and federal resources. We praise the town of Sisters for making firefighters and vacationers feel warmly welcomed during a tense, but intelligently handed crisis situation.

Assignment

Read for yourself, or join with your class colleagues in acting out the case role play as newscasters issuing bulletins on the rapidly approaching Black Crater Fire. Try out your acting skills in reading in a serious voice the days, dates, times, headings, and text as a newscaster. As you participate in this fast-moving drama, think about the information needs of the community and how you would meet them.

Write a one-page, single-spaced paper on what you, personally, would like and not like about being a public information officer (PIO) on call for a federal incident command. Or, participate in a class discussion about a PIO position, as your instructor directs.

Work individually, or in teams, as your instructor directs, and develop from the Lessons Learned that follow the class role play a priority-sequenced, at-a-glance, pocket card checklist that you would want to have in hand as PIO for an on call, federal-level firefighting incident command.

Class Role Play

Take turns reading the news briefs in this timeline. Act out using your news broadcaster voice. Include the day, date, time, heading, and text of each entry. Pause briefly between each news bulletin.

Cast

Newscaster #1

Newscaster #2

Newscaster #3

Newscaster #4

Newscaster #5

Newscaster #6

Newscaster #7

Newscaster #8

Newscaster #9

Newscaster #10

Newscaster #11

Newscaster #12

NEWSCASTER #1

Tuesday, July 25, 8:00 a.m.
Fire Burns on Black Crater

A wildfire estimated at between 50 and 70 acres continued to burn uncontrolled, this morning, on the south side of Black Crater within the Three Sisters Wilderness. The fire was discovered Monday morning after a Sunday evening lightning storm swept across about 10 miles southwest of Sisters.

Tuesday, July 25, 4:00 p.m.
Black Crater Fire Is Spreading

After 12 hours of relative calm, the Black Crater Fire was again spreading to the north and northeast this afternoon.

Wednesday, July 26, 1:00 p.m.
Black Crater Fire Triples in Size

The Black Crater Fire burning west of Sisters tripled in size yesterday and now is burning on 300 acres, according to fire information officer David Seesholtz.

NEWSCASTER #2

Wednesday, July 26, 10:00 p.m.
Black Crater Fire Holds at 400 Acres

Ash from the Black Crater Fire fell in town and surrounding subdivisions today. The fire is burning approximately seven miles southwest of town.

Thursday, July 27, 10:00 a.m.
Black Crater Fire Increases to 820 Acres

The Black Crater Fire revealed itself last night. Infrared aerial surveying of the fire showed the fire area to be 820 acres, up from the 400-acre estimate earlier in the day.

Thursday, July 27, 11:00 a.m.
Residents Advised of Evacuation Plans

Evacuation plans for the subdivisions of Crossroads and Tollgate, as well as other residential properties scattered in the area southwest of Sisters, have been developed in case the Black Crater Fire blows up and threatens these communities.

NEWSCASTER #3

Thursday, July 27, 1:00 p.m.
Black Crater Air Attack Is Underway

An air tanker and helicopter made retardant and water drops on the Black Crater Fire this afternoon as firefighters tried to keep the 820-acre blaze from spreading toward the Crossroads subdivision.

Thursday, July 27, 3:00 p.m.
Crossroads Is Being Evacuated

Fire officials and Deschutes County Sheriff deputies are evacuating the Crossroads subdivision and the Edgington Road area.

Thursday, July 27, 6:00 p.m.
Black Crater Fire Advances

A public meeting on the Black Crater Fire situation has been scheduled for 7:30 p.m. tonight at Sisters High School. The fire has advanced to within three-quarters of a mile of the demarcation line that would trigger an evacuation of Tollgate.

NEWSCASTER #4

Thursday, July 27, 9:00 p.m.

Governor Declares State of Emergency

The Black Crater Fire has grown to between 1500 and 1700 acres, and has forced the evacuation of approximately 600 residents of the Crossroads subdivision and another 70 or so from the Edgington Road area.

Friday, July 28, 11:00 a.m.
Black Crater Fire Grows to 2,684 Acres

The Black Crater Fire grew to 2,684 acres yesterday, according to an aerial infrared survey conducted last night. The fire is about one mile from a demarcation line that would trigger an evacuation of 1,500 Tollgate residents.

Friday, July 28, 11:00 a.m.
Forest Closure Announced

Fire officials have closed all National Forest lands west of Three Creeks Road. Forest service personnel are notifying campers and recreationists to leave the area.

NEWSCASTER #5

Friday, July 28, 1:00 p.m.
Winds Quiet in the Morning

The winds that fire officials fear could push the Black Crater Fire toward residences in the Edgington Road area and the Crossroads subdivision did not materialize as early as expected today, according to a meteorologist with the Northwest Oregon Incident Management Team.

Friday, July 28, 1:00 p.m.
"High possibility" of Tollgate Evacuation

Fire officials are saying there is a "high possibility" that Tollgate will be evacuated by tonight, and a "reasonable possibility" that the city of Sisters will be evacuated by tonight.

Friday, July 28, 5:30 p.m.
Black Crater Fire Burning Toward the North

The column of black smoke that loomed over the Black Crater Fire late this afternoon was from fire activity along the north rim of the fire. The fire, which is the number one priority fire in the nation, is now approximately 3,000 acres in size.

NEWSCASTER #6

Friday, July 28, 8:00 p.m.
Firefighters Have Made Progress

Firefighters held the eastern edge of the Black Crater Fire where it had pushed toward residential areas yesterday and forced the evacuation of the Crossroads subdivision and the Edgington Road area.

Saturday, July 29, 11:00 a.m.
Good Chance of Evacuation Today

"There is a good chance the Tollgate subdivision will need to be evacuated today or Sunday," Sisters/Camp Sherman Fire Chief, Tay Robertson, told a large crowd of homeowners at a public meeting this morning at Sisters High School.

Saturday, July 29, 5:00 p.m.
Tollgate Is Evacuated

The call went out at about 3:52 p.m. today to evacuate the Tollgate subdivision near Sisters.

NEWSCASTER #7

Saturday, July 29, 9:00 p.m.
Using Fire to Fight Fire

There is a 50–50 chance that the city of Sisters may be evacuated by late tomorrow morning, according to Black Crater Fire Incident Commander Carl West.

Sunday, July 30, 8:00 a.m.
Night Crew Makes Strong Headway on Blaze

A fire-fighting crew worked all night to secure an eight-mile section of the eastern and northeastern perimeter of the Black Crater Fire where it has been pushing hard toward residential areas. A burnout operation to rob the fire of fuel and to help firefighters secure a line around the head of the fire was successful.

Sunday, July 30, 11:00 a.m.
Winds Will Test the "Black Line"

Winds gusting in the 25 to 35 miles-per-hour range on Sunday will test the "black line" created in an all-night burnout operation on the Black Crater Fire, according to Incident Commander Carl West.

NEWSCASTER #8

Sunday, July 30, 3:00 p.m.
Firefighters Pound Blaze from Ground and Air

Fire crews are taking advantage of cooler temperatures and cloud cover to capitalize on ground gained during Saturday night's burnout operation.

Sunday, July 30, 8:00 p.m.
A "Good Day"

Firefighters built on the successful burnout operation conducted by the Saturday night shift to consolidate their grip on the Black Crater Fire today. "It was a good day," said Dale Gardner of the regional firefighting command.

Monday, July 31, 8:00 a.m.
Federal Incident Team Takes Over

The Northwest Oregon Interagency Incident Management Team is handing command of the Black Crater Fire to the federal Southern Area Blue Team, a management team from Georgia.

NEWSCASTER #9

Monday, July 31, 12:00 p.m.
Firefighters Are on the Offensive

Firefighters are on the offensive against the Black Crater Fire, mopping up and strengthening lines on the east side of the fire where it had pushed toward residential areas and forced evacuations of Crossroads, Edgington Road, and Tollgate. The fire is 20 percent contained.

Monday, July 31, 1:00 p.m.
No Word Yet on Evacuee Return

Despite significant progress on containing the Black Crater Fire, fire officials have not yet determined when evacuees can return to their homes in Crossroads, Edgington Road, and Tollgate.

Monday, July 31, 5:00 p.m.
Tollgate Residents to Return Home at 6:00 p.m. Monday

Captain Tim Edwards of the Deschutes County Sheriff's Office has announced that residents of Tollgate may return home at 6:00 p.m. tonight. Crossroads and Edgington Road remain under evacuation until further notice.

NEWSCASTER #10
Tuesday, August 1, 11:00 a.m.
More Evacuees Could Return Home Today

Residents of Crossroads and the Edgington Road area may be returning home on Tuesday afternoon, Black Crater Fire Incident Commander Mike Quesinberry told a smaller-than-usual crowd at Sisters High School. He said, "You folks will be back in your homes this afternoon."

Tuesday, August 1, 5:00 p.m.
Evacuation Order Lifted

As of 5:00 p.m. today, Crossroads and Edgington Road residents will be allowed to return to their homes, fire officials announced.

Tuesday, August 1, 5:00 p.m.
Sisters Community Rallies in The Face Of Fire

The Black Crater Fire rallied the community spirit of Sisters. As flames and smoke rolled closer to Sisters, people began to prepare for the eventual evacuation of their homes. Residents safe from the advancing fire started looking for ways to help. School officials put out the welcome mats. The Northwest Interagency Incident Management Team set up fire camp at Sisters Middle School, while the Red Cross established an evacuation center at Sisters High School.

NEWSCASTER #11
Tuesday, August 1, 5:00 p.m.

Weather Aids Black Crater Fire Fight

A lack of firefighting resources dogged the effort to fight the Black Crater Fire, but that effort was aided by the weather. Though some nasty winds played a large role in the blowup that forced evacuations of Crossroads and Edgington Road on Thursday, the weather overall was more cooperative, allowing firefighters two days in which to consolidate gains made in an all-night burnout operation on Saturday.

Tuesday, August 1, 6:00 p.m.
Firefighters Gain Upper Hand on Black Crater Fire

Firefighters seemed to have gained a strong hold on the 9,200-acre Black Crater Fire west of Sisters by this morning. Tollgate residents who evacuated Saturday were allowed to return home at 6:00 p.m. yesterday. Residents of Crossroads and Edgington Road, who had been out of their homes since Thursday, anxiously awaited news that they, too, could go home.

NEWSCASTER #12
Thursday, August 3, 1:00 p.m.
Black Crater Blaze Is 50 Percent Contained

Firefighters continued to mop up hot spots on the Black Crater Fire as they worked to complete the last eight miles of containment line around the 9,200-acre blaze. The fire is 50 percent contained.

Friday, August 4, 8:00 a.m.
Fire Containment Expected Sunday

The 9,400-acre Black Crater Fire is 70 percent contained, according to fire officials. Full containment is expected Sunday at 6:00 p.m.

Monday, August 7, 9:00 a.m.
Black Crater Fire Is 95 Percent Contained

The Black Crater Fire was 95 percent contained as of yesterday. Expected containment has been pushed back to August 11.

Lessons Learned

Black Crater Fire will be remembered as a model of cooperation between citizens and firefighting personnel at all levels of government. The incident provides a slate of lessons in public information management titled here as Points of Importance.

1. Treat each other with respect. The rapport between town residents and firefighters was exceptional, resulting in extraordinary cooperation and coordination.

2. Give residents access to all information as soon as it is available. Information was quickly disseminated through print, broadcast, telecommunication, and Internet channels.

3. Give information the priority of operational direction. In other words, "firefighting comes first" is an attitude, not a viable principle. Operations and public communication must have the same priority in order to have public support and cooperation.

4. Begin public briefings not with polite ramblings, but with up-to-the-minute details as in a military command briefing. Begin public meetings with details the public wants to hear first.

5. Make incident command the authoritative public information source. For example: www.NWOregonIMT.com was established and later moved to www.fs.fed.us/r6/centralOregon with a link to "Black Crater Fire."

6. Give tough-to-take instruction directly and completely. No filtering. No hesitation. For example, residents were told "Once the evacuation order is given, you will not be permitted back into the area."

7. Answer all questions. For example, one question was asked three different ways by three different people and each query was treated with respect as though it was asked for the first time.

8. Completely address areas of intense public interest, regardless of their importance or relevance. They will not go away. For example, questions about the location of power lines and the use of air support were asked at several public meetings and were answered each time.

9. Fully explain processes and procedures. For example, evacuation notification and procedures were explained in detail. How will residents be notified? Will there be a pre-alert? How much time will there be between the pre-alert and the evacuation order? Will the town be notified all at once or in phases and, if so, in what sequence? If residents work in Redmond or Bend and an order is issued can, they get back into Sisters? In other words, should they go to work tomorrow? What about their pets? Should they leave their doors unlocked? Will reverse 911 phone notification include cell phones?

10. Avoid jargon, such as moppin' in, moppin' up, hose ways, retardant line, structural crews, root out, transitional pattern, hot shots and hot shot crews, rehab work, and emergency restoration work.

11. Facilitate public confidence in leaders. For example, fire command was transferred from local to regional to federal command. For each change in incident command, the commander's first remarks need to instill public confidence in a new leader.

12. Consider the children. Emergency situations provide teachable moments for children, such as learning about firefighting and showing appreciation for firefighters by baking and handing them brownies.

13. Expect public information challenges. For example, the local fire chief said, "You can expect public information challenges in three areas: the situation itself, staffing, and technology."

14. Use opportunities to garner goodwill. For example, the Sisters fire chief said, "You can rest assured that we are taking good care of your property. We're even watering your plants while you are away."

15. Be particular in selecting a public meeting place and facility. For example, Sisters High School became the evacuation center—conveniently located; able to accommodate nearly the entire town of 2,000 people for meetings; and fully equipped with a sound system, computer projection equipment, laser pointer, large screen, chairs, rest rooms, and a radio station, Outlaw Radio 106.5 FM, with a feedback email address: KZSO@outlawnet.com.

16. Focus public meeting agenda on specifics. For example, brief people with military-type precision and detail. What exactly was accomplished today? How was it done? What resources were used? What's the plan for tonight and tomorrow morning? What additional resources are needed? Are we going to have them? If not, why?

17. Let experts speak. People don't want information from an incident command spokesperson. They want information directly from persons in charge, such as the sheriff, incident commander, meteorologist, fire behavior analyst, state fire marshal, Oregon Department of Forestry, Red Cross, local fire chief, or U.S. Forest Service.

18. Make public information a two-way exchange. Give people what they want to know, then have them listen to what they need to know.

19. Take advantage of existing communication resources. For example, Sisters High School radio station was used to broadcast public meetings live and replay them during the day along with interviews of experts on the fire team, and statements were given to *The Nugget*, Sisters' weekly newspaper, for posting on www.nuggestnews.com, and to the Bend Bulletin for posting on www.bendbulletin.com. Regional television was included.

20. Be respectful of every question and concern. For example, during one public meeting a woman from a recreational vehicle parked in the evacuation/information center parking lot said, "We don't have an FM radio; how will we know when it's OK to go back to our house?" The commander of the federal Southeastern Area Interagency Incident Management Team kindly replied: "I will come over and tell you."

21. Use visuals. For example, project web addresses and emergency help and information phone numbers on a big screen and give people plenty of time to copy them.

22. Use handouts. For example, explain the evacuation notification process that will use media releases, the incident team phone line 549-3211, the Oregon Department of Transportation number 511-8, phone calls to evacuees who register with the Red Cross, Outlaw radio 106.5 FM, police car sirens, and house-to-house door-belling.

23. Spike rumors. For example, an evacuee who was eager to get back into his home spread the word that houses were being looted. Authorities immediately challenged the rumor with accurate information.

24. Accept volunteered resources. For example, Clearchannel.com provided free wireless Internet connections at the Red Cross evacuation center, along with 20 drops throughout town, and it offered free long distance phone service.

25. Walk in the fire victim's shoes. For example, sit with people voicing their questions, concerns, and anxieties to fully appreciate the importance of providing information fast, accurately, and in great detail.

26. Be forthright and honest. For example, the lead PIO for the federal Southeastern Area Interagency Incident Management Team said, "Whether news is good or bad, you can count on us to tell you the truth."

27. Drop boundaries. Promote cooperation among local, state, and federal officials and the people they serve and the rewards will be bountiful. For example, when the Type II Northwest Interagency Incident Management Team turned command of the emergency over to the federal Type I Southeastern Area Interagency Incident Management Team, the Northwest team received a standing ovation from hundreds of residents and the federal team quickly came to regard Sisters as "the most giving and patient community."

28. Support each other. Meeting the challenge of a life- and property-threatening situation is a significant accomplishment to be recognized. For example, parents helped children make cookies and fudge and take it to fire fighters. Residents and merchants posted thank you signs around town. When one resident during a public meeting asked what more the town could do to show its appreciation to the fire teams, the incident commander said, "Just give 'em a smile and a wave."

29. Use multiple channels. For example, the Incident Management Team staffed a bulletin board briefing at the town park and ran a daily information trap line to key businesses and local government offices.

30. Keep the media informed. For example, the Incident Management Command conducted frequent and scheduled briefings, and took reporters and photographers on trips to the fire line. An incident management team treated the media as a partner to ensure that accurate information was conveyed to the public.

31. Consider related impacts. For example, the Incident Management Team, thinking of the economic impact the emergency could have on a small town, made a special effort to communicate with visitors and included them in the information trap line with a staffed, in-town sidewalk briefing.

32. Use a phone bank. For example, the Incident Management Team provided information through a phone bank and also used this channel to spike rumors with accurate facts. Out-of-towners used the phone bank to ask about the smoke and whether they should come to Sisters.

33. Use public meetings. For example, regularly scheduled public meetings at Sisters High School—the official evacuation center—gave residents, visitors, business owners, and evacuees the opportunity to get to know, eyeball to eyeball, the leaders of the fire suppression organization, particularly "the outsiders" of the Southeastern Area Incident Management Command. When first introduced, the incident commander said in a typical Southern drawl, "I may talk slow, but I fight fires real fast." Instantly, he had a close, winning rapport with the hundreds of people attending the meeting.

34. Accept help and resources. For example, the Incident Management Command could have ignored the Sisters High School principal when he offered the use of the school's radio station that was due to come on line at the fall start of school. Instead, the Incident Management Command partnered with the school and Outlaw Radio 106.5 FM became a major information source that taped and aired the public meetings repeatedly, along with interviews of fire officials from the interagency team. The station, thanks to the high school principal, just happened to be available—something that doesn't happen for most fire-fighting emergencies. When the public meetings were discontinued, the Incident Management Command continued to provide briefings on Outlaw Radio 106.5 FM.

35. Messaging must be consistent. For example, the information function was seamless, mainly because messages to the public were consistent with all sources within the interagency group. In contrast to the sharp, commonly seen bickering over turf among government agencies, collaboration between local, regional, and federal authorities, the media, and citizens in fighting the Black Crater Fire was commendable beyond everyone's belief.

36. Announce and celebrate success. For example, as one incident command official said, "I am not sure you could have a more comprehensive program." In return, the community hosted a pie and ice cream social for the firefighters.

12. Risk Communication: What Could Go Wrong?

Learning Outcomes

By the end of this case, you should be able to:

1. explain the difference between an ethical and a legal standard for organizations and public relations professionals;

2. generate and implement optimal communication strategies for releasing potentially volatile information to your publics;

3. understand the vital roles and ethical responsibilities of those who practice public relations to facilitate dialogue between an organization, its employees, and concerned public parties;

4. understand and provide examples of the importance of proactive communication, trust, transparency, collaboration, and social responsibility in effective risk communication; and

5. understand what could go wrong if proactive communication, transparency, improper protocols, and lack of collaboration are not present in risk communication.

Public relations consultants, in working for clients, often become privy to proprietary information, as well as to the private internal operations of businesses. Consultants are expected to respect confidential matters shared by clients. Not every consulting job has clear lines of responsibility, as you will see in this case. There are situations when the consultant may have difficulty defending the actions of a client to the publics affected.

The PR consultant in this case was hired to advise the manager of an industrial plant how to communicate the imminent installation of equipment that would add two more toxic substances to the 17 toxic substances currently in use. This communication is mandated by federal law.

The consultant tours the plant operations, interviews employees, and conducts a focus group discussion on safety with community leaders. The consultant's actual research findings are presented here in a class role play for you to enact with colleagues.

Assignment

Examine this situation from the perspective of the PR consultant hired for this job. Act out the case role play with your colleagues in the classroom and experience, vicariously, how it would feel to begin your research and encounter a series of increasingly startling, life-threatening discoveries. Then, write a single-spaced paper answering all of the following questions.

1. How would you organize and present your research findings?

2. What would you say to the plant manager who wants you to present your findings to him and his staff with no prior preview with the manager?

3. You were hired to advise the manager on how to communicate the use of two more toxic materials in addition to 17 already in use. How will you incorporate your startling discoveries into your presentation?

4. Will you limit your advice to an announcement?

5. Will you broaden your advice to cover safety concerns? If so, in what ways?

6. Is it your responsibility, as a consultant, to know what actions your client will take with the safety concerns you have uncovered?

7. Are you, as a consultant, bound to client confidentiality agreements under all circumstances?

Additional Notes

In the mid-1980s, the federal government made it the public's right to know about hazardous materials used in the work place. Companies using dangerous chemicals were mandated by law, under SARA Title III (EPCRA), to disclose their use of these substances by completing and making available reports which are reviewed for compliance by local, state, and federal governments. Information reported tells where hazardous chemicals exist and in what quantities. Initially, residents of many communities throughout the country were shocked to discover the risks posed to their personal health and safety by their industrial neighbors.

Today, the risks continue to exist; the public is less interested and informed and has abrogated the safeguarding of its health and safety to local, state, and federal agencies.

A fire chief gave this perspective: "Material Safety Data Sheets are of interest to local emergency planning committees, state emergency response commissions, and first responders; the general public is relatively uniformed, and largely uninterested. There seems to be a willingness to rely on government to protect people from bad things in their community. In my opinion, interest in chemical risks by the public peaked within the first decade of SARA Title III (EPCRA), and has since waned. Fortunately, my experience has been that industry still cares and is sensitive to public expectations."

While people have gained a right to know about the use of hazardous materials in the work place, they would be misguided to think that the risks in using toxics have been eliminated. Currently, they rely on employer and government oversight to ensure their personal health and safety in the workplace. Employees should seek information and know for themselves what hazards exist and how they are being managed.

Class Role Play

Cast

Narrator
PR Consultant Vince Brockwell
Plant Manager Harry Holderman
Employee Mike
Employee Arvin
Employee Rich
Employee Bill
Employee Bob
County Commissioner Iffert
Chamber of Commerce Executive Dorothy
Fire Chief Sonders
Police Chief Jefferies
Mayor Hunt
State Senator Winchester
State Representative Gritmeyer

Narrator

The PR consultant meets with the plant manager in the manager's offfice.

Plant Manager Harry Holderman

Vince, I asked you to see me because we are going to make an addition to the plant.

PR Consultant Vince Brockwell

And you want an announcement.

Plant Manager Harry Holderman

I wish we could do it without any fanfare.

PR Consultant Vince Brockwell

What are you going to add?

Plant Manager Harry Holderman

Just another piece of equipment.

PR Consultant Vince Brockwell

So why the serious look?

Plant Manager Harry Holderman

You know we already use 17 hazardous chemicals. Well, this will add two more and the community, by law, has a right to know. We made the big disclosure about our chemical use back in the mid-'80s. Now that the information is accessible, people don't seem to have as much interest. But this is going to wake the sleeping dog.

PR Consultant Vince Brockwell

This has always been considered a dangerous place to work, Harry. And I don't know that the perception has changed.

Plant Manager Harry Holderman

I'm afraid that's true. The head shed just wants to make money—at anyone's expense.

PR Consultant Vince Brockwell

Why don't I have some informal conversations with people inside and outside the plant? I'd like to interview some employees. I'm sure I could arrange a focus group of community leaders like the mayor, Chamber director, police chief. That will give us an idea of how people feel about accepting more risk.

Plant Manager Harry Holderman

You might wake the sleeping dog.

PR Consultant Vince Brockwell

Let's do this, Harry.

Narrator

The PR consultant, having made arrangements to interview employees in the most dangerous areas of the plant, begins with Mike.

PR Consultant Vince Brockwell

Mike, tell me about your job.

Mike

First thing to know when we go to work is which way the wind's blowing. If you smell a foul order, you know to run away from the wind. That's how we watch for chemical leaks.

PR Consultant Vince Brockwell

So what are you supposed to do in an emergency?

Mike

There've been spills. That should be a sign that we need some written procedures, but there aren't any.

Narrator

The PR consultant completes the interview and moves to another dangerous area of the plant and talks to another employee.

PR Consultant Vince Brockwell

Arvin, where do you work?

Arvin

Can I say, without getting in trouble?

PR Consultant Vince Brockwell

Sure.

Arvin

They say I work in the "powder house." My area is a danger zone.

PR Consultant Vince Brockwell

Is it like a bomb?

Arvin

Kind of …

PR Consultant Vince Brockwell

Are you worried about that?

Arvin

I was told that I would be safe. It's designed to explode up into the air and not out to the sides.

PR Consultant Vince Brockwell

What would you do in an emergency?

Arvin

I'd try to find the foreman.

Narrator

The PR consultant moves to another dangerous area of the plant.

PR Consultant Vince Brockwell

Rich, I see that you work with computer controls. This room looks like a military command center.

Rich

I'm working five different jobs now; each one has computers to work. Ya know, it's hard to get to know computers on five different jobs, especially when you don't really know the programs.

PR Consultant Vince Brockwell

So what do you do in an emergency?

Rich

There're no written procedures.

PR Consultant Vince Brockwell

So, you just …

Rich

You just wait until the situation gets bad enough to set off an alarm and see what the computer tells you to do.

PR Consultant Vince Brockwell

You're pretty much on your own.

Rich

Pretty much.

Narrator

The PR consultant talks to another employee.

PR Consultant Vince Brockwell

Bill, tell me about your job. What do you do?

Bill

I monitor equipment. I get a little nervous sometimes when the supervisor is gone for two or three weeks. Even when he's around, he's always tied up some place in meetings.

PR Consultant Vince Brockwell

What are you afraid might happen?

Bill

I worry about seeing a bad chemical reaction and not having anyone around to explain it.

PR Consultant Vince Brockwell

Like what?

Bill

Tanker trucks come and go. No one checks them in. They pull up to a tank, fill it, and leave. I've seen more than one driver put something into the wrong tank.

Narrator

The PR consultant walks over to a railroad siding.

PR Consultant Vince Brockwell

Bob, you work in a hazardous area of the plant. Tell me what it's like.

Bob

I do chlorine hookups.

PR Consultant Vince Brockwell

You unload chlorine from railroad tank cars.

Bob

Yeah.

PR Consultant Vince Brockwell

Is there a training program for that?

Bob

No. You know how it goes. One guy learns from another.

PR Consultant Vince Brockwell

So how did you learn?

Bob

From Hank.

PR Consultant Vince Brockwell

Who taught Hank?

Bob

Someone else. I know that's not good. If the first guy's not trained, no one does it right.

PR Consultant Vince Brockwell

Tell me. How would you feel standing around one of these tank cars while someone else does the hookup.

Bob

Not on your life, man.

PR Consultant Vince Brockwell

What would you do in an emergency?

Bob

You mean like in a chlorine attack? I can always count on three or four other guys for help.

Narrator

The PR consultant slowly lowers his head, closes his notebook, and heads for the office. Next, the PR consultant conducts a focus group session with the Chamber of Commerce executive, the fire and police chiefs, the mayor, a county commissioner, a state representative, and a state senator. He begins by focusing on the group's knowledge of plant safety hazards.

PR Consultant Vince Brockwell

As you know, I am working on behalf of the local plant management to assess the plant's relationship with the community and, in particular, communication regarding health or safety issues. Let's start with the subject of safety.

Commissioner Iffert

I don't think anybody knows whether it's safe or not.

Chamber Executive Dorothy

We know there are hazards down there.

Fire Chief Sonders

There could be problems with safety. There are potential hazards with the transportation of chlorine.

PR Consultant Vince Brockwell

What's your view, chief? Does your department have any concerns about safety?

Police Chief Jefferies

We're not aware of any particular hazards.

Mayor Hunt

We've seen people evacuated from that area twice. The chemical leaks tend to cause irritation. I don't think anybody outside the plant has had to be treated.

State Senator Winchester

The most obvious concern is the chlorine. It comes by rail right to the plant. Tank cars sit there on a side rail. I'm not aware of others, but they have some pretty heavy-duty stuff.

State Representative Gritmeyer

The plant is a very hazardous place to work. But they have worked at it, so it's much better than many small businesses.

PR Consultant Vince Brockwell

What do you think about the odors from the plant?

State Senator Winchester

Son, that's the smell of greenbacks!

State Representative Gritmeyer

That question is very difficult to answer.

Commissioner Iffert

In my opinion, the odors are from harmful stuff. But the plant represents a lot of money. So it's a trade-off. In all honesty, I don't think anybody knows what's coming out of the plant.

Chamber Executive Dorothy

I was caught on Park Street when they released something. I was scared! I thought I'd been gassed!

Fire Chief Sonders

Fortunately, practically nothing solid is coming out of the stacks. It's more like steam.

Police Chief Jefferies

I don't believe the odors are harmful. It's just part of the manufacturing process. There are environmental controls, and I'd assume they're operating in limits.

Mayor Hunt

It can't be too bad for ya. They spent millions to take particulate and harmful crap out of the air.

Narrator

The subject of the focus group changes to seeing where members get information about the plant.

PR Consultant Vince Brockwell

I would like to know how you keep informed about the plant and the management decisions that might affect the community.

Commissioner Iffert

Twitter, Facebook, our online news outlet. Sometimes even the newspaper.

Chamber Executive Dorothy

I talk to the plant manager.

Fire Chief Sonders

I go straight to the head of the company.

Police Chief Jefferies

I usually talk to employees.

Mayor Hunt

We've had real problems getting information. A lot of times we don't know what's going on until something is published.

State Senator Winchester

I go to the highest person I can find.

State Representative Gritmeyer

I've been wanting to talk to someone for a long time.

Narrator

The focus of the group changes again, this time to the plant manager.

PR Consultant Vince Brockwell

Let's talk for a minute about the plant manager. At the Chamber, do you know the plant manager?

Commissioner Iffert

Sure, I know him.

PR Consultant Vince Brockwell

How would you describe the plant's involvement in the community?

Chamber Executive Dorothy

It took a long, long time to persuade them to put someone on the Chamber board.

PR Consultant Vince Brockwell

What about you, Commissioner. Do you know the plant manager?

Commissioner Iffert

If I've met him, I don't recall.

PR Consultant Vince Brockwell

Chief, have you met the manager?

Fire Chief Sonders

I can't remember.

PR Consultant Vince Brockwell

What about the plant's involvement with the community in your area?

Fire Chief Sonders

I'd say their involvement is four or five on a scale of one to 10. The plant doesn't want to appear to run the town, so it keeps its involvement down.

PR Consultant Vince Brockwell

Have you met the plant manager, Representative Gritmeyer?

State Representative Gritmeyer

No. I haven't met him.

PR Consultant Vince Brockwell

How would you describe the plant's involvement in state legislative affairs?

State Representative Gritmeyer

I'd call it laid back at best.

PR Consultant Vince Brockwell

Would you agree with that, Senator?

State Senator Winchester

Their community activity is sporadic.
There's no corporate obligation. It's purely a business involvement with the community.

PR Consultant Vince Brockwell

Have you met the plant manager?

State Senator Winchester

No. Don't think he's involved much in the community.

PR Consultant Vince Brockwell

Has the manager had any contact with you, Mayor Hunt?

Mayor Hunt

Yeah. He's a busy guy. Their involvement with the community is limited. Either they don't see their value to the community, or they have made a decision to keep to themselves.

PR Consultant Vince Brockwell

Is there any plant contact with the police department?

Police Chief Jefferies

Not really. I don't know the manager.

Narrator

The subject of the focus session shifts to the matter of control, to see if the plant shares with the community, through local emergency services or some government agency, any sense of control over health and safety hazards.

PR Consultant Vince Brockwell

Chief, when the plant has to make a decision that affects the community, is there an opportunity for the community to participate?

Fire Chief Sonders

They just decide what they want to do and do it. We would like to have some input.

Police Chief Jefferies

We don't have a say in anything.

Chamber Executive Dorothy

I don't find things out until I read about them in the paper or see them on social media. If I didn't get the paper or check social media, I'd be completely in the dark.

PR Consultant Vince Brockwell

Mayor, have you been consulted by the plant?

Mayor Hunt

Well, not directly, I guess.

State Representative Gritmeyer

Don't ask me. I'm never called.

State Senator Winchester

I'm not sure what to say. Within the company there's some unpredictable behavior. Let's move on.

Narrator

The PR consultant now looks for evidence, such as a jointly developed emergency plan or track record of cooperation, that the plant could use to back up any claims or statements it makes about safety.

PR Consultant Vince Brockwell

Is there a plan for a major emergency?

State Senator Winchester

I think we're extremely well prepared.

State Representative Gritmeyer

I don't think we are. There's no plan.

Commissioner Iffert

There's no plan. No alarms. No evacuation plan or anything.

Chamber Executive Dorothy

Maybe that's an area we need to work on. There's always concern about what we would do in a major emergency.

Fire Chief Sonders

There're no major response plans in place, but there should be.

Police Chief Jefferies

No plan. No drills. No alarm.

PR Consultant Vince Brockwell

So what would you do if there was a gas leak?

Narrator

The police chief takes the PR consultant outside to his patrol car and opens the trunk.

PR Consultant Vince Brockwell

What are all these, chief?

Police Chief Jefferies

These are different gas masks or respirators. Five.

PR Consultant Vince Brockwell

How would you know which one to use?

Police Chief Jefferies

Oh, someone from the plant would call and tell me.

Narrator

The PR consultant, now in deep thought about what he has learned and about his responsibilities as a consultant, slowly closes his notebook and returns to his office. Having prepared his report, he takes it to the plant manager.

PR Consultant Vince Brockwell

Harry, I finished my interviews.

Plant Manager Harry Holderman

So, is this going to let the cat out of the bag?

PR Consultant Vince Brockwell

Look, Harry, this isn't about announcing new equipment. Good grief, man! You are sitting on a powder keg! The employees I talked to in the most dangerous areas of the operations are not safety trained. They're not computer trained. They're barely supervised. They've devised their own ways to stay safe. They're sitting at their workstations with a big, fat, false sense of security. What I … no …

Plant Manager Harry Holderman

What, Vince?

PR Consultant Vince Brockwell

No, I shouldn't be …

Plant Manager Harry Holderman

What? So constrained? Go ahead. Pound my desk with your other shoe.

PR Consultant Vince Brockwell

I can't believe the feds haven't shut this place down. Actually, I do know why they haven't. The whole town is protecting you. Without this plant, there wouldn't be a town.

Plant Manager Harry Holderman

So what did people in town have to say?

PR Consultant Vince Brockwell

For one thing, they don't know if the plant is safe or not. There's lots of doubt that it is and little interest in finding out—even among the emergency services, would you believe? What they know is what they read in the paper, see online, or what they hear over the fence from a friend in the plant.

Plant Manager Harry Holderman

It's a small town. Everybody knows everybody.

PR Consultant Vince Brockwell

Not you, Harry. Not everybody knows you! If you had to talk to people in this town, they'd want to see your ID. The fire chief can't remember if he ever met you.

Plant Manager Harry Holderman

Well, we have a lot to handle.

PR Consultant Vince Brockwell

I hope you have your own fire truck.

Plant Manager Harry Holderman

It's a good thing we're good friends, or I'd have thrown your butt out of here by now.

PR Consultant Vince Brockwell

Harry. Seriously. This is not good. Employees and the town's people are taking a big risk. They could die in their beds at night if those tank cars. … Are you prepared to handle an emergency? The town isn't. No alarm. No drills. No evacuation plan. You need to be prepared to manage and communicate in an emergency. You need to have some agreements up front, among yourselves and with others, about how you're going to function in a crisis situation.

Plant Manager Harry Holderman

It's not that simple, Vince. We've never gotten the resources we need. To the headquarters, we're nothing but a cash cow and all that counts is the milk.

PR Consultant Vince Brockwell

What about the company's responsibility to the town, to all the people who are virtually risking their lives to keep the cow productive? Surely, there must be some sense of social responsibility up there.

Plant Manager Harry Holderman

Not much I can say about that.

PR Consultant Vince Brockwell

Then what about the human values right here? How are you and your staff getting along with each other and the rest of the workforce? You must have some shared values.

Plant Manager Harry Holderman

We do, Vince. And that's really why I called you.

13. Hospitality Event Planning: IndyCar Racing

Learning Outcomes

By the end of this case, you should be able to:

1. know how to persuade stakeholders that an event is not just a party, but has real quantifiable returns for investors;

2. appreciate how business-to-business partnerships occur and develop skill in identifying and creating tactics that create ease in the relationship; and

3. understand, on some level, the psychology of investors and the appropriate communication strategies, including type, frequency, and delivery of key messages.

This case is an introduction to sports marketing with a focus on auto racing. It provides insight into corporate sponsorships of IndyCar Racing League teams and to how businesses participate in and profit from these high-profile activities. In professional sports, there are essentially athletes, owners, and fans. However, as you get into a particular activity, such as IndyCar racing, things get more complicated. There are many titles and groups of people to think about, including the racing team owner, the driver, the crew, the title sponsor and secondary sponsors (usually corporations), fans (at large), corporate fans, employees, customers, suppliers, investors, and the general media—plus the business aspects of financial and sports and trade print and broadcast press.

All of these interests surround the sport in a complex configuration of relationships and are drawn to it by an incredible aura of competitive excitement. The distinctions between these groups are basic and straightforward. Spectator sports generate tens of billions of dollars in revenue annually. This is clear indication of the tremendous involvement they draw from both business and consumers. Corporations purchase sports-related products worth billions of dollars annually, commonly in the form of advertising and sponsorships. Managing a title sponsorship can become a public relations responsibility with requirements similar to managing a multimillion-dollar business. This case is your opportunity to explore the hospitality event planning facet of sports marketing by seeing what your team can do with the title sponsorship of an IndyCar team.

Team Assignment

Chief Executive Officer Daria Malone has just signed a contract for Severe Clear Inc. to be title sponsor of an IndyCar racing team. Malone has always taken great pride in the strength of the company's relationships with customers. For the coming year, she wants to make a social connection with customers and, at the same time, make a lasting impression on them about the company's creative, customer-centered use of advanced technology. Severe Clear Inc., is a leader in cleaning, sanitizing, food safety, and infection control products and services. Malone has a personal interest in auto racing and, especially, in the way that IndyCar racing requires teamwork, precision, and the creative use of advanced technology to be a winner. She would like from the company's PR department a hospitality event plan to be used at each race of the IndyCar season, except for the Indianapolis 500, which is to be planned separately. Details of the assignment are provided in the case role play, which is followed by individual assignments.

Class Role Play

Cast

Narrator

Daria Malone, CEO

Christina

Chris

Maria

Ali

Nickie

Justin

Rachel

Marissa

Ruth

Babe

Joshua

Caitlin, PR Manager

Amanda

Richelle

Amber

Becky

Kristen

Narrator

CEO Daria Malone has called a meeting in the conference room with the company's PR department to make an assignment. Some staff members from sales, marketing, and product development also are in attendance.

Daria Malone, CEO

Good morning. I have an assignment that I think you are going to find interesting. Severe Clear has signed a contract to be the title sponsor of an IndyCar racing team. It will be a two-year investment. We have strong relationships with our customers. However, I would also like to have a strong social connection with our customers. And I believe we can do that with our sponsorship of an IndyCar racing team. Our drive to grow and exceed customer expectations is fundamental to this company. I think our customers would be even more impressed if we met with them, socially, to showcase our innovative use of advanced technology. Now, I don't mean putting products on display like we do in a trade show. I mean surprising customer guests at each race with an entertaining dinner show extravaganza that incorporates some of our newest products and services to make a lasting, overall impression that we are a leader in applying advanced technology for their businesses.

Christina

What specifically would you like us to do?

Daria Malone, CEO

I would like your PR team to prepare a hospitality event plan. I want it to be implemented at every venue of the IRL racing season, except the Indy 500, which we will plan separately.

Chris

I just found the IndyCar site. So you're talking about hospitality at 15 races?

Daria Malone, CEO

Yes—generally the same format for each one. I want to include a reception and a business dinner and show the evening before race day. That's when I want the company to make a lasting impression on them about our creative use of advanced technology to serve their needs.

Maria

Would that be for about 50 customers, plus company hosts?

Daria Malone, CEO

Yes, about 50 customers and 15 company hosts for the dinner. We will have some executives from headquarters, including me, plus our sales and service representatives from or near each venue. On race day we will have 50 customers, each with an additional guest, plus the same 15 company hosts. So, about 115 people total on race day.

Ali

We launched nearly 40 products and services this year. Which ones do you want to use in this hospitality plan?

Daria Malone, CEO

Remember, now, I want a show, not a display of individual products. But let's go ahead and talk about products and services that could be highlighted in the show. One product that must be included is our revolutionary utensil-washing system. Nickie, you've been working on that. Describe it for us.

Nickie

The Sperge is revolutionary! This system gives restaurants better control of their utensil-washing process. We can download operating data from the Sperge controller that can be processed and analyzed. The results can show restaurants how to reach higher levels of efficiency and reduced utensil-washing costs. We can also use the results to show how the Sperge reduces a restaurant's environmental impact. Is that cool, or what!

Daria Malone, CEO

I would also like to focus on the Severe Clear Hand Check Program. You know, in North America alone, more than two million health care patients get health care-related infections every year. Hand hygiene is the single most effective method for preventing these infections. Our program enables hospitals and health care facilities to comply on a consistent basis with federal hygiene regulations. So, we need to include the Hand Check Program. Let's see, Justin, I also want to include your new product for the food and beverage industry.

Justin

Yes! The Scruitiniser! We're just launching this system. This is awesome! Imagine getting excited about a sanitation system! This product cleans up salmonella on poultry product surfaces. Not completely, but dramatically. And you know what else? The solution can be reconditioned and used over and over again. That saves water, energy, and labor. And it complies with federal regulations on using it more than once. Awesome! Just awesome!

Daria Malone, CEO

I have to comment on your enthusiasm, Justin. It's part of our culture. We have talented. high-potential people, like Justin, in every area—from R&D to sales. We work in an environment of spirit, pride, determination, passion, and integrity. That's what drives results for our customers. It's the lifeblood of our company. Yes, ... well, there are two other products to include in our social relationship-building effort.

Rachel

What about Sanitair? We're introducing this new sanitizing agent next month to the dairy, beverage, and food processing industries.

Daria Malone, CEO

Yes! Excellent example of our innovative R&D.

Rachel

It's also registered with the EPA as a disinfectant for farms, poultry operations, and animal care facilities.

Marissa

Hey! What about the new bed bug treatment protocol?! That's brand new from the Nuisance Elimination Department. It's already cutting downtime by 25 percent for our hospitality customers. NED also has an improved version of the AirWatch unit. It uses a lot less energy to catch even more flying pests.

Daria Malone, CEO

I'd say that we have more than enough innovative examples for a great dinner show! We've always given our sales and service reps the technology and support they need to help our customers run clean, safe operations. Now we're going to add another dimension of support with our hospitality event program.

Ruth

So, you want our PR team to develop a special hospitality event plan using our new IndyCar sponsorship. And you want the centerpiece to be a dinner show extravaganza our customers will never forget.

Daria Malone, CEO

Yes. Here's what I have in mind: a reception, dinner and dinner show extravaganza the evening before race day for 50 customers and 15 company hosts ... on race day, there will be time for the 50 customers and their respective guests to use their credentials to explore the track ... have a continental breakfast at the transporter ... tour of the team's motor coach. We would probably want to use the area covered by the awning from the motor coach for serving lunch and having customers socialize with the team owner ... maybe getting an informal chalk talk from the driver about his strategy for the race.

I want to see in your plan a detailed description of the dinner show extravaganza concept. When you are thinking about show themes, you need to connect with how IndyCar racing requires teamwork, precision, and the creative use of advanced technology to be a winner.

Babe

What about during the race?

Daria Malone, CEO

For the race, we will have a chalet. It's a private, covered, hospitality area with food and beverages. During the race, guests can go back and forth between reserved stadium seats and the chalet. They are only about 100 feet apart. There will be live TV coverage of the race in the chalet.

Joshua

I assume that our sales and services reps will provide guest lists in each of the 15 cities. Do you want only customers and company hosts at the dinner? Can guests come to the race with an associate, spouse, or friend? And what's our budget?

Daria Malone, CEO

Only customers and company hosts at the dinner. This is a business meeting. Yes, customers may bring one associate, spouse, or adult friend to the race. No children under drinking age. As for budget, the motto we live by is, if we're going to do it, we're going to do it right. That's your budget.

Narrator

The meeting with the CEO adjourns. After the CEO leaves, PR staffers gather briefly.

Caitlin, PR Manager

Well, team. Now we are hospitality events planners for the 20XX IndyCar racing season. We need to do some preliminary research. We need to know more about our team and driver. We need to know what hospitality opportunities we have to work with in the sponsorship contract. Let's divide up the work, take three days for research, and regroup to begin planning.

Narrator

The PR team meets in their department conference room after researching sponsorship contract provisions and race track hospitality features and opportunities.

Justin

I checked out their website. I still need to make a list of the cities that are race venues. I also got a bio of our driver and background on the team.

Amanda

What about the dinner before race day? I started to research restaurants and hotel facilities.

Daria Malone, CEO

We don't have to be so traditional. We could have dinner catered. … maybe in an old car museum or some sports facility.

Richelle

What do we know about "transporters?"

Amber

They are large trailers, usually with two compartments—one above, one below. Get this. A hydraulic device lifts a race car to the upper compartment. There's room for two cars. Below is a machine shop where mechanics can make repairs to parts. Some transporters have an awning on one side to form a hospitality area, or a place where the pit crew can take a break.

Becky

I checked on motor coaches. The team usually has one. Some race car drivers have their own.

Kristin

Another feature at each track is the chalet, the private hospitality area with food and beverages. During the race, guests can leave a private section of the stadium and walk less than 100 feet over to the chalet, which has live TV coverage of the race. Sponsors also have theme parties.

Joshua

Don't forget the pace car! We can offer a few of our very special guests rides around the track in one of the pace cars. The drivers can treat guests to some impressive speeds.

Justin

I found out that most teams make two or three pit passes available to guests ... no more than three at a time, even during the race. Some teams give guests a personal device that lets them listen to the owner and driver talk to each other during the race.

Christina

It's customary for a driver to give a kind of chalk talk to guests. The driver shows the track on a board and explains the strategy for the race—how turns must be taken, how certain unsafe drivers have to be dealt with or avoided. This is not a contact sport like NASCAR. The engines in these cars are so expensive that many are leased from manufacturers. The cars go more than 200 miles an hour. There's no front bumper, guys. The driver's toes are about eight inches from the front tip of the car.

Ali

Something else we can use are show cars. Teams have a couple of these. They are actual racing cars, but without engines. They can be used for display in lobbies, outdoor parties, country clubs, and shopping malls. There is usually a team representative on duty, who might let people sit in a car or have their picture taken in or next to the car. On very special occasions, the driver might make an appearance and pose with people for pictures and sign autographs. [The PR team meeting wraps up.]

Individual Writing Assignments

For this case, each team member is to complete a different one of the following items that might or might not be included in the design of your plan.

1. Write a colorful, 100-word description of your IndyCar racing team's driver to be used by a speaker to introduce the driver at a hospitality event.

2. Write in stellar terms a description (200 words) of your IndyCar racing team, its record of accomplishments, and how a race car team relates to Severe Clear's business to be used on the company's website and in various program materials.

3. Write a 150-word business rationale to justify the investment in sport marketing by Severe Clear. Include the total number of customers and the sales regions to be influenced by the sponsorship. Base the rationale on comments made in the role play by CEO Daria Malone.

4. Look up B2B. Understand what it is and create an infographic for your group to use. Try not only to describe it, but to put elements of this case directly into the infographic.

5. Write an electronic news release announcing that Severe Clear has decided to sponsor an IndyCar racing team. It must include two quotes of meaningful substance from CEO Daria Malone.

6. Write a response to a letter from a Severe Clear stockholder who criticizes the company's investment in sponsoring a race car team and would like the money used to pay dividends to investors. Use a fictitious name for the stockholder.

7. Assume that after each race, Severe Clear sends an email to guests it has hosted at a track announcing who took the top three positions, providing a few race highlights, and reinforcing their connection with the company. Write the message using any past race for details and assume that your team took first place on the podium.

8. Draft and storyboard a video for internal use introducing the company's IndyCar team and driver and stimulating employee interest in the sponsorship.

9. Create a social media plan to be utilized leading up to each event using Instagram, Twitter, Facebook, and Snapchat. Also, create a Snapchat filter for the races that will promote your driver and Severe Clear.

10. As a group, create an event plan using many of the communication tools above, and adding notes and timelines leading up to the typical events discussed in this case. Remember to use many of the additional findings that were noted in the public relations team meeting.

14. Government Relations: Give and Take Away

Learning Outcomes

By the end of this case, you should be able to:

1. understand the role of a lobbyist and how the function is, indeed, of a public relations capacity;

2. grasp the role of a ghostwriter and how the function is, indeed, of a public relations capacity;

3. grasp the rules, procedures, and requirements involved at different levels of government and government relations, and learn to appreciate the importance of understanding the aforementioned components; and

4. develop a clear understanding of how and why a company needs to commit to monitoring government activity for the effects that it can have both socially and monetarily.

Citizens elected to positions in state government—from state representative to governor—have a responsibility for the state's economic health. States compete among each other to attract investments, such as the building of a plant or a headquarters relocation that will strengthen a state's economy by providing revenues in wages, taxes, and local purchases. State competition includes providing incentives, such as tax credits, infrastructure improvements and additions, land packages, expedited permit processing, and worker training programs. Companies base their site selections, in part, on these state government incentives.

In this case, some members of a state's legislature are proposing to rescind an incentive once given to companies that selected the state for their operations. The chief executive officer of the company you serve is not about to stand idly by and give up the incentive that was promised to his company.

Background details of the case as well as team and individual assignments follow. Your team comprises the public relations department of ChannelGate Electronics Inc. located in Overton, Anystate. Norman Gate, ChannelGate CEO, has instructed your department to see that the state legislature does not approve H.B. 3540, a proposed measure that would rescind tax credits granted to electronics companies as an incentive for locating their operations in the state. Gate wants to see a PR plan that develops for his company enough political clout to eliminate H.B. 3540 from further consideration by legislators. He wants his company to be operating with the benefit of tax credits indefinitely.

Additional Notes

Six elected representatives of the Anystate state legislature are sponsoring a measure that would amend legislation passed in 2005 that gave ChannelGate in Overton and six major electronics firms in Circuitville tax credits for an understood indefinite period as an incentive for locating their operations in the state. The incentive amounts to a 50 percent credit on each firm's state business and occupation tax. The six state representatives are working aggressively to eliminate the tax credit granted to the electronics firms because of the state's dire financial position.

The managements of ChannelGate and the other six affected electronics firms were surprised and upset about the initiative to eliminate what once was promised as an incentive for the firms to locate in Anystate. The annual contribution of the seven electronics firms to the state's economy in terms of wages, taxes, and local purchases, totaling $552 million, far exceeds the tax credit totaling $24 million. The firms question how reneging on the incentive would look to other firms considering Anystate as a place to locate a business. The CEO of ChannelGate, Norman Gate, insists that his PR department block any measure to take away the firm's tax credit. Your team is ChannelGate's PR department and has responsibility for government relations, specifically. You are your department head and a registered lobbyist in Anystate.

You begin to assess the situation. First you consider home base. Your area of the state is represented by three elected officials—two members of the House of Representatives (Alfred Peabody and Charlie Bismark) and one member of the Senate (Holly Green). When your firm was considering Overton for its operation, Mayor Helen Fish and the entire city council welcomed ChannelGate with open arms. Included in the grand welcome was the Overton Chamber of Commerce headed by George Harman and the Overton Economic Development Council headed by Sandra Dollars, as well as the town's many service clubs, particularly the Rotary Club of Overton led by 86-year-old Charlie Dobetter. As you assess the situation, you are thinking about developing as much political clout as possible by bringing these key contacts and possible coalitions together on the issue to rally to your cause.

Looking beyond home base you consider that ChannelGate is a member of the Association of Anystate Businesses, a statewide organization of businesses headed by Randy King, and that your CEO, Norman Gate, is a member of the influential Anystate Business Roundtable in Appleton, led by Executive Director Butch Bartolli. Your state representative, Alfred Peabody, is a member of the Revenue Committee of the House of Representatives. The governor of Anystate is Elsie Greenbach.

The elected officials sponsoring the measure to eliminate the B&O tax credit are Bruce Fisher and Allen Giverback of Plum Valley, Molly Wantsmore and Jim Glover of Artichoke Hill, and Byron Bick and Karen Greedy of Crabapple. Your CEO is so upset about the situation that he wants you to send individualized emails to every member of the House.

The measure to eliminate tax credits, H.B. 3540, is expected to be sent to the floor for a vote of the House of Representatives sometime within the next three weeks. A public hearing on the proposed measure is scheduled one work week from today at 3:00 p.m. in the state capital.

As a seasoned lobbyist and head of your PR department, you know that it is best always to take the high road—to work as a statesman, to argue positions on the basis of their merits. You know to attack the issue and never its supporters because opponents today might be needed as allies tomorrow. It is not unusual for a lobbyist to argue an issue intensely with an opponent in a public hearing and relax afterwards with the same opponent at dinner. You proudly regard maintaining respectful relationships as a mark of good statesmanship.

Team Assignment

The CEO wants PR plan that develops for his company enough political clout to eliminate H.B. 3540 from further consideration by legislators. His goal is for his company to be operating with the benefit of tax credits indefinitely. Your plan must be developed right away and must include provisions for orchestrating support from individuals and organization heads who will testify in favor of maintaining the tax credits during a public hearing on H.B. 3540 scheduled one work week from today at 3:00 p.m. in the state capital.

Individual Team Member Assignments

Each team member is to complete a different one of the following items that might or might not be included in the design of your plan. Before you begin, refer to the following material from author Tom Hagley about his experiences as a ghostwriter so that you best understand this capacity. As you see, the CEO of ChannelGate Electronics needs to be perceived as a strong and persuasive leader, so you will want to read about how professional writers can help executives create a commanding presence.

1. Write a one-page letter from your CEO to the head of the Association of Anystate Businesses presenting your case and urging the organization to take a position against H.B. 3540. Write an email message from your CEO to be sent individually to every member of the Anystate House of Representatives urging them to oppose H.B. 3540.

2. Write a one-page memo (legislative alert) from your CEO to ChannelGate employees presenting your case, urging them to write to their elected representatives in the House and asking them not to consider H.B. 3540.

3. Write a one-page information sheet to be used electronically as a PDF file in assembling a coalition to defeat the proposed measure. It should give information about H.B. 3540, identify its sponsors, provide reasons for opposing H.B. 3540, and offer instructions for contacting members of the House. This should be a persuasive document in the form of an issue bulletin.

4. Write text for a pocket card with facts about H.B. 3540, reasons why it should not be considered by the legislature, instructions for contacting members of the house, and your organization's contact information.

5. Write a one-page letter from your CEO personally addressed to individuals and organizations that supported incentives, originally, such as a tax credit, to recruit your company to locate in the state. The letter should express appreciation for their support in recruiting your firm, describe the current situation with the proposed H.B. 3540, and actuate them to contact the CEO to confirm that they will testify in support of retaining tax credits at a public hearing scheduled for (make up the date) at the state capital.

6. Write 90 seconds of opening testimony against H.B. 3540 to be given by Norman Gate before members of the House Revenue Committee chaired by Representative Oscar Harrison.

Further Research: Ghostwriting

We probably will never have a definitive answer to the question: Does every CEO have a ghostwriter? CEOs who have good writers are not inclined to talk about it. However, many CEOs do have talented, highly-skilled ghostwriters. And for reasons that will become obvious, having such writers is an invaluable capability.

A highly-skilled ghostwriter can give a CEO a commanding presence in any situation.

In any situation? A commanding presence? How do ghostwriters do that? How do they know what to write? How do CEOs find talented ghostwriters?

Tom Hagley himself can help you discover answers to these questions because he was a ghostwriter for corporate executives of Fortune 500 companies for more than 30 years.

In what kinds of situations do ghostwriters give CEOs a commanding presence?

Highly-skilled ghostwriters give CEOs a commanding presence before members of the board, industry analysts, shareholders, customers, employees, journalists, government officials, potential investors, and many other important audiences.

How are ghostwriters able to give CEOs a commanding presence in such diverse situations?

Highly-skilled ghostwriters are able in what they write to give CEOs a commanding presence in virtually any situation because they:

1. have experience working with CEOs and have learned to think like CEOs;

2. are able to assimilate the mind-set of CEOs and can write in ways that reflect their character, values, beliefs, and goals;

3. are adept researchers, able to gather even the most complex and technical information, organize it, and translate it into plain English;

4. keep abreast of management trends and jargon and incorporate current management thinking into their writing to help keep CEOs on the cutting edge;

5. provide CEOs with ideas and concepts that help shape policy, crystallize visions, solidify goals, and articulate positions; and

6. stay connected with and analyze the attitudes and beliefs of important CEO audiences and, in their writing, enable CEOs to effectively influence the attitudes and beliefs of these audiences.

How Do Ghostwriters Know What to Write?

Ghostwriters usually get their direction directly from the CEOs.

Talented ghostwriters require surprisingly little direction from CEOs, provided that the CEOs give their writers ample opportunity to get to know and understand who they are, what they stand for, and where they are heading.

Once a working relationship is established with a ghostwriter, a CEO is able to make assignments in terse form and expect, with little or no further discussion, first class results in an appropriate form, which might be a keynote speech, a formal letter, informal remarks, testimony, a presentation narrative or script, a position paper, a bylined article, or just a list of talking points.

With a good ghostwriter, all that a CEO needs to say is, I would like:

- to make these three points before this audience in a 20-minute presentation

- a bylined article on this subject for this magazine

- a position paper on this issue to submit to this congressional committee

- talking points in preparation for my interview with this reporter

- a draft of my letter to shareholders for the annual report

- a technical paper and scripted presentation with visuals to give before this trade conference

- a response to this shareholder's letter

- a proposal on this for the board

- informal remarks for the upcoming employee awards dinner

- a persuasive argument in opposition to this issue for my meeting with the head of this government agency

How Do CEOs Find Talented Ghostwriters?

Shopping for a ghostwriter is not something done easily by an executive recruiter or by a human resources director. Ghostwriters can come from various disciplines, such as public relations, marketing, law, human resources, and finance.

However, first and foremost, ghostwriters are highly skilled editors, writers, and researchers. They are good listeners and interviewers. They have strong intuitive qualities. They have a sense of what leadership is all about. They respect and appreciate the value of corporate reviews and clearance procedures. And, above all else, they have good chemistry and unshakable trust with CEOs.

Many CEOs do have ghostwriters. Many CEOs have more than one. For busy executives, good ghostwriters are an invaluable resource, an indispensable capability.

15. Public School Emergency Response: Violence at South County High

Learning Outcomes

By the end of this case, you should be able to:

1. understand how studying cases can help to critically train the public relations professional, as one can learn retrospectively from others to inform future professional actions;

2. contrast the potential outcomes of negative situations by analyzing the alternatives of communication decisions and processes;

3. grasp how existing tools, such as videos and speakers, can potentially be used to inform necessary audiences; and

4. develop a clear understanding of expected emotions in audiences and construct a plan to best meet the needs of said audiences.

School districts have a responsibility to develop crisis plans. However, the range of traumatic events that districts experience has increased significantly over the years from temporary disruptions to highly publicized events. Educators are greatly challenged to obtain the training needed to deal effectively with today's diverse range of crisis situations. While many schools have plans to deal with the unexpected, their plans must employ more than a top administrator and a small response team. Today's problems require broader involvement with all members of the school community. They require the involvement of outside support services, from fire and rescue to professional counseling. They require plans with provisions to meet the physical and psychological needs of individuals in every stage of a crisis situation—from trauma through recovery.

This is the case of a peaceful school environment that unexpectedly exploded with emotions, taking administrators, faculty, staff, parents, and even many students by surprise. The role play that follows will lead you through a dramatization of what actually happened. A high school principal who had no training in crisis management or communication tried unsuccessfully to deal with a mounting crisis that led to a gathering of more than 600 parents who were frightened for their children's safety and, highly upset over the principal's mismanagement of the situation, attempted to take control of solving the problem.

Team Assignment

In this case your team will be a school district's public relations staff. The class role play contains all the case details. After conducting the class role play, we will turn back the clock and assume that the parent meeting had not been called. Your assignment is to develop for the principal a crisis communication plan for responding immediately to unanticipated incidents. If your team decides that a parent meeting should be part of your plan, but with certain alterations, that is permissible. Stay within PR responsibilities and remember that safety, training, policy enforcement, and building operation and maintenance are human resource functions at the high school and district levels and thus should not be included in your communication plan. Of course, recommendations could be made in regard to those things. Individual team member assignments follow the role play.

Your challenge begins when the principal calls the PR department at school district headquarters and asks for your assistance in responding immediately to unexpected incidents. He has not asked for a recovery plan; everything is in crisis mode. When you meet with the principal at the high school, the principal says, "We have a serious situation and I think I should call an emergency meeting of parents this weekend. This is overwhelming to me. I'm not trained for this. I just want the high school operation to be back to normal as quickly as possible."

To turn things around, you will have to focus not only on the situation, but on two important dimensions of leadership—courage and trust. The case provides an opportunity to show how your team would support a leader, the high school principal, in ways that would strengthen his courage to stand up and do what's right. It also provides an opportunity to show how your team would support the principal in ways that would enable him to regain the trust that people would want in order to let a leader, the principal, guide them through a difficult situation.

Class Role Play

Cast

Narrator
Sally Edwards, Parent
Tom Edwards, Parent
Nadel Harper, Parent
Paul Burdick, High School Principal
Irritated Parent No. 1
Irritated Parent No. 2
Irritated Parent No. 3
Irritated Parent No. 4
Irritated Parent No. 5
Irritated Parent No. 6
Irritated Parent No. 7
Clark Cantwell, Reporter
Rose, Teacher
Ellen, Teacher
Alex, Science Teacher

Narrator

A stream of several hundred cars flows into the parking lot at South County High. Doors slam shut, one right after another, as parents leave their vehicles and head for the walk to the auditorium. A journalist asks an officer to reposition her patrol car and turn on the strobe lights for a more dramatic camera shot. Tom Edwards and his wife Sally are among the parade of parents.]

Sally Edwards, Parent

Tom, I'm worried. We've never been called like this to attend a meeting. Oh, my, an "emergency" meeting they said on the phone! Tom!

Tom Edwards, Parent

(trying to be reassuring)
Now, Sally, let's not jump to conclusions. It's probably just a precaution.

Sally Edwards, Parent

Precaution!

Tom Edwards, Parent

Calm down, dear. It's probably about some party that got out of hand.

Sally Edwards, Parent

Get real, Tom. It's not about six-pack shenanigans down on the Chattahoochee. These days it's about hostage taking, sniper attacks, murders, terrorists, and bombings. Oh my, Tom!

Narrator

The Edwards reach the auditorium entrance with others. No one is at the door to meet the anxious visitors, which adds to an already empty feeling in the pits of nervous stomachs. Tom Edwards takes a seat, turns his head to the left, and is eye to eye with Nadel Harper, another parent.

Tom Edwards, Parent

Hello. I'm Tom Edwards. This is my wife Sally.

Nadel Harper, Parent

(looks with a raised eyebrow)
Hey!

Tom Edwards, Parent

Do you know what this is about, Nadel?

Nadel Harper, Parent

(gossipy voice)
Well this is what I heard from Gloria and Trudy Shonemocker …

Sally Edwards, Parent

(to her husband in a hushed voice)
What'd she say, Tom? What'd she say!

Tom Edwards, Parent

She must be the school gossip, bless her heart.

Narrator

Sometimes people say, comically, that in the South you can say whatever bad things you want about a person as long as you follow it with "ain't he special" or "bless her heart" as Edwards said, "She must be the school gossip, bless her heart."
The principal's finger thumps over the sound system. It's more an expression of nerves than a test of the microphone. Thump. Thump … Thump. The high school principal speaks.

Paul Burdick, Principal

(staring not at the audience of 600 parents, but down at notes on the podium)

Several years ago, we established a program for diversity in our school …

Sally Edwards, Parent

(talking loudly to her husband, Tom)
He could have at least said hello. He makes us come to this meeting at nine o'clock on a Sunday morning and doesn't even acknowledge that we're here.

Paul Burdick, Principal

(continuing his remarks)
Included in our diversity program were students, faculty members, administrators …

Narrator

An irritated parent stands to address the high school principal.

Irritated Parent No. 1

(assertively interrupts the speaker)
Paul darling, would you mind just telling us why we are here?

Irritated Parent No. 2

(also interrupting, assertively)
Yes! What's the big emergency? What's this all about?

Paul Burdick, Principal

(raising his eyes slightly, not looking very far into the audience)
Yes, I'm getting to that. Last Wednesday, a boy, 19 years old, who is not a student, drove into the parking lot in a pickup truck flying two Confederate flags. His name is Jack Sanders. He got out of the truck, and for no apparent reason, mumbled something and assaulted an African American student. He entered the school wanting to reclaim his jacket that he gave to a girlfriend, a student at South County. The girlfriend gave the jacket to another student, who saw a Ku Klux Klan patch on the jacket and cut it off. Before Sanders could

find his jacket, he was escorted off the campus and arrested for assault.

Irritated Parent No. 3

(interrupting the principal)
So, what's the big emergency, Paul?

Paul Burdick, Principal

Yes, I'm getting to that. That incident on Wednesday started students talking about race, freedom of speech, wearing a KKK or any patch, the boy being apprehended and sent away from the school.

Narrator

The principal fidgets with the microphone.

Paul Burdick, Principal

(thump, thump, thump on the microphone)
Thursday morning, we discovered random acts of vandalism around the school.

Irritated Parent No. 4

Like what? What kind of vandalism?

Paul Burdick, Principal

Yes. Well, 62 bird feeders were found glued solid to a paint bench in wood shop. In the home ec room the door to a refrigerator was glued shut, and so were the doors to all of the storage cabinets. Thursday afternoon we had some trouble during band. Students got into another argument.

Irritated Parent No. 5

What kind of trouble, Paul? We didn't give up a Sunday morning for nothing. What exactly happened in the band room?

Irritated Parent No. 6

(shouting out)
I'll tell you what happened! I heard from Nadel that a tuba got thrown out a window. A trombone slide was wrapped around someone's neck ...

nearly strangled him. A student got struck in the head with an oboe and was taken to the hospital.

Irritated Parent No. 7

(interrupting, excitedly)
I heard teachers and two parents just stood and watched. That's when Jamie got hit in the head with the oboe.

Irritated Parent No. 1

(interrupting)
My daughter said she ran down to the office to call home. She said they wouldn't let her use the phone, said it was school policy.

Paul Burdick, Principal

Listen up now, and let me tell you what happened in the band room. An argument over free speech started among several students. That's not true about the tuba or the trombone. There was no damage.

Irritated Parent No. 2

What about the oboe?

Paul Burdick, Principal.

One girl did get bumped in the head with an oboe, but it wasn't a serious injury and she was not taken to a hospital.

Irritated Parent No. 3

(shouts out two questions that shock the audience)
What about the gun reports? Are you going to tell us about the gun reports?

Sally Edwards, Parent

(screams, gasps repeatedly for air, calls to her husband)
Tom! Oh, Tom, dear! They've got guns!

Paul Burdick, Parent

Yes. I'm getting to that ... I mean, no, I wasn't going to bring that up. We checked those reports thoroughly and found no basis for them. Believe me. No guns. Now let me finish telling you what happened. By Friday, it was pretty intense around here. So in the morning I told students that I would like to meet with anyone who would like to talk about their feelings and what was causing the unrest. About 60 students met with me at the back of the cafeteria. There were some heated exchanges among several students. The meeting ended about 1:00 p.m. As students moved into the main part of the cafeteria where about 1,000 students gather for lunch, someone let out a very nasty racial slur. That led to shouting, pushing, and shoving. Two male students started punching each other. A girl tried to break up the fight and her arm was broken. She was taken to the hospital. One of our staff members called 911 and the police came and were able to calm things down. Now you have the whole story. I'd like to introduce Jeri Johnson, my secretary, who will collect questions. I would like those of you who have questions to write them on a slip of paper. We will pick out the most important ones to answer because we can't answer every question.

Irritated Parent No. 4

(barking at the principal)
NO! We're not going to do that! And YES, you are going to answer questions. We are staying until every one of our questions is answered!

Irritated Parent No. 5

I'm not sending my child to school until I know exactly what's behind all this and that it's safe for my child to be in school!

Irritated Parent No. 6

(interjecting)
So, what's the plan, Paul? How is the school going to deal with this? What are you going to do to make this place safe for our children?

Paul Burdick, Principal

Yes. I'm getting to that. That's why I called this meeting. We used a phone tree to notify everyone. I know we didn't offer a reason for the meeting.

I hope that didn't alarm anyone. We are thinking about banning any clothing that disrupts education. We are also planning to have security personnel, and city police visible and in uniform, and two metal detectors at the main doors.

Irritated Parent No. 7

(interrupting)
How many entrances are there?

Paul Burdick, Principal

There are six.

Irritated Parent No. 7

Then we want six metal detectors!

Irritated Parent No. 1

(with an expression of disgust)
There doesn't seem to be any plan.

Irritated Parent No. 2

(stands up)
If you don't have a plan, we'll give you one. So, here's the plan, Paul. We want every measure necessary to secure the safety of students. We want an 800 help line for any student who is troubled about anything. We want to review the dress code. I'm sure many of us parents are willing to volunteer to …

Paul Burdick, Principal

I appreciate that. We also want to involve the students in helping to solve this problem.

Irritated Parent No. 3

(interrupting)
That's the last thing we need. This is for adults to straighten out.

Irritated Parent No. 4

I don't agree with that.

Clark Cantwell, Reporter

Excuse me, Mr. Burdick. I'm Clark Cantwell from the Spotlight News. I would like to know …

Paul Burdick, Principal

(interrupts)
I'm sorry Mr. Cantwell. The press wasn't invited. This is, well, it's a private meeting with parents.

Clark Cantwell, Reporter

You can't be serious! A private meeting? At a public school? With parents! A student riot! You might not want to answer my questions, but you can be sure that every comment made today will be in tomorrow's paper.

Narrator

The meeting finally adjourns after nearly three hours of emotionally charged dialogue. Parents feeling frustrated and upset are leaving the auditorium. Small groups gather outside talking. The Edwards walk toward the parking lot.

Sally Edwards, Parent

So, we're called to an emergency meeting, given no useful information on the phone or at the meeting.

Tom Edwards, Parent

This is shocking! There was no indication of any kind of festering problems. It's the largest high school in the district. It's in a safe town.

Sally Edwards, Parent

Everyone seemed to be getting along. What's the minority population, John?

Tom Edwards, Parent

About 10 percent, I think.

Sally Edwards, Parent

Paul Burdick doesn't do very well under pressure. I thought he was going to have a heart attack.

Tom Edwards, Parent

He tried to avoid telling us about the incidents. He went on and on about diversity. He ducked the gun reports. He tried to duck the press.

Sally Edwards, Parent

Worst of all he didn't address our biggest concern—safety.

Tom Edwards, Parent

I thought his action plan was … well, it wasn't even a plan. He didn't have a plan!

Sally Edwards, Parent

What about the way he tried to control questions! He says write down your questions and we'll pick the ones we want to answer.

Tom Edwards, Parent

Where was the district? I can't believe no one came from the district. Where was the superintendent?

Sally Edwards, Parent

Probably at the WaffleHouse.

Tom Edwards, Parent

(closing the car door)
Heads are going to roll, Sally. Heads are going to roll.

Sally Edwards, Parent

We're not sending our daughter back until this mess is straightened out.

Tom Edwards, Parent

Yes, dear. That's for sure!

Narrator

Standing in a hallway near the auditorium are three teachers talking about the meeting and wondering if any parents are going to let their children go to school on Monday.

Rose, Teacher

This is a mess. I don't know what's going to happen on Monday.

Ellen, Teacher

I'd say we're all a little short on facts.

Alex, Science Teacher

Does anyone know exactly what happened? How accurate are these stories? Is that true about the fight in the band room?

Ellen, Teacher

I'm in the room next door. Things have been kicked up a notch.

Rose, Teacher

Why didn't Mr. Burdick anticipate what parents were going to ask? Why the big emergency meeting? Seems like we could have taken the initiative to head off the rumors. We still could. Parents are begging for some plan of action.

Alex, Science Teacher

I'd like to know more about pressure behind all this pent up emotion. What's forcing the steam out of the volcano? What's happening at the core? Is a really big eruption imminent?

Ellen, Teacher

Poor Mr. Burdick. He's no coward, but he let fear get the best of him instead of letting it bolster his courage. He needs to step up to the tough questions, be more open with people. He was so nervous he didn't see how desperately parents wanted him to talk about keeping their kids safe.

Rose, Teacher

No question. He missed an opportunity. The school has to be more responsive. There are too many unanswered questions for parents, for us, for the students. Parents trust Burdick. He's always shown respect and compassion for everyone. He

just needs to be clear, to give everyone a chance to work on the problem.

Alex, Science Teacher

Well, he had better be quick about it. This mountain is puffing steam. The magma is moving.

Ellen, Teacher

It's not like the district to get so caught off guard. Knowing the superintendent, there will be an action plan on the table before anyone sleeps tonight.

Rose, Teacher

I think you're right. We'll see details on building security, notification procedures, intervention. There will be an investigation of the current issues, open forums for kids and parents, and individual counseling. I know this superintendent. She's thorough. We'll have a plan that lets everyone know that the problem is being managed.

Alex, Science Teacher

I hope you're right. I'm telling you, the mountain is …

Ellen, Teacher

That's enough about the volcano, Alex.

Rose, Teacher

Oh, what do you expect from a science teacher?

Alex, Science Teacher

I'm serious. This is earth shaking.

[End]

Discussion Points: Situation, Crisis, and Risk Communication

Situation

- Called emergency meeting
- Addressed broad issues
- Tried to minimize the incidents
- Ducked gun reports
- Overlooked priority concern—safety
- Offered inadequate immediate action
- Tried to control discussion—censor questions
- Tried to ignore the press
- Did not insist on parent/student involvement in solution
- School district headquarters offered no support, physical presence

Crisis Communication Principles

- Tell it all
- Tell it fast
- Tell it truthfully
- Take charge
- Own up to responsibilities
- Lay out immediate action steps
- Validate actions
- Determine who needs what
- Address everyone's concerns
- Assist the media
- Communicate frequently, regularly

Risk Communication Principles

- Provide information from a trusted source

- Source must have a record of credibility

- Address emotion first, then risks

- Answer all questions

- Ignoring even one of the four principles above could ignite outrage

Individual Writing Assignments

Each team member is to complete a different one of the following items that might or might not be included in the design of your plan. It is up to you to decide what the content should be for each element.

1. Write opening remarks (2-minute duration, 250 words) for the high school principal to make in appropriate tone (attitude toward the subject) and voice (personality) before a student assembly that would establish a climate for everyone to be able to work through the school's racial unrest in a sensible manner.

2. Write a letter from the principal of South County High School to parents explaining the unexpected incidents and using key principles of risk communication to assure them that the situation is under control.

3. Write remarks (2–3 minute duration, 250–350 words) for the South County High School principal to use in explaining to the local newspaper's editorial board what happened, why it happened, and how the situation is being managed.

4. Write a memo from the high school principal to faculty and staff to be placed in mailboxes in time to be read Monday morning that explains what happened, why it happened, how the situation is being managed, and how to handle questions from students, parents, the media, and others.

5. Write a script for the principal to use in recording an announcement recapping recent unrest and appealing to students to embrace diversity.

6. Create a question and answer sheet for school faculty and staff to use in responding to queries by anyone interested in the current situation. The sheet should cover what happened, why it happened, and how it is being managed.

7. Write a phone script to be read by a school secretary with a message from the principal inviting leaders of South County High's Parent Teacher Organization to meet with him to discuss what happened, why it happened, and how it is being managed.

8. Design a talking sheet (long enough to do the job) for the principal to use in advising leaders of South County High's Parent Teacher Organization about what they could tell parents that would help them keep their children safe at school. For content, search the Internet information about violence in schools and related subjects.

9. In order to educate the students (and potentially parents), construct a social media plan using only memes and existing videos about acceptance, racism, authority, or any other topic that you feel needs to be addressed. Use all social media platforms that you deem appropriate. Create a positive hashtag to be used in the social media efforts. Consider the use of a YouTube channel as well.

10. Research possible local speakers (use your own location for the exercise) to come into the school to talk to the students about acceptance, racism, authority, or any other topic that you feel may be imperative to address. Make a bio sheet including at least five potential speakers to present as a suggestive tool to the principal, faculty, Parent Teacher Organization, and the like.

16. Community Opposition: Metha-DON'T Put it Here

Learning Outcomes

By the end of this case, you should be able to:

1. understand the importance of proactive communication in a potentially volatile situation and comprehend how to best foster preparedness for such communication;

2. appreciate how to develop a risk and crisis communication plan that relieves a volatile situation and ultimately provides acceptance for your client;

3. recognize the terms *thought leaders* and *opinion leaders* and develop strategies for appealing to and utilizing these types of people; and

4. comprehend how core values play in to forming public opinion and develop an understanding of how to appeal to those core values.

It would be nice to be called before something becomes a major problem; too often, it doesn't happen that way, as in the case of Metha-DON'T. The complete slogan, Metha-DON'T put a methadone clinic in this community, was borrowed by protestors from another town that tried unsuccessfully to block the placement of a clinic in its community. Your public relations agency has been hired by Pivotal Directions Inc. (PDI), an expanding methadone clinic operator, to do what should have been done at inception—win acceptance for establishing a methadone treatment clinic in a community. The mishandling of this situation takes this organization back to square one, requiring that it follow federal guidelines and conduct a community relations and educational effort before moving in and opening its doors. Conducting such a program would be a challenge in itself. Recovering from public outrage, handling misinformation, and answering crippling rumors while simultaneously conducting a successful outreach program will be a monumental challenge for your agency and your new client, PDI.

Your agency team is scheduled to meet with the executive management of PDI for an in-depth discussion of PDI's expectations of your services, especially about how progress will be tracked and results will be evaluated. The meeting will be held at PDI tomorrow afternoon, so your team will be working late to prepare for the discussion. Prepare? Oh, yes. If you want this business for your firm, you need to show the client that you have a knowledgeable interest in its goal.

Team Assignment

The goal is for PDI to be operating a methadone treatment clinic in Lighthouse Bay with community acceptance. Your PR agency's job is to develop with PDI a PR plan to recover from the initial public rejection, educate residents on the importance of providing methadone treatment and, ultimately, winning acceptance for establishing a treatment facility in Lighthouse Bay to serve this area of the state. For case details, read the memo from the new clinic director, Harold Clifton, to his boss, Ted Blake, who asked for a status report on the situation in Lighthouse Bay. Also conduct the role play of a public information meeting during which outraged residents refused to listen to Clifton. See the individual team member assignments. Most importantly, read Chapters 1 and 5 of Publication No. (SMA) 95-3050 by the U.S. Department of Health and Human Services about siting treatment programs and the NIMBY (Not In My Back Yard) Syndrome following the individual team member assignments.

Lighthouse Bay/Methadone Treatment Clinic Memo

January 18, 20XX

TO: Ted Blake
FROM: Harold Clifton
RE: Lighthouse Bay Situation Report

Ted, you asked for a report on the situation here at Lighthouse Bay to use for possibly orienting a PR firm on our unsuccessful attempts to win public acceptance for siting one of our methadone treatment clinics in this community. I have tried in this report to provide an objective view of what has transpired over the past months. There is no question. We need professional help.

People learned about the clinic from an article in the *Lighthouse Community Beacon* that said that the county had approved its location on Sea Drive near the high school. Citizen concerns about the clinic caused one of the county commissioners to ask state officials to hold a community forum about the facility before it opens its doors. The state Division of Alcohol and Substance Abuse announced that it would hold a public information meeting on the clinic, February 1, and a public hearing, February 22.

I was completely surprised at the information meeting. People acted outraged and demanded that we put the clinic in some other town. Every time I tried to talk about methadone and methadone treatment, the audience interrupted and shouted all sorts of accusations. They were angry about putting the clinic near the local high school. As you know, we met with a resident while we were looking for a site for the clinic. We said, at the time, that we would be willing to meet with residents. By not doing enough to ask for their input during the planning stage for the clinic, we apparently have made them feel as though we do not value their opinions. They seem madder about being excluded than about having the clinic, which they know nothing about. The only thing that some know is that methadone is a drug for treating heroin addiction.

Believe me, I tried to explain. They don't know what goes on inside a clinic and they are afraid that drug dealers are going to hang around trying to sell to people fighting addiction. You know, I tried to tell them nicely that the decision to put the clinic in Lighthouse Bay was already made and that they can't do anything about it. Here's a link to an audio file of the meeting. [Treat the role play as the audio file.]

An editorial in the *Beacon* argued that the fears of residents were unfounded and that helping addicts recover can bring benefits to the community. Unfortunately, the writer referred to the methadone clinic as a "meth" clinic. As you know, Ted, a lot of people believe that methadone is related to methamphetamine, so the editorial just reinforced the belief.

Several community leaders took their concerns to county government and said the community was committed to preventing the clinic from opening on February 15. Feeling the pressure, the county asked state government officials not to move ahead with the clinic until PDI provided a community outreach plan. They got attention. State officials put the clinic on hold. I thought that would calm things down, but I found out that residents were planning to demonstrate on the day of the clinic's open house.

You saw the letter we got from the county commissioners recommending that we "start over in our search for a viable location for the clinic."

In preparation for the public hearing scheduled by the state for February 22, residents began posting fliers with the slogan Metha-DON'T, as well as writing emails to the local media. They also established an elaborate website. We haven't had anything about this on the PDI website.

The public hearing on February 22 didn't go well. Instead of digging in our heels, I think we should have apologized for not doing more to keep the community informed and state that we would like to involve the community more. Instead of arguing, we should have done more informing, specifically educating people. I don't think anyone realizes that there are more than 1500 heroin addicts in this county.

The commissioners got another letter from residents, this time insisting that they delay any decisions regarding the certification of the clinic until PDI has demonstrated that it can effectively meet state and local standards for community relations. They said they would take their votes elsewhere if the commissioners failed to act on their behalf. The county then issued a cease and desist order to prevent PDI from moving into the clinic and offering treatment. This showed just how serious the county is about making sure that the community's fears are adequately addressed. The order stated that no PDI employee was allowed inside the clinic. Unfortunately, Ted, someone saw me inside preparing for the open house. That's when we canceled the open house to show the commissioners that we were willing to comply with the county's order. It was crystal clear that we were not going to open the clinic without first presenting a community relations plan that was acceptable to residents.

PDI then got a letter from School Superintendent John Pupil. He said that he wasn't concerned about the clinic's proposed proximity to the high school, but rather about traffic if the clinic had several hundred people coming for treatment every day, before and after work. We hadn't met with the superintendent and decided to make a visit. It was clear that he was siding with the community. He asked about security. He wanted to know about PDI's experience at other sites. He said the school already has its hands full with families where one person works and the other is in prison or some type of rehabilitation program. He wanted to know how many patients will be drawn in from outside the town.

Shortly after our meeting with Superintendent Pupil, we caught wind of a rumor that an active drug addict was involved in a local drug-related crime spree. We're not sure how it started.

So here we are, weeks behind schedule, on the wrong side of the community, and under government pressure to produce a community outreach plan. We need desperately to get into the good graces of the community and to show county commissioners how we intend to comply with federal guidelines on community relations and education.

Class Role Play

Presume this role play to be the audio file referred to in Harold Clifton's status report.

Cast

Narrator

Ron Alder, Department of Alcohol and Substance Abuse (DASA)

Lauren Butterworth, Homes on the Bluff Association

Harold Clifton, PDI Clinic Manager

Deputy Sheriff

Helen Coats, DASA Clinic Certification Manager

Irate Resident #1

Irate Resident #2

Irate Resident #3

Irate Resident #4

Irate Resident #5

Irate Resident #6

Irate Resident #7

Irate Resident #8

Unnamed Resident

Methadone Client

Narrator

Harold Clifton, manager of the new Pivotal Directions Inc. clinic, walks toward the community center and tries to be friendly with a town resident. He smiles and says hello, but the resident frowns and turns away. In the center, people look and sound agitated. They are talking in loud voices, picking up or ignoring PDI handouts from a table near the entrance. Ron Alder from the state Division of Alcohol and Substance Abuse, calls the meeting to order.

Ron Alder, DASA

(taps microphone)
May I have ... May I ... Please ... Ladies and gentlemen ...

All Irate Residents

(purposely ignore speaker; jabber loudly among themselves)

Ron Alder, DASA

(serious, assertive)
Hello. It's time ... ladies and gentlemen ...

All Irate Residents

(boo the speaker)
Boo! Boo! Go back to where you came from! Go back! Go back! Go back!

Ron Alder, DASA

(persists; crowd settles down)
Please! Let's ... let's be respectful and get things under way.

Ron Alder, DASA

This meeting was called by the state Division of Alcohol and Substance Abuse. The purpose is to provide information about placing a methadone clinic in Lighthouse Bay.

Irate Resident #1

(interrupts, shouting)
Who decided we needed a clinic?

Irate Resident #2

(shouting)
We don't-a-want no meth lab here!!

Irate Resident #3

(shouting)
Yeah! I mean no! We don't!

Irate Resident #4

(stands up and sternly instructs the speaker)
Just tell us what we have to do to keep the clinic out of here!

Ron Alder, DASA

Could we please just give our speakers a chance to talk? Thank you ... thank you. The first person on the agenda is Harold Clifton. He's the new manager of the clinic.

Harold Clifton, PDI Clinic Manager

(steps up to the microphone)
I have some prepared remarks that I would like to read. But first I'd like to ask you to think kindly about the people who really need this clinic ... people who are fighting different addictions ... people who ...

Irate Resident #5

(shouting)
Take your druggies and treat 'em someplace else! Go back home and take PDI with you!

Irate Resident #6

Where did this idea come from, anyway? Who decided we needed drug treatment?

Ron Alder, DASA

(steps back up to the microphone)
The Division of Alcohol and Substance Abuse held a hearing here a year ago. We took comments about the need for a methadone clinic.

Lauren Butterworth

I'm Lauren Butterworth. I'm here for the Homes on the Bluff Association. I never knew about a hearing held last year.

Ron Alder, DASA

Well, we didn't exactly have a hearing on a specific site in the Bay.

Lauren Butterworth

Well, you should have.

Irate Resident #7

(shouts out)
Darn right! Go Lauren!

Lauren Butterworth

The county, the state ... you people did not do due diligence when you selected this location.

Irate Resident #8

(shouts)
Tell 'em Lauren!

Ron Alder, DASA

At last year's meeting, that's when it was decided a clinic was needed.

Irate Resident #1

That's when who decided? The secret Sneak It In Here Club?

Ron Alder, DASA

There were 28 people at the hearing.

Irate Resident #2

(with great sarcasm)
Wow! Nearly the whole county!

Lauren Butterworth

Well, the state, the county, and PDI must have had a cozy little get together. No one around here knows about any such decision. You left the citizens out of the loop. And it looks like you did it deliberately!

All Irate Residents

(start chanting)
Metha-DON'T! Metha-DON'T! Metha-DON'T! Metha-DON'T!

Ron Alder, DASA

Please! Please! Let's try to be orderly. Please, we have a speaker with important information.

Harold Clifton, PDI Clinic Manager

(steps back to the microphone)
The purpose of the clinic is ...

Irate Resident #3

(interrupts)
We know your purpose, Clifton. It's to make money off the druggies. Look for addicts somewhere else.

Harold Clifton, PDI Clinic Manager

(losing his patience; uses a reprimanding voice)
Listen friends, the decision has been made. Like it or not, we're going to hold an open house and start treating people.

Narrator

The crowd jeers. Irate resident #4 stands, raising up a book as if winding up to throw it at the speaker. She faces off with a deputy sheriff.

Deputy Sheriff

Hey, it's my job to throw the book at people.

Irate Resident #4

You think I'm a problem? Just wait 'til the felons start lining up. How big is your jail? You better start fluffin' pillows, big guy.
(Irate Resident #4 retreats to her seat)

Harold Clifton, PDI Clinic Manager

About 8 to 12 percent of our clients will be from this area.

Irate Resident #5

Eight to 12! So 90 percent of these addicts are coming from outside our area! From where? Oystershells?

Irate Resident #6

Put the clinic in Oystershells!

Irate Resident #7

Yeah! Put it across the bay!

Irate Resident #8

I'm really upset about this. I can't believe you want to put this clinic next to the high school!

Drug dealers are going to be all over the place trying to sell to your addicts.

Irate Resident #1

This is terrible. What have they been smoking at DASA?

Narrator

Helen Coats, state certification manager for medical clinics, steps up to the microphone. Harold Clifton is relieved to be out of the spotlight and walks over to a chair and sits down with an exhausted and somewhat exasperated expression.

Helen Coats, DASA

I hear your anger and your frustration and I'm not discounting that in the least. I have some prepared remarks and I'm going to set them aside. There are several requirements that aren't completed. Part of what we are concerned about is mitigating concerns that you have.

Irate Resident #2

With all due respect, we don't want to hear what they're going to do to make us like them. We just want to know what we have to do to make them leave.

Irate Resident #3

(looks over at County Commissioner Jack Hokesman)
We can vote certain people out of office. Find another site for the meth lab, Jack!

Ron Alder, DASA

We're not talking about a meth lab. Methadone is a legal replacement for heroin.

Lauren Butterworth

So you're replacing an illegal drug with a legal drug. Is that some kind of cure, or do the legal druggies just have a new master?

Ron Alder, DASA

Methadone is legal when a licensed clinic controls it. When it's taken daily in a maintenance dose, it allows people addicted to heroin or prescription pain pills to manage their addiction and lead normal lives.

Harold Clifton, PDI Clinic Manager

(stands and comments)
We have 12 other methadone clinics. The one here will only serve insured patients and those who pay privately.

Irate Resident #4

That's nice. We would feel much better having only white collar felons.

Ron Alder, DASA

I have licensed every methadone clinic in the state. In the 20 years that I've been doing that, we never received a single complaint from a citizen or a neighborhood.

Irate Resident #5

Ah. That explains why you don't bother to tell people where you're going to put them.

Irate Resident #6

If you've been doing this for 20 years, you shouldn't have any trouble putting this one someplace else!

Narrator

A methadone client in the back of the room tries to explain that people using methadone under a doctor's supervision can live normal lives.

Unnamed Methadone Client

Excuse me. I take methadone and I drive a cab. A lot of public transportation employees take methadone. We aren't unstable people. We can drive. We feel perfectly normal. And you're perfectly safe in my cab.

All Irate Actors

(begin chanting)
No addicts. No addicts. No addicts. No addicts. No addicts. No addicts.

Harold Clifton, PDI Clinic Manager

(stands, once again)
Some of our clinics are treating Iraq war veterans. They got addicted to pain pills when they were getting treated for war injuries.

Unnamed Resident

Please don't talk about veterans like they're drug addicts.

Irate Resident #7

Listen everybody. I've heard about all I need to hear. If you think this is outrage, you haven't seen anything.

Ron Alder, DASA

I want to thank ...

Narrator

The crowd starts gathering belongings, talking in aggressive tones about stopping the clinic. Harold Clifton turns to Ron Alder. He's dumbstruck over how hostile people can be. Ron Alder, DASA, says quietly, "We should have had some formal public involvement. That's what they're angry about."

[End]

Individual Team Member Assignments

Each member of your team is to select and complete a different one of the following writing assignments:

1. Prepare notes for your first client meeting with PDI. Research the Internet for brief answers to the following questions. What is a methadone clinic? What services does one provide? Methadone is an addictive drug; is it safe? What is methadone maintenance treatment? What's the difference between methadone and meth? Who are the clinic's clients—addicts? Are they dangerous people? Why or why not? Do methadone clinics' clients attract drug dealers?

2. Read PDI's situation report in the memo from Harold Clifton to Ted Blake and write an assessment of how you see the situation as a PR professional. Express yourself in no more than a typed, singled-spaced, one-page document.

3. Search the Internet for recent news stories and comments that might have a bearing on work for your new client, PDI (a fictitious name). Basically, environmentally scan the situation at hand.

4. Assume that your team decided to create a website for the Pivotal Directions clinic to be established in Lighthouse Bay. Make a list of critical information revealed in the case and what you would show on the home page to instantly direct visitors to what they want and need to know.

5. In this case, the writer of an editorial in the local newspaper referred to the Pivotal Directions clinic as a "meth" clinic. Compose an email to the writer showing how you would correct the error in a manner that would be accepted by the writer as constructive, not critical.

6. As a member of your PR team, you have volunteered to write as part of your proposed PR plan an explanation about how you would search social media to identify community leaders in the Lighthouse Bay area (use your own city for this exercise). Identify methods that you would use, what you would be searching for, and keywords you would be using. Then, decide which individuals to reach out to and determine how you would potentially get them to become advocates. Write and design a memo with photographs and findings.

7. It is imperative that a PR professional, whenever possible, does crisis prevention. This is an extensive brainstorming process, often resulting in a hefty document, that can detail what is to be done when a crisis occurs and pushes those involved to find possibilities of potential crises within their respective organizations. Make an outline for how a PR professional should construct a crisis communication plan, and also discuss as a group at least ten other potential crisis situations that could occur when the aforementioned clinic opens and is fully functional. Educating clients upon this process is invaluable, as it puts them in a forward-thinking position and gives them a basic plan to follow if a crisis does occur.

Siting Drug and Alcohol Treatment Programs: Legal Challenges to the NIMBY Syndrome

Technical Assistance Publication (TAP) Series 14

DHHS Publication No. (SMA) 95-3050
Printed 1995

U.S. DEPARTMENT OF HEALTH AND HUMAN SERVICES
Public Health Service
Substance Abuse and Mental Health Services Administration

Rockwall II, 5600 Fishers Lane
Rockville, MD 20857

Introduction

All neighborhoods and, most families in the United States today have witnessed or suffered the tragic effects of alcohol and other drug abuse. In 1990, a *Washington Post*-ABC News poll found that 40 percent of Americans believed that drug abuse was the most serious problem facing the Nation.[1] While many people recognize the pervasiveness of alcohol and other drug problems, however, such widespread concern has not always resulted in communities welcoming alcohol and other drug treatment programs into their neighborhoods. Community opposition—commonly known as the NIMBY (not in my backyard) syndrome—often prevents or delays the siting of a treatment program. This manual examines the legal remedies available to treatment providers who wish to challenge discriminatory zoning and siting decisions that result from the NIMBY syndrome.

The NIMBY syndrome is not new, and it does not arise solely in opposition to alcohol and other drug treatment programs. Community resistance is often mobilized to prevent the opening or expansion of many types of health and social service facilities, including shelters for the homeless, group homes for the mentally ill, halfway houses for ex-offenders, and health-related facilities for persons with acquired immunodeficiency syndrome.

The opening of an alcohol or other drug treatment program, regardless of treatment modality, is often met by community resistance. Neighborhood opposition has delayed or prevented the siting of many treatment programs and even disrupted the relocation of existing programs. Unfortunately, even if a program ultimately prevails, the fight can be costly, not only in terms of resources, but in its

---

1   Noted in National Association of State Alcohol and Drug Abuse Directors (1990), *Treatment Works*, p. 3.

effects on the clients as well. In one instance, a New Jersey town's campaign of harassment against a recovery home caused each of the home's residents to relapse.[2]

A community may battle to keep out alcohol and other drug treatment programs for a number of reasons. Residents may fear that property values will decline, and merchants may be concerned that crime will increase. The community may believe that a treatment program will bring in "outsiders"— perhaps outsiders of a different class or ethnic group. The community may believe that there is already an over concentration of services in the vicinity, or it may simply confuse the problem's solution with its manifestations. One provider remembers an opponent to his program stating: "This program shouldn't be here. There's already a homeless shelter and a crackhouse down the street."

In almost every instance, a community's fear of having an alcohol or other drug treatment program located within its borders is unfounded. In reality, treatment programs pose no legitimate danger to the health or welfare of the residents, nor do they draw substance abusers and pushers to the area. In fact, alcohol and other drug treatment programs improve neighborhoods by helping people get well.

If a locality attempts to keep out a treatment facility through discriminatory zoning ordinances and practices, these actions may be more than just unreasonable: they also may be unlawful. Federal disability-based antidiscrimination laws (including the Fair Housing Act, the Rehabilitation Act and the Americans With Disabilities Act), the equal protection clause of the fourteenth amendment to the U.S. Constitution, and many individual State laws have been used successfully to overturn the actions of local governments that preclude the siting of both outpatient and residential alcohol and other drug treatment programs.

This manual discusses ways in which an alcohol or other drug treatment provider can use the law to challenge the NIMBY syndrome or overcome it through other means. This manual is intended to provide technical assistance to treatment providers. While it is intended to be comprehensive, it is no substitute for professional legal advice on a specific situation. The interpretation of the laws may vary slightly from State to State, and the case law is always evolving. Therefore, it is essential that the treatment provider consult an attorney throughout the siting process. The information in this manual is presented in the following chapters:

- "Chapter 2—Zoning and Other Requirements That Affect Siting" provides general information on zoning ordinances and other codes that affect program siting. While these regulations vary from locality to locality, this chapter offers information helpful to understanding the bases for zoning ordinances and decisions. It explains variances and special use permits, and it summarizes the procedures that such applications might entail.

- "Chapter 3—Legal Challenges to Siting Barriers" describes the Federal laws and constitutional protections that a program can use to challenge a locality's refusal to allow the siting of a facility. These laws include the Fair Housing Act, the Americans With Disabilities Act, the Rehabilitation Act, the equal protection clause of the 14th amendment to the Constitution, and State zoning enforcement procedures. This chapter also includes a review of the case law developed under each statute.

---

2   June 1993 telephone conversation between Robb Cowie and Steve Polin, General Counsel, Oxford House, Inc.

- "Chapter 4—Applying the Legal Principles" demonstrates the application of the legal principles outlined in Chapter 3 to two representative case studies for in-patient and outpatient programs.

- "Chapter 5—Building the Case: To Site or To Sue" starts with the point that lawsuits may be won or lost long before they are filed. Using a model developed by the National Institute on Drug Abuse, this chapter provides advice on finding allies in the community, assuaging neighbors' fears, and averting local opposition. It also helps programs assemble information and documents throughout the siting process, which may later prove crucial to building a case.

The primary message of this manual is that while some communities may continue to oppose the opening of new programs, alcohol and other drug treatment providers should not be discouraged. There are various ways short of going to court to defuse, confront, and overcome the NIMBY syndrome. Furthermore, if a treatment provider must file suit, the provider should be confident in the knowledge that in case after case, in the face of groundless and irrational community fears, treatment programs have won the right to open their facilities and treat substance abusers in need.

...

Building the Case: To Site or To Sue

Siting an alcohol or drug treatment facility does not have to lead to a legal battle. Many treatment providers have overcome the not-in-my-backyard (NIMBY) syndrome through outreach and educational efforts that have dispelled neighbors' misconceptions and fears about treatment and persons in recovery, leading opponents to reconsider their resistance. Other providers prefer to go about siting their facilities as quietly as possible, hoping not to stir up any attention that could lead to opposition. If opposition does arise, these providers use the threat of litigation to dissuade the community from taking any discriminatory actions. A provider should make every effort to site a program without resorting to legal challenges, while keeping in mind that community and official responses to its efforts may be valuable evidence if it ends up in court. This chapter discusses the nonlegal strategies that have proved to be particularly effective in defusing neighborhood hostility. It also provides suggestions on steps that a provider should take and information that it should gather throughout these efforts in the event that legal action is ultimately required.

Reaching Out to The Community

For many programs, outreach is the key to opening new facilities and avoiding prolonged and difficult disputes with neighbors. By being aware of and sensitive to community concerns, many programs are able to turn opposition into acceptance, making the siting of the facility easier for community residents, for the treatment program, and ultimately for the program's clients.

To assist programs with such outreach and educational efforts, the National Institute on Drug Abuse recently developed a resource manual entitled *Overcoming Barriers to Drug Abuse Treatment*.[3] Based on extensive research and the experiences of treatment providers, communities, and single

---

3   National Institute on Drug Abuse (1992), *Overcoming Barriers to Drug Abuse Treatment*, Rockville, MD: National Institute on Drug Abuse.

State agencies, the manual recommends that a program do its homework on a community in which it plans to site a facility, approach the community and its leaders openly, dispel myths about alcoholics and other drug abusers who are in recovery, and try to help community residents understand what treatment is and the benefits that it provides. The following guidelines are based on the principles outlined in the National Institute on Drug Abuse manual and suggestions from treatment providers who have waged successful community outreach and education campaigns.

Knowing the Community

Before proceeding with its plans, a provider should become familiar with the particular character and attitudes of the community in which it intends to site a facility. The provider should determine who is likely to understand the need for treatment and to lend support for the proposed facility. Natural allies could include teachers, the police, human service providers, and charitable organizations. The provider should also determine who the likely opponents are, such as real estate developers and homeowner associations.

If the provider is planning to site the facility in a specific neighborhood due to its high incidence of drug abuse, it should try to assemble statistics that demonstrate the need for treatment in that area. Such data may also be valuable in litigation to demonstrate that excluding the program would have a discriminatory effect on the neighborhood or that establishing the program would contribute to the general welfare of the region.

Finally, the provider should determine who the important "formal" (mayor, councilpersons, zoning board of adjustment members) and "informal" (religious and business leaders) decisionmakers are, as well as the factors that might influence their support. The provider should consider the timing of its efforts; political leaders are often more sensitive to community pressure during an election year. It should also determine whether there have been battles in the past over the siting of similar facilities. This information could be useful to prove a pattern or tendency to discriminate against persons with alcohol or other drug problems. The more a provider knows about the community before it starts the siting process, the better its chances of success.

Cultivating Community Support

The provider of a proposed treatment facility should attempt to meet with as many community leaders as possible, even those who are not directly involved in approving the facility. Program representatives should speak to block and tenant associations, business groups, and churches, as well as local government officials. Often, NIMBY opposition is triggered by a community's belief that it has not been fully informed or consulted. By meeting with leaders throughout the community, the provider can ensure that all interested parties have been included.

One way the provider can overcome community distrust is to have leaders and residents from other communities in which it provides services discuss their experiences with members of the new community. It can arrange meetings between mayors, members of community boards, and police departments, or it can have a homeowner meet with the families who live close by the site of the proposed facility. There are two advantages to this tactic: the community is more likely to trust and identify with others in its position, and the treatment provider's ability to turn out support from other communities in which its programs are located represents a tremendous vote of confidence.

Another key to successful siting is to build strong relationships with the local media. The National Institute on Drug Abuse has developed public service announcements that emphasize the effectiveness of treatment, which community programs can provide to local television and radio stations.

An especially effective means of cultivating community support is to form an advisory board that includes community leaders. Giving community leaders a role in the planning and operation of the facility can stem fears and reassure residents that the program has proper oversight. One treatment provider in California was able to overcome local resistance by placing a leader of the community group opposing its facility on the program's board.

To the extent that these efforts do not win community approval, they provide a fertile ground for gathering evidence of discriminatory intent. Documenting the comments of residents and local officials and the media's characterization of the program or its residents are critical if the provider has to build a legal case and to prove that disability was considered inappropriately in a siting decision. In addition, if local officials refuse to meet with the provider or discuss its proposal, it can evaluate whether this behavior reveals a bias, particularly if officials routinely meet with groups that try to site other types of facilities.

Carefully Selecting a Site

One of the most important decisions a provider will make is determining where to locate a facility. It must take into account not only the zoning ordinances that govern the property, which may affect the type and size of facilities that can be constructed or sited, but also additional factors that can determine the degree of community resistance that it may encounter.

For example, if the provider decides to build a treatment facility close to a school or in an area already saturated with similar services, it could face difficulties that it would not have encountered if it had chosen a different site that still met its needs. The provider may succeed in ultimately siting its program in the original location, either through extensive negotiations or litigation, but adopting strategies to avoid such costly efforts should be emphasized.

Obtaining Legal Advice

A provider should obtain legal advice as early as possible when selecting a site for its program. An attorney should be able to identify all the zoning, health, and safety requirements that apply to the prospective facility under the zoning ordinance. The attorney should also be able to determine whether any requirements are facially invalid or will have a discriminatory effect or whether a reasonable accommodation would enable the provider to satisfy the ordinance requirements.

The attorney can also threaten to file a lawsuit to the extent that local officials are not willing to work with the provider to find an appropriate site, are bowing to community pressure to not site the program, or are applying the zoning ordinance erroneously. Officials often change their positions when informed about legal precedents that prohibit the decisions and actions that they are considering. Sometimes, local officials need the "cover" provided by legal precedents to make the right decision.

Legal help may also be available from public or private fair housing enforcement groups. For example, the Department of Housing and Urban Development provides funds to approximately 25 fair housing agencies to enforce the Fair Housing Amendments Act. In addition, protection and advocacy agencies exist in all States and provide legal assistance on discrimination in housing to individuals with disabilities.

It is important to remember that this manual is only a guide on the legal challenges that may be available. It is necessary to have an attorney who will be able to evaluate the provider's particular situation for possible statutory or constitutional violations.

Planning a Facility Carefully and Being Prepared To Make Accommodations

Many communities are concerned that proposed development projects will not "fit in." Many projects, including commercial developments, are delayed for this reason. A provider should take community concerns into account and modify whatever aspects of the new facility it can to meet their concerns. Again, the provider might be able to challenge successfully official or community requests to modify particular features on the ground that such requirements will have a discriminatory effect or are inappropriately based on the disability of future residents. However, if such challenges can be avoided without burdening the program, the provider should accommodate the requests.

Altering the size or appearance of a facility in order to make it architecturally consistent with neighboring buildings might make a community more receptive. Changing the name of the program might reduce opposition. For example, a program agreed to substitute "rehabilitation" for "alcoholism" in its name in order to win approval.

Planning and zoning boards, as well as fire and health inspectors, may require numerous technical modifications for a new or expanded facility. Such requirements may be legitimate, or they may be used as a pretext to block the opening of the program. Regardless of the motivation for the requirements, the program is obligated to bring the facility up to them to the extent that they are warranted by the unique needs of the individuals who will be using the facility. Again, an attorney would be useful to help evaluate which requirements are necessary versus those that could be construed as unnecessary and discriminatory hurdles.

Educating the Community

Many communities have tremendous misconceptions about treatment programs and the people they serve. As noted above, a critical component of any siting effort is to dispel these myths through community education. It is important that local decisionmakers and residents understand that treatment programs help communities by reducing many of the costly problems associated with active alcohol and other drug abuse and that treatment enables former users to return to productive lives.

A community board or zoning commission hearing, which is a standard element in most siting processes, presents a provider with an excellent forum to speak directly to its opponents and to demonstrate that its treatment program will be effective in treating alcohol and other drug abuse. The provider should explain the goals of the program, how it works, and why the disputed site has been chosen. Having an individual in recovery attend the hearing and describe how treatment has benefited his or her life may be useful.

Many communities resist treatment programs because the fear that active users and dealers will be drawn to the neighborhood and that crime will subsequently increase. The provider can address these fears in various ways. For example, it could explain to the community—

- How treatment encourages abstinence and prevents clients from relapsing,

- How the program monitors client drug use through urinalysis and other measures, and

- The program's rules of conduct, including how it enforces curfews and supervises individuals who are allowed to travel outside the program site.

The provider might also agree to participate in anticrime activities in the neighborhood. This would demonstrate its commitment to maintaining a safe community.

Another common fear is that the presence of a treatment program in the neighborhood will cause property values to decline. One way the provider can address this issue is to examine property values in other neighborhoods in which treatment programs operate. The single State alcohol and other drug agency may have conducted a study on the impact of alcohol and other substance abuse treatment on local property values that will provide assistance.[4] Even if the provider cannot obtain such information, it can still explain that its program will provide an important service that can only improve the community.

The hearing process also serves several important purposes if litigation becomes necessary (the provider should therefore obtain a transcript or a recording of the hearing proceedings):

- The provider can gather statements from residents and local officials who oppose the siting, which will be useful to prove that the locality is acting with a discriminatory intent to exclude persons with alcohol or drug problems.

- The provider can create a record that proves that it has responded to any of the neighborhood's legitimate health and safety concerns. To the extent that an adverse decision is then based on these concerns, the provider can demonstrate that they are simply pretexts for an underlying discriminatory intent.

- The provider can perhaps get the local officials to identify their reasons for opposing the project and then evaluate whether or not those reasons are legitimate. Moreover, if the reasons for opposing the project change over time, the provider can perhaps demonstrate that these reasons are simply pretexts to obscure an underlying desire to exclude individuals with alcohol and other drug problems from the community.

- The provider can identify ways to modify the locality's practices and procedures in order to accommodate the program's needs and demonstrate why such modifications will not impose a burden on the locality or alter the nature of the neighborhood. If the locality refuses to provide an accommodation by claiming an undue burden, the provider will have a record to demonstrate that such an accommodation is reasonable.

Demonstrating Willingness To Be Part of The Community

There are a number of tangible benefits that a provider of treatment services can offer a community to demonstrate its commitment to being a good neighbor. First of all, it can offer what it does best: provision of alcohol and other drug treatment. It can perhaps guarantee that local residents will have priority in receiving services. In addition, the program counselors can go into local schools and community centers to provide prevention and outreach services for youth, or they can work with the police and the courts to assess persons arrested for driving while intoxicated.

The provider can also propose to be a resource in other ways. Staff and residents can work as volunteers at the local nursing home, clean the park, or rebuild an abandoned apartment house. Representatives of the program can get involved in civic groups. The provider can pledge to hire from

---

4   The Bazelon Center for Mental Health Law (formerly the Mental Health Law Project) in Washington, DC, has extensive information on housing discrimination, including a bibliography of social science research on the economic and environmental impact of group homes on neighboring property.

within the community and make purchases from local merchants. Whatever it chooses to do, it is important that it show that it is willing to have a stake in the community.

To the extent that the provider's efforts to reach out are rejected or met with hostility, it can use these responses as further evidence of community opposition to site its program on the basis of the disability of the individuals who will eventually use the facility.

Initiating Legal Action

While the above recommendations have proved to be helpful to many programs, they certainly do not guarantee success. A provider must continually evaluate whether there is any likelihood of winning approval without initiating legal action. An attorney can help the provider determine when it may be necessary to discuss with local officials the legal protections that prohibit discrimination on the basis of disability and to discontinue conciliatory efforts.

If the provider decides to take legal action, it should consult an attorney to determine the best approach to take. It will need to determine the following:

- What legal claims it has and the strength of its case

- Whether it wants to sue in State or Federal court or file an administrative action under the Federal antidiscrimination laws

- Whether it wants to ask the Attorney General to become involved in the matter so that it can benefit from the Federal Government's resources and expertise in developing and litigating cases.

If the provider has few resources to pursue litigation, it should not walk away from the problem. The Federal antidiscrimination laws authorize the party that wins a suit to recover attorney fees and the costs of litigation. The provider may be able to find an attorney who will take its case without a large investment of funds if the prospect of winning and recovering fees exists. The provider may also choose to pursue the administrative complaint procedure that exists under the antidiscrimination laws, particularly that under the Fair Housing Amendments Act, because the administrative agency will conduct the investigation and gather evidence on the provider's behalf without cost. While the remedies may differ under an administrative complaint procedure and a civil court action, the provider can still accomplish its primary goal of siting its program.

Conclusion

In the search for effective ways to deal with the Nation's alcohol and other drug problems, it is often ironic that communities and local officials waste precious resources and time fighting the establishment of treatment programs. However, effective models exist for winning community and official approval to site new programs and expand facilities, and when those efforts fail, strong legal protections exist to fight discrimination.

It is also important to remember, however, that once a treatment program has opened its facility, either through legal action or through a persuasive educational campaign, the battle is not over. Fences must continually be tended and repaired. Studies show that communities that opposed treatment programs generally become more accepting over time, as they see the benefits that the programs bring.

However, neglecting community relations, even for a short time, can open old rifts or create new ones that can make future operations or expansion difficult.

17. Fundraising: What in the World Would You Like to Share?

Learning Outcomes

By the end of this case, you should be able to:

1. understand how transparency and social sharing play into a quality fundraising program;

2. contrast the use of social media in strategic communication as compared to personal communication;

3. grasp the rules and requirements involved for many of the logistical design elements on varying social media platforms; and

4. develop a clear understanding of verbiage and writing principles that result in persuasive calls to action and potentially evoke emotion.

A development officer at a major university thought about the importance of staying in touch with donors especially during economic downturns. She appealed to faculty members to think of gift ideas in the range of $1,000 to $3,000 that friends, alumni donors, and other prospective donors would find of interest to support. She encouraged one-time funding opportunities that would be of special value and even lead to long-term investment and giving. Her examples included things such as sending a student to Ghana, endowing a scholarship to support study abroad, supporting a weekend workshop, or endowing a workshop series. The opportunities would be relatively small donations with immediate impact and long-term potential that the donors may continue to support such endeavors. Her appeal sparked an idea from a faculty member who suggested a program called What in the World Would You Like to Share? While the proposed program captured the interest of areas throughout the university, it also created a challenge in how to launch it. For this case, assume you are one of a small group of students in the school of journalism and communication who has decided to assist the development office in announcing the program.

Team Assignment

Your task is to develop a public relations plan to announce the program What in the World Would You Like to Share? to three audiences: students, faculty, and potential donors.

Additional Notes

What in the World Would You Like to Share? is a personalized way to learn something firsthand and share the knowledge gained with many others.

In this program, students have an opportunity to propose experiencing something in the world that they would like to share with others. Examples include things such as attending a session of the United Nations; observing the news operation of CNN in Atlanta; interviewing a world leader or a celebrity; visiting with a family in Ghana; discussing fundraising challenges with the director of a raptor center in Alaska; interviewing a foreign ambassador to the United States; meeting to discuss an issue with an Environmental Protection Agency official in Washington, DC; meeting with the head of an advocacy organization, such as the National Resource Defense Council; and many other diverse educational experiences students are encouraged to propose.

An important part of the application process is for students to describe the experience they would like to have and specifically how they will share their experience with others based on a detailed paper they are required to submit upon their return. Their participation in the program requires the oversight of a faculty advisor.

Through this program, students engage in both a learning and a teaching experience. As Bill Moyers has said, "Sharing is the essence of teaching." Students also learn what is required to be effective ambassadors to their school.

Donors supporting this program are contributing not only to the university, but also to an even higher cause of promoting personalized sharing of knowledge through human interactions around the world. A unique aspect of the program is using social media to keep in close touch with potential donors. Donors who agree to participate in the program receive, electronically, opportunities to fund student proposals. Students are required in their proposals to package their experience as an irresistible funding opportunity clearly stating the benefits to a donor, the student, and the school. Using electronic means, the development office surprises donors with messages to their smart phones, Twitter, Instagram, or Facebook accounts about recently approved and available, amazing student proposals, which donors can select to support, instantly. Donors also receive flash reports of student experiences in progress and also those completed.

Participants in the program join the ranks of what Bill Moyers calls "public thinkers."

Individual Team Member Assignments

Each team member is to complete a different one of the following items that might or might not be included in the design of the team's plan.

1. Write an email message announcing the new program to students in a way that attracts interest and motivates them to further research the program.

2. Write a blog of no less than 150 words about the program that attracts student attention and stimulates buzz about students' potential proposals.

3. Decide on an experience that you would like to share with others through the program and summarize it in no less than 150 words as an irresistible funding opportunity for potential donors that could be conveyed by electronic means. Describe how the proposed experience would be of benefit to you, a donor, and the university.

4. Create a meme to easily illustrate the idea articulated above. Ensure that it is formatted for use on all social media platforms.

5. Explain how Twitter, Facebook, and Instagram could be used to get students to express things they would like to share with others as a way of promoting the program. Brainstorm about what this social media plan would entail. Include possible hashtags.

6. Write a script of no less than 200 words for announcing the program at luncheon meetings of business, trade, and civic organizations whose members could be potential donors.

7. Write a social media news release announcing the program that would be posted on the development office website.

8. Explain in a memo to the development officer how the program's irresistible funding opportunities could be conveyed electronically to potential donors and how donors could simply decide on the spot to fund a student proposal and notify the development office instantly to reserve the selection. Research Internet giving sites and propose one as a model to be followed for donor pools (projects that will have multiple donors).

9. Write a backgrounder on the program, using your imagination to embellish the description with creative examples and convey in what ways the program could be effective.

10. Create a Facebook cover photo design (research required size) that can be used by those who are hoping to have their projects funded. Create a different design for the development office's use. Test them on an existing Facebook account to ensure that it is correct.

11. Research LinkedIn and determine how it could best be used to reach influential donors.

12. Create a Snapchat filter to be used on campus to create more buzz about the campaign.

18. Corporate Communication: DOWNSIZED!

Learning Outcomes

By the end of this case, you should be able to:

1. understand how to use business sense to make a logical argument, even when emotions are involved;

2. comprehend and differentiate how several different audiences will evaluate the same information and which information will be the most important to each respective audience; and

3. grasp how reviewing cases from the Public Relations Society of America and other credible professional organizations help to expedite and inform good decisions in challenging communication endeavors.

Additional Notes

This is a case of closing a major production facility. It is representative of a phenomenon commonly referred to as downsizing that ran rampant in the 1980s and 1990s and continues to appear, especially in the manufacturing sector.

What is downsizing? It's the act of reducing the size and complexity of an organization. How is it done? It's usually done by any one or a combination of the following: decreasing the number of employees, closing facilities, exiting selected markets, dropping product lines, or shedding activities unrelated to a firm's core business. In business, this activity is given various names, such as restructuring, reengineering, reorganizing, redesigning, and reinventing.

Why do organizations downsize? Reasons frequently offered: escalating domestic and or global competition, increasing costs, declining markets, weak economy, increased use of technology. Reasons never offered: overstaffing, overestimating, overspending.

What are the benefits of downsizing? We have yet to see a definitive answer to this and other questions. If jobs are eliminated to improve a company's competitive position, will employee morale and/or productivity also improve? If a company reduces its workforce and sheds activities outside its core business, will its stock price increase? If a company simplifies its operations, will there be an actual cost savings? Will reducing a workforce temporarily and rebuilding it when market conditions improve automatically restore an organization to its original strength? Are the benefits of downsizing shared by everyone in an organization? Benefits have to be assessed on a case by case basis. In general, benefits are arguable. Nevertheless, the practice continues. What is known is that the process imposes multiple pressures that produce stress that is real and can be harmful and expensive. These effects can be mitigated to a significant extent through thoughtfully planned and professionally implemented communication and by heeding the lessons learned by others who have experienced the process.

Team Assignment

The team Assignment is to develop a public relations plan for closing Houston Operations, one of eight production plants owned and managed by Supercore International Inc., a leader in the design and production of structural products for commercial buildings. Background information for this follows, as does a role play of the chief executive officer's assignment to the PR director and another of discourse among executives of a core group in a private communication planning meeting. Information for individual team member assignments will be found in correspondence among core group members.

Individual Team Member Assignments

Each team member is to complete a different one of the following items that might or might not be included in the design of the team's plan. It is up to you to decide what the content should be for each element.

1. Develop a news release announcing closure of Supercore's Houston Operations.

2. Write a script for a video message from Houston Operations Manager Bill Cabot to employees announcing the company's decision to close the plant indefinitely.

3. Draft in no more than 300 words the business rationale for closing Houston Operations.

4. Draft a Q&A sheet addressing employment matters to be placed on the plant's website.

5. Draft an email message announcing the plant closure to be sent to Supercore's distribution centers.

6. Draft a Q&A addressing the plant closure for use by supervisory and management staff throughout Supercore International.

7. Develop a script for a video news release for use on television business news about Supercore's downsizing and how it will benefit the company.

8. Find external resources about job searches and employment opportunities and construct a special page on the company's intranet to be devoted to those who will be job searching. This should be all encompassing, as it will be a goodwill effort to help those who will be losing their jobs.

9. Construct a quiz for those who will be asked questions about the closing to ensure that they fully understand the information conveyed to them, and that they have the key points and critical details memorized.

Class Role Play #1

Cast

Chief Executive Officer George Waters
Public Relations Director David Maple
[Monday meeting, July 8, 20XX; CEO George Waters' office.]

CEO George Waters

I want to talk to you about a move we are about to make. This is highly confidential. You are among a select few to know about this decision.

PR Director David Maple

I understand.

CEO George Waters

We're going to close the Houston plant. This will affect about 200 employees. I want to do this in keeping with the reputation we have for upholding quality and acting responsibly. I want this announcement made, and I want Houston to be operating with minimal negative effects from the closure on the overall business.

PR Director David Maple

I'd like to know more specifically about the rationale for closing this particular plant.

CEO George Waters

Tom Oaks will give you those details. I want the announcement to be made in three weeks.

PR Director David Maple

Who will I be working with?

CEO George Waters

There will be a core group of five, including you.

PR Director David Maple

Will that include the plant manager?

CEO George Waters

Yes. I've known Bill Cabot for more than 15 years. I trust him completely. He'll do what's right for the company. You can work with Bill, Tom, Gayle, and Harvey. I want to have a communication plan from this core group by noon Friday.

[Meeting adjourns.]

Class Role Play #2

Cast

VP Operations Tom Oaks
VP Marketing and Sales Gayle Hopkins
VP Human Resources Harvey Collins
PR Director David Maple
Tuesday meeting of core group, July 9, 20XX; in a conference room; manager Houston Operations, Bill Cabot, is not included in this meeting.

VP Operations Tom Oaks

David, communication planning is your area. How should we prepare for this announcement?

PR Director David Maple

We don't have a track record in closing plants. Not this company. In fact, this will be our first experience. But other companies have closed more than one facility and have good advice to offer. I called the resource center of Public Relations Society of America in New York. Had them send articles about Fortune 500 companies that have learned about announcing plant closings. Ten lessons. These points go beyond communication, but they're all important considerations.

VP Operations Tom Oaks

A lot of people are going to take an interest in this announcement, not just employees.

PR Director David Maple

That's a good place to begin, Tom. Let's talk about audiences. Within the organization we have Houston Operations employees, including sales, customer service, and estimating personnel. Externally, we have Houston's customers and certain suppliers. In the community, we have community leaders, and government representatives on the local, county, state, and federal level. And we have the media—local, business, financial, and trade press. We're privately owned so we don't need to worry about investors. This points to the first lesson learned by others: We need to be first to communicate fully to everyone concerned.

VP Human Resources Harvey Collins

It's going to take some time to reach all of those groups.

PR Director David Maple

It has to be done all at once. I'll show you how we can reach everyone in a single morning. That's the function of a good plan.

VP Marketing and Sales Gayle Hopkins

So how do we decide what to tell these different groups?

PR Director David Maple

Key question, Gayle. We have to have a crystal clear business rationale for the decision to close Houston. That rationale will be the basis of every communication. Our credibility with all of these audiences depends on the soundness of our rationale for closing the plant. Tom, if you will provide me with the basic information, I'll draft the rationale. If we can't explain the business reasons for a closure to ourselves, we can't expect anyone else to understand why the facility must be shut down. The rationale will be at the heart of every communication we develop. In our next work session, tomorrow, we need to decide on message points for each audience—Houston employees, customers and corporate-wide employees, field sales reps, distribution center managers, the media, and the community.

VP Marketing and Sales Gayle Hopkins

What about Bill? Isn't he supposed to be working with us?

PR Director David Maple

That happens to be third on my list of lessons learned. It's essential to have full support of the plant manager. George said we can trust Bill Cabot completely and that he will do what's best for the company, even though he will be retired in the process. Bill will get an audio file of this meeting. We would have to alter our strategy if we had a manager who might take issue with the decision or resist talking about the decision. Most people would rather avoid confrontation and controversy. A plant manager who has been operating for years in the comfort zone of a routine operation could have a tough time with this. He suddenly gets thrust into having to confront people within and outside the plant on a difficult subject. It's much easier, even with someone as loyal as Bill, to follow a comprehensive, agreed upon plan.

VP Human Relations Harvey Collins

One of your points must focus on the 200 employees who will lose their jobs.

PR Director David Maple

Yes. Every Fortune 500 company I read about emphasized the importance of putting a high priority on human needs. You will need a Q&A on HR stuff, Harv. We're talking about job information …

VP Human Relations Harvey Collins

I know, … relocation opportunities, if any; early retirements, jobs training. We're going to want to provide financial and career counseling, family counseling, psychological counseling for managers. We will need to provide letters of recommendation, help with resume writing and whatever placement services are needed. You know this announcement can also cause people to jump ship. We need to make sure we identify and contact people we want to keep elsewhere in the organization.

PR Director David Maple

Another lesson learned is to protect against demoralization elsewhere in the organization. Employees easily identify with one another. How the Houston employees are treated will be of interest to every employee in the company. They will draw conclusions about how they might be treated. That reinforces the importance of having a sound business rationale for the decision to shut down. Another thing we have to protect is the safety and security of everyone at Houston. It's another lesson point. What's the physical layout at that plant?

VP Operations Tom Oaks

If it's what you're thinking, the operation is wide open. Someone could walk in …

VP Human Relations Harvey Collins

Like an emotionally distraught employee?

VP Operations Tom Oaks

Yes. Someone like that could walk right in the front door and have dozens of production people in his or her sights. We'll take a look at security. We also have to think about the unlikely possibility of vandalism, looting, sabotage, and any other form of reprisal. David, according to my notes, that's six points.

PR Director David Maple

I have four more. One is keeping the planning confidential with a core group, which we have. Another is having a comprehensive plan. We're working on that. Once we have a plan, we have to commit to following it. The plan will have to have contingency provisions for dealing with problems like leaks and rumors. A third one is in your area, Harvey—meeting all local, state, and federal laws for closing a facility. The fourth is leaving the community in a way that it would welcome our return in the future. This closure will impact the local economy in terms of revenue from wages, taxes, and local purchases. The community needs to understand our decision and not feel that it could or should have done something to secure the plant's future. We might even consider gifting the community some property, park equipment, or public improvement.

Let me wrap up this part of our meeting with a summary of lessons learned:

1. Have a crystal clear rationale.

2. Work confidentially with a core staff.

3. Follow a comprehensive plan.

4. Place a high priority on human needs.

5. Have full support of the person in charge of the facility to be closed.

6. Meet all local, state, and federal requirements.

7. Protect against demoralization elsewhere.

8. Ensure safety and tight security.

9. Leave the community in a way that it would welcome our return.

10. Be first to communicate fully to everyone concerned.

VP Operations Tom Oaks

We have to regroup tomorrow, here, nine o'clock.

[Meeting adjourns.]

PR Director David Maple's Plan

[Tuesday night, in office.]
Maple is reviewing his research on plant closings from PRSA headquarters in New York. The experience in plant closings by more than a dozen Fortune 500 companies reveals 10 important communication points. Maple decides to present them at Wednesday's planning meeting in a PowerPoint presentation. He finishes the last slide and checks his email before leaving the office. There's a message from VP Operations Tom Oaks and a file attachment. Message: The information you wanted for drafting the rationale is in the attached file. Maple opens the file, which is in a memo format.

Information for Writing Business Rationale

Supercore International Inc.

CONFIDENTIAL

JULY 9, 20XX

TO: DAVID MAPLE
FROM: TOM OAKS
COPIES: George Waters, Harvey Collins, Gayle Hopkins, Bill Cabot
RE: BUSINESS RATIONALE FOR HOUSTON CLOSING

Following is the information you will need for developing a statement of our business rationale for closing Houston Operations. Supercore International Inc. has provided the standard of quality in structural products for commercial buildings in countries around the world for more than half a century. We are a leading international supplier of custom designed products and systems. We have 51 facilities. They employ 5,221 people in North and South America, Europe, and Asia.

We have been the market leader in North America and have been steadily increasing market shares in Europe and Asia. However, business conditions in our major market, specifically the United States, are causing us to adjust our production capacity. The U.S. commercial building market is experiencing a major recession. Volume of construction business has dropped dramatically over the past five years. Many parts of the country are overbuilt in commercial construction. Contractors are constrained financially. Financing for construction projects is hard to get. Supercore and its competitors have seen their market drop 37 percent in five years. Industry analysts expect that it will be another 18 months with a further decline next year before this market begins to turn around. Competition for the reduced volume of business has put enormous downward pressure on pricing. That, plus the cost of maintaining excess production capacity, caused us to assess what could be done to reduce operating costs and still maintain the same high level of sales and service to our customers.

We decided our production capacity had to be brought in line with market conditions. By the end of this year, Supercore will consolidate its manufacturing operations in the United States, reducing the number of production plants from eight to seven. Houston Operations was the likely candidate for an indefinite closure. The Southwest has had the weakest construction environment in the country for the past five years, and this has led to a substantial decline in the plant's sales volume from levels 10 years ago. The depressed regional economy, resulting from a major decline in oil prices and a rash of major bankruptcies, together with an oversupply of commercial buildings, has severely reduced market demand for our products. Houston has been operating significantly under capacity for several years. Work there can be handled easily by our other facilities.

Actually, the Southwestern market is relatively small and isn't expected to improve much in the foreseeable future, which is another reason we focused our decision on Houston. But the main reason we selected Houston over other plants was that its closing would be least disruptive in terms of the company's ability to serve its national dealer network. We will serve the Southwest as effectively and aggressively as ever using the same sales organization. The Houston area sales districts and their distribution centers will become part of our Southeastern Area operations.

We are confident that reducing our production plants from eight to seven will leave us ample capacity to supply customer needs for the coming years. Even with the closing of Houston Operations, Supercore will continue to be one of the largest international producers of structural products for commercial buildings. We are generally considered to be the industry's quality leader with service that outperforms our competition.

Our outlook is positive, despite current market conditions. Commercial building represents a big market in the United States and around the world. Our brand has enjoyed a major market position and we have always been a full participant in economic recoveries. We see excellent market potential in Europe and in developing parts of the world. We have built our organization not on business but on relationships with employees, suppliers, customers, dealers, the media, social and environmental activists, and with the communities and countries in which we operate.

* * *

David, that should give you something to work with in developing our business rationale statement.
T.O.

Meeting Transcript of Lessons Learned by Others

Wednesday Morning Meeting, July 10, 20XX, Conference Room

Participants
VP Operations, Tom Oaks
VP Marketing and Sales, Gayle Hopkins
VP Human Resources, Harvey Collins
PR Director, David Maple
(Manager Houston Operations, Bill Cabot not included in this meeting)

PR Director David Maple

Tom, I read your memo. Thanks for the information for the rationale. Last night I gleaned more helpful information from my research on lessons learned by other companies. This information focuses directly on communication. In the interest of time, I'll quickly cover 10 points that I have summarized in a PowerPoint presentation.

1. Announce the closing according to a plan. The logistics of getting key messages to a diverse number of audiences all at one particular time requires meticulous planning and scheduling. We must have a plan and follow it through to the last detail.

2. Use prepared Q&As. When it comes to work like this, I know from experience that only birds can wing it. We will need a Q&A on each major subject area and we will have to supply them to everyone who has a responsibility for communicating the information.

3. Spike rumors. We need to offer every company communicator guidance on how to spike rumors and deal with news leaks.

4. Stay in touch with the media. A plant closure is a major news item. We can expect calls from the local, business, financial, and trade press. We can minimize calls and conversations by developing a news announcement that anticipates and responds to what journalists will want to know about the closure. This will help ensure the accuracy of what is reported. No matter what we do, there will always be more questions, so it's essential that we stay in touch with the media until all information needs are satisfied.

5. Assess audience reactions. The point here is that effective communication is a two-way process. We communicate. We listen. We respond to feedback. And the process continues until we're satisfied that the communication is complete and accurate.

6. Respond to problems. When an announcement is planned properly, people involved in the announcement activities develop a sense of ownership and commit to identifying and dealing with problems to help ensure a successful outcome. We want everyone involved in this announcement to have confidence in the plan and all the information they need so they will feel compelled to help head off potential problems.

7. Communicate frequently with employees. When an organization gets into a stressful situation, especially one that pertains to health, safety, or job security, people need face time with their leaders. They need to be in touch to have a sense that someone is in charge and providing direction. So, it's important for managers and supervisors to be in touch on a personal, face-to-face basis even when there is nothing new to communicate.

8. Show concern and commitment. The way in which we make the announcement in Houston needs to show everyone affected by it that the company is taking

an action that is absolutely necessary and that we are doing it with compassion, understanding, and a commitment to make good on every promise.

9. Generate positive follow-up publicity. We have opportunities to follow the announcement with positive news by publicizing successful personnel placements and any goodwill gestures to the community like a donation of property or park equipment.

10. Leave the community in a way that would invite our return. We need to make sure community leaders and government representatives are not blind-sided by the announcement, and that they are well informed and prepared to respond to questions from their constituents. We need to make known that we will continue to serve the Southwest market with products and services from our other facilities. We need to reposition, not sever, our relationship with the community.

These are the 10 communication points derived from the lessons learned by others.

VP Marketing and Sales Gayle Hopkins

Well, we're going to look to you for how we apply this. What do you need from us so we can get down to the specifics of developing the announcement plan?

PR Director David Maple

Gayle, I need you to provide key message points we want to make to distribution center managers, to field sales personnel, and to customers. We'll have to talk to Bill about the message points for Houston plant employees and key suppliers. Tom, I will need from you and Harvey message points for employees company-wide. I think I have what I need to draft the news announcement and the message points for community leaders and government representatives.

If you all agree, I think we should take some time now to rough out a timeline that will become our communication schedule. Then, let's meet again tomorrow morning, Thursday, July 11th. I will have a draft announcement plan and timeline for us to review. We should have a final draft by the end of the day. Tom, do you want to schedule a meeting with George for Friday, July 12th?

VP Operations Tom Oaks

I'll do that. Let's get it on the schedule.

PR Director David Maple

We need to bring Bill into the planning group. Why don't we have him join us on Monday, July 15th?

VP Human Relations Harvey Collins

We have a lot of stuff to review, probably revise, and get approved. It might be good to schedule a three-day work session.

PR Director David Maple

What about doing that next week, Wednesday thru Friday, July 17th through 19th?

VP Operations Tom Oaks

That should include review and approval of an operations shutdown plan and timetable.

PR Director David Maple

It's also the time we should decide if this core group needs to be expanded and who that should include.

VP Human Relations Harvey Collins

I will have the retention plan ready. We can do a final review of government requirements for a closure. We can review the employment information Q&A. I will also have a description of employment assistance services we will be providing. And we can review security arrangements.

PR Director David Maple

We can finalize the communication plan and timeline. It will contain contingency provisions for handling news leaks and rumors. The business rationale and news announcement need to be reviewed and approved, as well as the communication to all of the various stakeholders. For the announcement, I would see notifying the general managers of each of our operations by phone on July 26th and sending them information kits via courier to arrive the same day. We'll get Bill's opinion on how soon to notify key staff in Houston. We should courier information kits to sales reps and distribution center managers. I think we should schedule the announcement for Tuesday, July 30th. On announcement day, we need to cover the following something like this:

- Bill Cabot personally notifies supervisors

- Houston supervisors notify employees and distribute letter from Bill

- Facility managers company-wide distribute CEO letter to employees with business rationale attached

- Bill meets with Houston customer service representatives and estimators

- Headquarters faxes sales reps company-wide with instructions to notify Southwest customers by phone

- News release to headquarters personnel (electronically) and to Houston media, and via news distribution service to state wires, national business, and financial and trade media

- Bill and selected staff members call community leaders and local government representatives

- Houston faxes government representatives at state and federal offices

- Houston mails news release and letter to Houston customers and suppliers

- In the days following the announcement, Houston will be operating counseling services and employment assistance, and we should be looking for opportunities to generate some positive publicity.

David Maple's Notes for Writing the News Announcement

- Dateline should be from headquarters, Thyme, Illinois, July 30th, 20XX

- Indefinite closure of structural building products plant to bring production capacity in line with market conditions and consolidate our manufacturing resources in the United States by reducing the number of production plants from eight to seven

- This adjustment will enable us to reduce operating costs and still provide the same high level of sales and service to our customers

- With the U.S. commercial construction market in the midst of a major recession, the market for the company's products has dropped by approximately 39 percent nation-wide over the past six years

- Will be another 18 months, with a further decline in the coming year, before this market begins to turn around

- Supercore International will retain the same Southwest sales organization and distribution centers in Houston, Denver, and Wichita; these centers will be supplied by production facilities in Tennessee, Illinois, and Alabama

- Closure expected to be completed by year's end

- Will affect approximately 200 employees

- Some employees will have an opportunity to relocate to other Supercore International facilities

- The company will provide employees with a severance pay package and job placement services

- Houston has always had highly skilled, productive employees; closure is regretful; we will work hard to help them find other employment

- The plant started operating in 1980

- Business grew rapidly

- Ran at near capacity during the building boom of the early 1980s

- Houston was well situated to serve the Southwest and, in particular, the Texas markets, which had major levels of construction back in that period

- This period was followed by a virtual collapse of building activity in the region

- Supercore gave Houston Operations some of the company's international work and jobs from other parts of the country; it still operated below capacity levels

- Depressed conditions hit other regions and Houston's operating level was reduced further

- Market conditions caused us to assess our situation in the United States

- Supercore made a thorough analysis and concluded that of the eight production facilities, closure of Houston Operations would have the least effect on the company's ability to serve our customers nationally

- Conditions are what they are and we have to adjust our production capacity

- Houston plant was built in 1979

- Supercore International Inc. is a leading international producer of structural building products and systems for the nonresidential market

- Headquartered in Thyme, Illinois

- Supercore International has 50 facilities employing approximately 5,000 people in North America, Europe, and Asia

David Maple's Notes for Writing Q&A

We'll be asked why we're closing one of eight U.S. plants to bring production in line with market conditions.

Some may think we're overreacting; they'll try to point to indicators that we're coming out of the recession. But commercial construction business in the United States is in the midst of a major recession. Construction work has dropped significantly over the past six years. Supercore and other manufacturers have seen their market drop by approximately 39 percent in the past six years. It will be another 18 months before this market begins to turn around.

Not everyone understands why construction is in worse shape than the general economy. There's been substantial overbuilding in many parts of the country. Building activity is down substantially. Developers are constrained financially. They are unable to attract capital for projects.

We'll get plenty of questions. Why Houston? Fact is, the Southwest has been the weakest section of the country for construction for the past six years. Why? Breakdown of the energy belt economy with the big drop in oil prices, consequences of the savings and loan crisis, and lots of bankruptcies. It's likely to be a weak market for the foreseeable future. But the major reason behind selecting Houston was that it would have a minimal effect on our overall operation.

We have been in Houston so long that it will probably seem to some that we are pulling out of this market. So we need to be direct in letting people know that we're going to serve this market as well as ever before. We will continue to operate our distribution center in Houston. That center and those in Denver and Wichita will be supplied by production facilities in Tennessee, Illinois, and Alabama. These plants can handle additional volume.

About 200 employees will be affected by the closure. Some will be given opportunities to relocate to other facilities.

Severance. We'll get some questions about the package. It has two elements. Employees will be offered incentive pay to work until their individual assignments have been completed. All employees will get a severance amount whether or not they work until their jobs end.

We might be asked about a possible employee buyout. That's not possible. We're not interested in selling these assets. We may have use for them elsewhere in the future.

The end date? Closing date? We haven't set an exact date. We have to allow enough time for transferring work to other plants. Should be able to have everything done before the end of December.

As for other plants ... people will be wondering if other plants will be closed. The answer is no. According to our market outlook, we think this adjustment of reducing our U.S. capacity from eight to seven plants will give us the right size capacity to supply customers for the near future.

We know this is going to have an impact on the local economy. We'll get questions about that. The Houston plant has contributed about $20 million a year in wages, taxes, and local purchases.

There will probably be people who expect us to somehow make up this deficit, this loss of income to the community. What can we say? We've been a solid contributor to the local economy for many years. We've provided good paying jobs. But business conditions no longer support this plant. We're in a position that many others are in. We can't justify our cost of operating here and there's no way to continue contributing to the economy.

We'll probably get asked about the possibility of reopening the plant in the future. The closure is indefinite. The Southwest building market is severely depressed. We expect it to be that way for quite some time.

Someone will probably persist and ask if it will ever be opened again. But who could possibly know what conditions will be in the future? We can't make any projections, let alone commitments.

We have had such a good relationship with local and state government representatives that some of them are going to be wondering if there is anything they can do to change our decision. But there isn't anything they can do. The decision is based on business conditions in the Southwest and around the country.

I suppose someone could wonder if putting this plant here was a mistake in the first place. That certainly isn't true. It really took off in the mid-1980s and was well situated to serve the Southwest. Texas had lots going on then. Major construction projects were under way. But that period didn't last forever. Things pretty much collapsed. Who could have predicted this?

Employees at Houston had nothing to do with the decision. They are good, smart, hardworking individuals. They were always making suggestions on how to improve things, both quality and production. Other employers should take a hard look at the talent that will be available from this plant.

Employees at our other plants might wonder if any of them might get bumped by a relocated Houston employee. First of all, there will be a limited number of relocations. We place a high value on our human resources and will be very thoughtful in any placements.

That brings up the matter of employees who are not relocated. We will provide employment services, like preparing resumes, training for job searching, and how to interview. We'll be talking to local employers to describe the kinds of work people have been doing for us and how their skills might relate to other business operations. We'll give employees time off for job interviews. We will make a concerted effort to help everyone as much as we can.

The announcement may seem abrupt and someone might ask if we couldn't have given more notice. But we made the announcement as soon as we finished our analysis of the market situation. With the closure targeted for year's end, employees will have an opportunity to work and be looking for other jobs for many weeks.

Let's see, we made the decision to close the plant in June, after our study was completed and assessed. The final decision came in mid-July. So there weren't any unusual delays in going through the process and making it known publicly.

The Houston plant … we'll secure it, probably move the equipment, and eventually sell the property.

The Houston plant was built in 1979. It started up in 1980.

It produces structural building products and pre-engineering building systems for the nonresidential market.

It's not a union plant.

As for the outlook, we'll see an even greater decline in the market in the coming year and it will be at least 18 months before things begin to turn around. We will be stepping up our sales and marketing efforts. When things pick up, we'll be in position to participate in the recovery as we have in the past.

Information for Writing the Q&A

Supercore International Inc.

CONFIDENTIAL

JULY 10, 20XX

TO: DAVID MAPLE
FROM: HARVEY COLLINS
COPIES: George Waters, Tom Oaks, Gayle Hopkins, Bill Cabot
RE: INFORMATION FOR Q&A ON PEOPLE RELATED ISSUES

Following is information you can use in writing a Q&A on people related issues:

There will be severance pay for salaried and hourly employees. At the time of termination, each employee will receive a base severance payment. It will amount to the person's weekly pay times the individual's years of service up to 25. Partial years will be prorated.

There will also be an incentive severance payment for individuals who work up to a time we specify or to when their particular job ends. Employees who qualify will be given $1000 if they have less than two years of service and $2500 if they have two or more years of service. The incentive will be paid when their jobs terminate.

The severance base pay and incentive pay will be payable to employees who are offered relocations to other plants, even if the individual does not accept the relocation offer.

Anyone who resigns before their jobs end must give us two weeks' notice in order to get their base severance pay. There's some flexibility on this requirement depending on circumstances.

Acts of misconduct related to the company, customers, or other employees will disqualify a person from receiving severance payments.

We will get questions about benefits. Benefits end with job terminations. Hourly and salary employees may continue their medical insurance at their own expense according to COBRA provisions. We'll have more on COBRA later.

As for retirement benefits, individuals who qualify for retirement or early retirement under either hourly or salary retirement plans can do so and receive retirement benefits. We'll have more details on this later.

We will be pressed hard on how many Houston employees will be transferred to jobs in other facilities. Actually, we don't know at this point. We have to see what's needed at other plants and we'll have to see who is willing to relocate of those who could be offered the opportunity. As soon as the announcement is made, other plants will be assessing their personnel needs. We will have a more accurate idea when we have reports from the other seven plants. It won't be a large number.

Likely transferees will be employees in managerial, supervisory, or technical jobs.

We'll probably be asked where the relocations could be. Most likely places would be Cilantro, Tennessee; Sage, Illinois; and Rosemary, Alabama.

As for when transfers might be made, I would say beginning in September and going through the end of the year.

Unfortunately, most employees will not have an opportunity to transfer. There's no cut-off date for employment. It will be different for each individual. It depends on how their work relates to the transition and if they accept the incentive to work as long as we need them. We will try to be more specific about this in the coming weeks.

If an employee wants to be transferred—and that refers to salaried employees in managerial and technical jobs—they will be given an opportunity to complete a form that will be sent to appropriate personnel for consideration.

It's different for hourly employees. A transfer might be possible for jobs with specialized skills. However, the individual would be responsible for moving expenses.

H.C.

Supercore International Inc.

CONFIDENTIAL

JULY 10, 20XX
TO: DAVID MAPLE
FROM: BILL CABOT
COPIES: George Waters, Tom Oaks, Gayle Hopkins, Harvey Collins
RE: INFORMATION FOR MY MEMO TO HOUSTON EMPLOYEES

David, I'd appreciate a little help with writing my memo to the Houston employees. I've known many of these folks for more than a dozen years. If you would rough out something I will personalize it. Some of the points I'd like to include are:

- Very difficult; we have operated like a family

- Proud of the teamwork we've shown

- Struggled through some lean times together, but always recovered

- Personally believe the decision to close was justified from a business assessment

- Need to support each other as we prepare for looking in new directions

- Can't help but wonder, why us? But there's nothing we could have done to alter the outcome. That's clear when we face the facts:

  - Supercore has too much underutilized production capacity and will have for some time to come

  - The market our plant serves is the by far the softest in the country

  - Prices have eroded, profits are down, no way to cover the cost of operating this facility

  - Unfortunately for us, our customers can be easily served by other plants

  - The Southwest distribution center will serve to anchor Supercore's business in this market

  - I'll be talking with everyone in smaller groups as we move forward; we'll go over personnel concerns.

I know we all have mixed emotions over this; we will have to make a special effort to rely on our professionalism to maintain the teamwork needed to work through the shutdown process.

We have always given our customers a level of quality that always meets and often exceeds company standards; they deserve our continuing commitment and a smooth hand-off to our other plants; you know the rapport we have enjoyed; nothing has changed in that regard; we will continue working together in an open, straight-forward, totally honest relationship.

In all honesty, I have to admit this is the most difficult memo I have ever had to bring myself write.

See what you can do with that. Thanks, David.

B.C.

Supercore International Inc.

CONFIDENTIAL

JULY 10, 20XX

TO: DAVID MAPLE
FROM: GAYLE HOPKINS
COPIES: George Waters, Tom Oaks, Harvey Collins, Bill Cabot
RE: INFORMATION FOR MY MEMO TO DISTRIBUTION CENTERS

I appreciate your help with this communication, David. I am providing the main points that I think should be written in my memo to be sent to Supercore's distribution center managers.

- You were notified this morning about the company's decision to close Houston Operations

- I talked by speaker phone to the staff at the Houston distribution center; as you know, that facility will remain in operation; Southwest Area Sales will also remain as usual

- We're all going to have our own thoughts about the shutdown and we're certainly entitled to that

- We have a responsibility to fully understand and be able to discuss the business reasons for the decision

- Urge you to read and study the business rationale in your information kits

- As members of the sales organization, our biggest responsibility is to maintain our current business and make every effort to keep from losing any business as other plants begin to supply Houston customers

- To protect our position will require a stronger than ever commitment to the company and its strategic direction

- I know we are up to the challenge

- No matter how we plan, there will be some rough situations—some not easy or even possible to see

- Will place great demands on our ability to work together

- Can't emphasize enough the importance of reading and studying all of the materials in your information kits; you must know this material well enough to show complete confidence in Supercore's decision about Houston

- We need time to go over the transition plan in detail; plan to attend a meeting of all distribution center managers at headquarters on Friday, August 2nd, at 11:00 a.m. in the main conference room, your attendance is mandatory; we have a big job ahead of us and I know we can handle it when we tackle it as a team

That's about what needs to be said, David. I'll look forward to your draft.
Thanks.
G.H.

Supercore International Inc.

CONFIDENTIAL

JULY 10, 20XX

TO: DAVID MAPLE
FROM: TOM OAKS
COPIES: George Waters, Gayle Hopkins, Harvey Collins, Bill Cabot
RE: INFORMATION FOR MEMO FROM CEO TO ALL EMPLOYEES

David, we'll need a memo written from George Waters to all employees. I would see it containing these points:

- For a company that holds its employees in highest regard, putting business realities ahead of our personal relationships is extremely difficult

- I have a responsibility to our organization to keep us in a strong, competitive position

- Market conditions, as we all know, are heavily taxing our ability to generate the sales necessary to earn some return on investment; in the United States we have experienced swings from no orders to 'round-the-clock production

- The bottom line is we have to face the reality of bringing our capacity in line with market conditions that are expected to remain depressed for the foreseeable future

- Because the situation is serious, I asked for a thorough market study and comprehensive study of our production capacity and operating options; it became evident that the way to restructure with minimal effects on our overall business is to shut down the Houston plant

- It is with deep regret that we have to pursue a decision that will affect nearly 200 hard-working employees, some of whom have been with us for more than a dozen years; we will provide severance and employment services, including working with Houston employers to make local placements wherever possible

- So that everyone is able to know the details behind our decision to close Houston, I have included with this letter to all employees a copy of our business rationale for this action

- You will see clearly from the rational that Houston has always been a top performer and closure is entirely due to market conditions

David, let me have a draft by tomorrow. George asked for a draft ASAP. Thanks. T.O.

19. Marketing Communication: Campus Café

Learning Outcomes

By the end of this case, you should be able to:

1. create a plan for gathering and utilizing research to compare branding efforts (the messages controlled by a company or organization) to the external perceptions of the company or organization (the true brand);

2. understand how to use the aforementioned research findings to inform and direct strategy;

3. understand the importance and differentiation of market segmentation in creating PR plans and strategies;

4. practice developing specific, measurable, and achievable objectives based on research; and

5. grasp how public relations creates competitive advantage and can be quantified for use in improving or even reviving an organization.

Additional Notes

The purpose of this case is to develop skills in research as a strategic part of developing a public relations campaign for a specific audience.

Some coffee houses are highly successful. This is a case of a coffee house company in trouble. Happy Roasters Cafés Inc., a fictitious name, was incorporated more than a decade ago with the aim of giving people a way to step out of their busy lives into an environment wafting with good smells, good tastes, good music, and good spirits. Like many previously successful businesses, Happy Roasters lost its focus. Much like a plane with a stalled engine, a free fall began, but there was a chance to regain control. Its stock began to plummet. Market leadership fell to competing with fast-food franchises. The business pursuit appeared to be revenue growth rather than profitability. Things such as automation over custom brewing, overcrowded stores with high-priced merchandise, and the aroma of freshly ground coffee being accessible only through push-button vents on packaged beans became customary. The company was in a tailspin with industry analysts crying out advice: "Train your people." "Improve the food." "Improve the coffee." "Brighten up the stores." "Stop opening stores." "Forget about growth; fix your problems."

It is in this downward spiral that Happy Roasters is hiring public relations firms to drive sales by market segment. Your PR firm has a contract to promote retail sales at Happy Roaster Cafés located near college and university campuses. Your proposed plan must be backed by research that was specifically designed to inform and validate your strategies. Your proposal must creatively capture the interests and meet the needs of college students. Your proposal must refocus the company on its original aim to give people a way to step out of their busy lives and into an environment wafting with good smells, good tastes, good music, and good spirits. Your PR firm's role, in this case, has been expanded from "communication" to "marketing communication," which means that you are expected to consider the total sales environment, including physical layout, customer service, collateral merchandise, pricing considerations, and promotional programs. Your firm is to develop a proposal for which the company will pay $10,000. The proposal timeline must allow for conducting ample research and then planning implementation.

Team Assignment

To be clear, your PR firm is to develop a marketing communication plan to promote retail sales at Happy Roaster Cafés located near colleges and universities. Strategies in the plan must be directly linked to, and driven by, the research findings. This research must be specifically designed to garner information that will be proposed in the plan, and the plan should show results in 12 months, preferably sooner.

Individual Team Member Assignments

If you are working this case as a team, each team member is to select a different one of the following individual writing assignments that should pertain to the same coffee house. Choose one near a college campus:

1. Visit the company's website and read its business purpose or mission statement. Visit the coffee house and through personal observation determine how well its operation lives up to the company's mission statement. Write your findings and conclusions in a one-page, 1.5-spaced report titled Coffee House Research—Personal Observation.

2. Search the online archives of the local newspaper. Study the content of stories mentioning the coffee house and determine the image (positive and negative) of the coffee house or company projected by the article(s). Write your findings and conclusions in a one-page, 1.5-spaced report titled Coffee House Research—Media Content Analysis. Include a list, by date and headline, of articles covered in your analysis.

3. Search the Internet and find at least six blogs by different bloggers in which the company is mentioned. Study the content of the blogs and determine why the company is mentioned and in what context. Write your findings and conclusions in a one-page, 1.5-spaced report titled Coffee House Research—Content Analysis of Blogs.

4. Search Twitter, Instagram, and Facebook for mentions of the company and determine why the company is mentioned and in what context. Be sure, when you find probable hashtag indexing, to look deeper into those hashtags for more potential content. If the company has Snapchat, begin to monitor their story and also visit the location to see if they offer and/or fluctuate filters. Write your findings and conclusions in a one-page, 1.5-spaced report titled Coffee House Research—Content Analysis of Social Media.

5. Conduct personal interviews of 10 students and get their views on what would make the coffee house more attractive to students. Write your findings and conclusions in a one-page, 1.5-spaced report titled Coffee House Research—Personal Interviews.

6. Research survey construction. Work to construct a survey that seems similarly understood by all who pretest the tool. Multiple revisions may be necessary as the survey is discussed with those who are interpreting the questions. Ensure that it seems to measure what you are trying to gauge.

7. Conduct an on-the-street survey of 20 students to determine where they usually go to buy a cup of coffee, what type of drink they buy, and why they patronize that particular vendor. Write your findings and conclusions in a one-page, 1.5-spaced report titled Coffee House Research—Survey College.

8. Conduct the same exercise as above (the surveys) at a location further from campus, and talk to those who are noncollege students. Write your findings and conclusions in a one-page, 1.5-spaced report titled Coffee House Research—Survey Non-College. Compare the results of the two groups to better understand the college students' perspectives.

9. Research the company's policy on sponsoring events, activities, and organizations. Write your findings and conclusions in a one-page, 1.5-spaced report title Coffee House Research—Sponsorships.

10. Look at the controlled messaging that the coffee house studied above disseminates, including in store, on social media, and on their website. Decide what the top three to five key messages seem to be by observing the aforementioned

controlled communication. Compare these intended messages to the results above (the perceptions) and discuss the differences and similarities. Focus on which key messages do not seem to resonate with external audiences.

11. Propose a strategy based on the findings above. Brainstorm and discuss as a large group.

20. Online Community Engagement: Culture of Secrecy

Learning Outcomes

By the end of this case, you should be able to:

1. analyze a problem on levels above the immediate situation;

2. research beyond traditional practices to find other ways to solve a problem;

3. learn to respond to a Request for Proposals (RFP); and

4. understand the benefits and application of online community engagement.

Author's note: There are six superscript reference numbers in the following case which refer to the QR codes at the end of the case study.

The state of Washington is struggling with strong public opposition to a proposed oil terminal at the Port of Vancouver, which precedes another expected fight over a coal terminal proposed by the Port of Longview. Government officials, including the governor, who is the ultimate decision maker in these public disputes, will continue to face months of demonstrations, packed hearing rooms, and media events opposing these and other proposals unless a better way is established for these Washington ports to engage the public. Collectively, the ports are members of an association; specifically, a trade association, with the aim of advocating for and furthering the common interests of the ports.

The state, not wanting to have more surges of hot public discourse spiraling up from port districts to the governor for decisions, is looking for ways to foster coexistence between port districts and communities. In that regard, the state has issued an RFP (hypothetical) for a plan that will serve as a road map for the Washington Public Ports Association (WPPA) to lead its members in making community engagement an integral part of professional port management, thereby improving relations with the people who live in their districts and who pay port taxes.

To compete for a contract, according to the RFP, firms must present, in person, a plan that is easily understood and plausible to the reviewers. It must have the appearance of truth and reason. It must seem credible, believable, and worthy of approval. The plan must clearly demonstrate a firm's comprehensive understanding of why the Port of Vancouver is at such odds with the public—just as other ports could be (and mostly will be) in the future. The plan must demonstrate a solid working knowledge of online community engagement, methods and technology.

Team Assignment

Your public relations firm has decided to respond to the state's RFP and to compete for a contract. Presentations are due 15 working days from today.

This means that your team will have to pitch a plan and pitch the firm's capabilities relative to the plan implementation. To begin, your team has called on various members of your firm, as well as outside friends from city and state government, to participate. This is not a brainstorming session for creative ideas, but a round table discussion to acquire knowledge and to research information. The desire is to gain a better understanding of port districts and their dealings with communities in which they operate.

Read or act out with your class colleagues the role play of the round table discussion to obtain details of the case. The annotations refer to Quick Response Codes at the end of the role play to scan and to help expedite further research. Following the role play are objectives to help guide you in developing a plan for the WPPA.

Class Role Play

Conference Room Round Table Discussion

Cast

[12 Participants; affiliations omitted as being unnecessary.]
Oakley
Charlie
Azariah
Landry
Skyler
Justice
Armani
Frankie
Lennon
Dakota
Emerson
Casey

Dakota

Let's get under way. I want to thank our friends from local and state government for joining us. We all know the community's experience with the Port of Vancouver over the proposed oil terminal. So that will serve as a good case for us to refer to in our broader discussion of port management.

What we'd like to get from this round table is to see what we know and to determine what more we need to know to win the state's RFP. The plan we develop, according to the RFP, must serve as a road map for the Washington Public Ports Association to lead its members in making community engagement an integral part of professional port management, thereby improving relations with the people who live in their respective districts and who pay port taxes.

Let me say that no question is too elementary to ask. So, I will begin by asking, What is a port district?

Charlie

It's a strange animal ...

Dakota

How so, Charlie?

Charlie

A port district is public in that it's supported with tax dollars. But it's mainly a business charged with a mission to make a profit. You can call it a public enterprise.

Casey

Who pays port taxes?

Armani

Everyone who lives in the port district.

Justice

In the case of Vancouver, does everyone pay a port tax?

Armani

Yes. Because the city forms the port district's boundaries.

Emerson

So, is the port responsible to the city?

Armani

No. Actually, it's responsible to itself.

Skyler

What?

Lennon

I pay the port tax. I elect one of the commissioners. I expect the commissioner to represent me.

Dakota

Armani, why do you say the port is accountable to itself.

Armani

Residents of the port district, like Vancouver, for example, elect three port commissioners, one from each of three territories within the district. They should be responsible to their constituents, but therein lies a problem. In the case of the proposed oil terminal, the Vancouver port commissioners seemed to be acting in defiance of their constituents.

Dakota

I think we need to know more about the port's regard for the public interest.

Skyler

There is something here that we don't understand.

Landry

People don't take an interest in ports until there's something they really care about. Meanwhile, they go on electing port commissioners every six years.

Skyler

Maybe people need to start taking more interest in the business of the ports.

Justice

I've been following the Vancouver case. I wondered a lot about why the commissioners seemed to have no regard for the public interest. A friend of mine is a commissioner on the board. I couldn't understand how he could be so dead set on building an oil terminal that people don't want.

Well, I did some checking. I started with the Washington Public Ports Association. The WPPA publishes a guide for new port commissioners. It's very obvious that the overarching theme of the guide is that the ports are responsible to themselves. Their mission is industrial development—to undertake projects and make a profit doing it.

There's virtually nothing written about operating in the public interest. In notes at the back of the guide, there is one line about keeping the public informed.

Skyler

So following the WPPA guide, a commissioner might say, "We want you to know that we've decided to build the nation's biggest oil terminal right here on the Columbia River."

Justice

Yes, according to the guide, that's keeping the public informed. To ignore the public seems arrogant, or cavalier, especially for a project with such huge ramifications.

Oakley

Huge is right. Listen to how the City of Vancouver described the oil project in testimony before the state's Energy Facility Site Evaluation Council.

"Vancouver, the host jurisdiction for the Facility, is staunchly opposed to approval of the Application. Tesoro's proposal involves the construction of the largest oil terminal in the country, which will handle the equivalent of 1,667 tanker trucks per day of highly flammable Bakken and diluted bitumen crude oil. This proposal is directly counter to Vancouver's vision for itself as a vibrant urban community and threatens the safety of its approximately 165,000 citizens."

Frankie

It's no wonder people were angry. Who can blame them for protesting in all the traditional ways. They wanted to be heard. They have every right to be heard.

Azariah

And what about people outside the district? There are hundreds of people in the county who are affected by the port's decisions, but who have no vote in the election of port commissioners. They are completely out of touch with the port district. To see the number, just subtract the population of the city of Vancouver (port district) from the population of Clark County. These are the disenfranchised. Also

figure the geography. These folks live miles away from the port offices and hearing rooms. They should, at least, have communication with the port.

Frankie

Is there anything we should know about communication here?

Skyler

I was impressed to learn that the Vancouver School District, which reaches beyond the city's borders, each year collects and reissues electronic devices, like computers and iPads, to nearly all 23,000 students in grades 3 thru 12. All of the district's school buses have WiFi for students. It's hardly a community that is out of touch, certainly not with the school district.

Emerson

It isn't exactly fair to criticize the port commissioners for ignoring the public interest. Actually, they are just doing their job according to state law.

Article VIII, Section 8 of the Washington State Constitution authorizes the use of public funds by port districts "in such manner as the legislature may prescribe for industrial development of trade promotion." There is no mention in the law about operating in the public interest.

RCW 5306.030 empowers port district commissions to designate the Washington Public Ports Association as a coordinating agency "through which the duties imposed by RCW 5306.020 may be performed, harmonized or correlated." There is no mention in the law that obligates the WPPA to operate in the public interest.

Port districts, under state law, are supported with public funds with the mission to initiate industrial development projects within their respective districts. Port commissioners are elected by residents of their districts—every six years, for example, in the Vancouver port district.

Charlie

We need to know if all of the state's port districts are operating like the Vancouver district, making decisions and springing them on the public. The local newspaper called it a culture of secrecy. If so, any community engagement plan will have to address the job of replacing a culture of operating out of the public view with a culture of engaging public interest in port business.

Lennon

This is going to be a big challenge to commissioners. They will have to convince citizens that they sincerely care about public opinion, that citizens can trust that commissioners will listen to the community, treat residents as constituents, and engage them in timely discussions of prospective projects.

Charlie

Promoting community engagement where there hasn't been any must be initiated at the state's highest level—the governor's office. The governor, himself, must make this a priority and show an honest interest in public engagement.

Dakota

The governor has turned to us professional communicators. The state wants a plan to serve as a road map for the Washington Public Ports Association to lead its members in making community engagement an integral part of professional port management thereby improving relations with the people who live in their districts and who pay port taxes.

Once again, I want to thank our friends in local and state government. Your input has been invaluable to this round table discussion.

We will continue to work on the state's RFP. Justice, I would like you to select and lead a team to pursue this project.

[Meeting adjourns.]

Tips for Developing the Proposal

- To win the RFP, your plan must pitch the plan, and pitch your firm's capabilities. In which of the 10 components of a plan would it be best to do that? In the plan's Introduction? To pitch your firm's capabilities in the Introduction, you could point out that R. Buckminster Fuller—an American architect, systems theorist, author, designer, and inventor who published more than 30 books, coining or popularizing terms such as "Spaceship Earth", *ephemeralization*, and *synergetic*—said, "You never change things by fighting the existing reality. To change something, build a new model that makes the existing model obsolete." In this case, the existing model comprises traditional methods of protest—demonstrating, packing hearing rooms, attracting media. The new model, something better, is the practice of community engagement, one of your firm's strong capabilities. You could also point out that transforming a culture from secrecy to transparency to embrace community engagement requires, in this case, strategic communication, another one of your firm's strong capabilities.

- The focus (or target audience) of the plan must be on the Washington Public Ports Association. The state's RFP asks for a plan that provides the WPPA with a road map to lead its members in making community engagement an integral part of professional port management, thereby improving relations with people who live in their respective districts and who pay port taxes. Note that any change in the way a port district is managed would have to be accepted and endorsed by the district's locally elected port commissioner(s).

- To write a goal for a plan, you would have to know something about associations in general. One way to do that is to Google "what is the role of an association." You will find common functions for trade associations, like the WPPA, are to further a profession, to promote, to maintain, to reward. A goal for a plan for this case could be: For the WPPA to be actively promoting, maintaining, and rewarding the practice of community engagement by Washington's port commissioners.

- Following is guidance for writing objectives and strategies for this case.

  – Objective #1 could be: To promote community engagement to the state's port commissioners so they learn about and accept community engagement as an integral part of the port management profession. Strategy A, telling how the objective could be accomplished, could be: One way for the WPPA to promote acceptance of community engagement among the state's port commissioners is ... (for example, sponsoring a statewide conference). Strategy B could be: One way for the WPPA to promote acceptance of community engagement among the state's port commissioners is ...

  – Objective #2 could be: To maintain interest in community engagement among the state's port commissioners so they keep it top of mind and apply it as part of the port management culture. Strategy A, telling how the objective could be accomplished, could be: One way to keep community engagement top of mind and applied among the state's port commissions is ... (for example, to create an interactive website). Strategy

B could be: One way to keep community engagement top of mind and applied among the state's port commissioners is …

- Objective #3 could be: To reward the practice of community engagement among the state's port commissioners so they make it part of their bid for reelection. Strategy A, telling how the objective could be accomplished, could be: One way to reward the practice of community engagement among the state's port commissioners is … (for example, to offer a certification program). Strategy B could be: One way to reward the practice of community engagement among the state's port commissioners is …

- For this case, you may use any or all of these tips as written and simply expand on them with details to complete your plan to win the state's contract.

Additional Resources: Quick Response Codes (QRCs)

There are six superscript reference numbers in Case 20 that refer to the QR codes below.

1. Citizens Oppose Port of Vancouver Oil Terminal

2. Citizens Oppose Port of Longview Coal Terminal

3. City of Vancouver Legal Brief Opposing Oil Terminal

4. Queensland Model Community Engagement Guidelines

5. Washington Public Ports Association Commissioner Resource Guide

6. Washington State Law Authorizing Port Districts

Index

CPSIA information can be obtained
at www.ICGtesting.com
Printed in the USA
FSHW021638140121
77703FS